STATES OF VIOLENCE

STATES OF VIOLENCE

Politics, Youth, and Memory in Contemporary Africa

Edited by
Edna G. Bay and
Donald L. Donham

UNIVERSITY OF VIRGINIA PRESS

Charlottesville and London

University of Virginia Press
© 2006 by the Rector and Visitors of the University of Virginia
All rights reserved
Printed in the United States of America on acid-free paper
First published 2006

1 3 5 7 9 8 6 4 2

Library of Congress Cataloging-in-Publication Data

States of violence : politics, youth, and memory in contemporary Africa / edited by
Edna G. Bay and Donald L. Donham.
p.   cm.
Includes bibliographical references and index.
ISBN-13: 978-0-8139-2569-1 (cloth : alk. paper)
1. Violence—Africa.   2. Africa—Social conditions—1960–   3. Social conflict—Africa.
I. Bay, Edna G. II. Donham, Donald L. (Donald Lewis)
HN780.Z9V577 2006
303.6096'09045—dc22
2006006847

CONTENTS

THE SOCIAL CONSTRUCTION OF FORGETTING AND REMEMBERING VIOLENCE

PREFACE

In 2000 Dr. Harriet Zuckerman, senior vice president of the Andrew W. Mellon Foundation, invited applications from Emory University for the John E. Sawyer Seminar Program. In the foundation's words, Sawyer Seminars support comparative research "that would (in ordinary university circumstances) be difficult to pursue, while at the same time avoiding the institutionalization of such work in new centers, departments, or programs."

As incoming director of the Institute of African Studies at Emory, I convened a working group of faculty and made an application that was funded, titled "Contending with Conflict: A Comparative and Historical Approach to Three African Cases." Our plan—no doubt too ambitious—was to pair discussion and analysis, over three successive semesters, of three African cases with structurally similar non-African examples: (1) the political transition and endemic violence in South Africa during the 1990s with that in Russia and Eastern Europe; (2) the communal and religious strife in contemporary Nigeria with that in India and Sri Lanka; and (3) the Rwandan genocide of 1994 with the Nazi murders of European Jews during World War II.

In each of these pairings our overarching question focused upon, in Weberian language, local constructions of theodicy, that is, how ordinary people, caught up in the sweep of history, interpret violence and suffering. How did collective memories of the past, formed and transmitted in textbooks, over the radio and television, and through museums, provide scripts for conflicts? How did people deal with trauma, the violent destruction of life, livelihood, and environment? How did they cope with displacement? Alternately, how did they persevere in home areas, creating new economic and political arrangements, forging outlets for tension, "forgetting" enmities?

These conversations, which were both stimulating and frustrating, brought visiting scholars together with Emory faculty and graduate students from anthropology, history, Jewish studies, law, Middle Eastern studies, religion, and political science. The stimulation resulted when suddenly new vistas opened up and unanticipated connections began to be appreciated; the frustration when specialists from each side of the pairing felt that they were only beginning to learn enough of the opposite case to ask intelligent questions as the semester closed.

As it would happen, the events of 11 September 2001 both disrupted the seminar and offered a horrendous example of just the kind of events that we were struggling to understand from the point of view of people who experience them. As our conversation deepened, we became increasingly suspicious of a developing trend in recent scholarship toward constructing violence as an interdisciplinary subject, one for which general approaches and even theories can be developed. No doubt, historical comparison of the type we were attempting revealed a series of broad commonalities in how human beings cope with what might be called violence, but it emphasized as well, and perhaps more so, just how historically and culturally relative violence is.

As a final event of the seminar, then, we decided to concentrate upon African conflicts themselves, not because comparison had been unhelpful but because in the end we felt that understanding of violent events of the kind we sought required a kind of radical contextualization that was made easier by historical commonalities. The papers gathered here represent a selection from the conference held in the fall of 2003.

After I left Emory to join the faculty at the University of California, Davis, Edna Bay became director of the Institute of African Studies, and she brought this long and complex project to final fruition. She and I are indebted to the Mellon Foundation and to a very long list of faculty, postdoctoral fellows, and graduate students at Emory, to visiting scholars who presented papers over three semesters, and finally to those who presented papers and served as commentators at the final conference. Edited books are always collaborative projects, but this one extends in particularly thick and ramified ways.

In thanking those who helped us, we would like to highlight the efforts of fellow Emory faculty who were organizers of the three Sawyer Seminars: Matthew Payne and Randall Packard, of the Department of History, who organized the Russia–South Africa series; Joyce Fleuckiger, of the Department of Religion, and Sidney Kasfir, of the Department of Art History, who planned the India-Nigeria sessions; and Shalom Goldman, of the Department of Middle Eastern and South Asian Studies, who worked with me on the Rwandan-Holocaust series.

We would also like to thank the participants in the conference not represented in this collection, whose stimulating comments greatly enriched our discussion and enhanced our collective insights: John Anene, Frederick Cooper, Alicia Decker, Madeleine Fullard, Kent Glenzer, Sharon Hutchinson, Jok Madut Jok, Nelson Kasfir, Sidney Kasfir, Kristin Mann, Catharine Newbury, Matthew Payne, Heike Schmidt, James Straker, Muhammad S. Umar, and Luise White.

Most importantly for the project as a whole, we would like to thank Robert A. Paul. Bobby, as we know him, was dean of the Graduate School when this project was initiated. Without his continuing support, first as graduate dean and later as dean of Emory College, this project would never have taken place. Being a dean, like overseeing a program at a foundation like Mellon, means creating the conditions for others' work. In appreciation of his leadership, we would like to dedicate this book to Bobby Paul.

DONALD L. DONHAM

STATES OF VIOLENCE

Introduction

EDNA G. BAY

An effort to be contextually faithful is the only
healing to which an historian can legitimately aspire.

—John Lonsdale, "Authority, Gender, and Violence"

FIFTY years ago the threat of violence engulfed colonial Kenya. White settlers feared, and expected, guerrilla attacks on isolated homesteads. Kikuyu feared denunciations by employers, reprisals by government forces, and betrayals by neighbors. "Mau Mau," a term without precise meaning in the Gikuyu language, captured international attention as a violent upheaval directed against a target whose exact nature has been debated by Kenyans and by historians ever since. The name nevertheless entered the popular Western lexicon as a synonym for irrational and unrestrained violence. "Mau Mau," in the imagination of Europe and North America at the time, evoked Joseph Conrad's earlier allusions to deep savagery in the heart of Africa. Yet it conjured up an even more terrifying specter, the inability of even a well-meant colonial effort to bring order out of primordial impulses to violence. Fifty years later, these popular readings of the terror of Mau Mau seem curiously forward-looking, pointing to contemporary suggestions that non-Western peoples, and Africans in particular, have a propensity to indulge in violence that is ultimately incomprehensible, a thesis most infamously linked to the writings of Robert D. Kaplan (1994).

"Mau Mau" and its meanings, to which I will return, in fact focuses attention on the elements incorporated in the studies of Africa presented here: the nature of violence, its association with states and with youth, and its changing

1

constructions in collective memory. Invoking Mau Mau is also a reminder that much violence in contemporary Africa has roots associated with colonial and postcolonial states, and with cultural norms about self-actualization and proper relationships between genders and generations.

The authors of these studies were among the more than two dozen participants in the culminating event of a series of seminars sponsored by the Andrew W. Mellon Foundation at Emory University in 2001–3. Designed by the faculty of Emory's Institute of African Studies under the leadership of Institute Director Donald Donham, these Sawyer Seminars focused on the question of conflict and violence in a comparative framework, pairing three African examples with differing but parallel cases: political transitions and violence in postapartheid South Africa compared with post-Soviet Russia; genocide and related wars in Rwanda compared with the Nazi Holocaust; and contemporary communal and religious strife in Nigeria compared with religious conflict in India. The three semester-long seminars were followed by a final conference on African violence that was both multidisciplinary— drawing together anthropologists, historians, sociologists, and political scientists—and comparative, informed by perspectives from other world areas. The reflections that form the bulk of this introduction are drawn from the discussions and debates that surrounded that four-day conference. Thus, this introduction will occasionally call attention to the ideas of one or more of the broader number of scholars who took part in our deliberations. Our scope is far from comprehensive geographically, as a quick glance at the contribution titles will indicate. Nevertheless, our debates yielded observations and insights with parallels for many other African sites. Some of the comparisons they evoked are reflected in this introduction and suggest possible lines of interpretive inquiry for a number of other questions related to violence.

Violence as a Problem of Intellectual Inquiry

Violence, long assumed by historians to be a phenomenon worthy of study under normalizing rubrics like warfare and rebellion, has become an academic subject of interest in its own right. Yet violence is an elusive subject for scholars in multidisciplinary settings. Definitions are hard to pin down: Is violence physical or bodily force alone, and force directed toward whom? Should definitions of violence include the structural violence of poverty, or of institutions that place individuals in disadvantaged classes or in disadvantaged gender or racial and religious categories? Can political and domestic violence be equated? Who has the right to define and describe violence? Donald Donham, in his meditation on violence as reality and concept, as event and word, provides a working definition for these essays: force that threatens bodies and the bare life of bodies. He points out that violence is always culturally defined, along with its implicit moral condemnation. Indeed, coercive power and legitimate force are euphemisms for acceptable violence conducted by states; discipline and correction are equivalents in domestic parlance. Both are related to authority and its recognition, which give legitimacy to certain forms of violence. But can the levels of the private and public be linked?

Methodologically, the study of violence evokes dramatically different approaches. Historians classically analyze violence as a focus of conflict, a method of resolution, a moment of social and political definition and decision. Viewed from afar, violence marks major shifts, brings clarity to the confusions of history, and is perhaps too easily separated from suffering. Anthropology, in contrast, struggles with the personal immediacy and pain of violence. Participant-observer methods that are central to anthropology catch practitioners in ethical predicaments. How does one set out to study violence, which by definition is not wholly predictable? To participate in or observe violence places the researcher in impossible moral dilemmas, for the realities of being present virtually force witnesses to take sides. Donham goes a step further to analyze the ambivalence of too close an association with violence, the voyeuristic fascination with what some have called the pornography of violence. How can scholar-witnesses not be caught in a whipsaw between attraction and revulsion?

Political scientists, too, must confront their relationship to incidents of violence. Conflict is related in turn to policy and policy-making processes, to governance issues, to political control and power. As Frederick Cooper observed during the conference, scholars in the face of violence walk "a tight-rope between scholarly detachment and human engagement." Africanist scholars, despite their protests that shapers of foreign policy ignore their work, in fact do impact the thinking of those involved in national and international organs associated with African countries, including leaders in African states. Reflecting on warfare in Sudan and the activism of scholars who have observed and written about it over more than two decades, Sharon Hutchinson pointed out that scholarly mistakes may not have impacts in academic circles but that violence and terror can and do hurt people. What are academics' responsibilities to peoples whose lives they may impact violently through their work?

The subject of violence in Africa today, as in the Kenya of the 1950s, is informed, too, by the continued existence of folk constructions of Africa as a site of unbridled and irrational violence. This supposed African exceptionality makes a publication such as this a delicate enterprise. Violence, our participants agreed, is neither natural nor endemic to African cultures. When violence occurs, however, it often, but not always, begets violence. Yet as Donham points out, violence is not inevitable. Violence alone therefore is not a useful domain of inquiry. It is only through a close study of context that violence in Africa can be analyzed and understood. Yet if violence is not predictable, there are nevertheless patterns associated with it that may be discerned and examined. It is to those patterns that we now turn.

The State

The Kenyan Mau Mau Emergency serves as an extended metaphor for the state processes that are reflected in the essays included in this collection. The Mau Mau movement's fighters, young men and a few women, made sporadic attacks from the cover of forests in the White Highlands of Kenya. Like all guerrilla fighters, they depended for food and supplies on people, often women, who remained in villages and towns. Their immediate targets were various: white farmers, government installations, and black Kenyans and Kikuyu in particular who worked with the state or against whom the fighters felt grievances. Initially labeled terrorists, as if the word itself were sufficient explanation, the forest fighters were also said to be linked to the nationalist movement, which disavowed them yet found the fact of their rebellion useful in the long run.

The fighters were relatively rapidly defeated militarily, but they were captured only gradually, while at the same time large numbers of Kikuyu who participated only marginally were killed or taken into custody by colonial authorities. Meaning and memory were central concerns of the state, which in the 1950s detained thousands in an early attempt to achieve what by the end of the twentieth century would be called deprogramming. There was no need, for Kenyans have ever since endlessly debated the meanings of Mau Mau. Was it primordial rebellion against change promoted by a modernizing, civilizing state? Was it heroic nationalist protest against a colonial state in which a relative handful of Kikuyu sacrificed themselves for the sake of the nation? Was it the reaction of landless Kikuyu to developmentalist demands following the end of World War II? Was it a Kikuyu civil war in which the landless sought property from the landed? Explications by the fighters themselves in dozens of articles and memoirs have not achieved resolution, let alone grants of land for the fighters. However, the name of their force, the Land and Freedom Army, points to their concerns. Land, appropriated by the state and granted to settlers, had been an issue in the central highlands of Kenya for the entire colonial period. Freedom, it is often assumed, meant freedom *from* colonial rule, but it may also have meant freedom *to* act.

Luise White (1990) first called scholarly attention to the debates over domesticity held by fighters in the forest and described at length in their writings. John Lonsdale (2003) has expanded White's description into a compelling argument about what he terms "intimate unease." For Lonsdale, what concerned the Mau Mau fighters was what concerns all human beings always: the quotidian questions of freedom to live, to procreate, to build if not wealth at least a modicum of comfort, and to build a reputation and honor in a community. Freedom to live does not imply an atomistic existence; it is limited voluntarily by the need for "insurance," the support and protection of kinsmen, neighbors, and political protectors. It is also limited by the resources available to any given individual. These private strivings take place within a public hierarchy of gender, generation, and class. It was the nature of that hierarchy, which was made up of elaborate webs of relationship running vertically from home to nation, from individual to state, that preoccupied the forest fighters and became the subject of their debates. And that web and its nature continues to leave peoples everywhere engaged in debates about how life can and should be lived, about order at home and political structure in the state, about the intricacies of blood ties and the problems of international migration and global business. In short, intimate unease fosters debates about order and morality, about what can be tolerated and what must be changed. And concern about change or its absence is often associated with outbreaks of violence.

Mau Mau occurred in the context of the late colonial state, and in the case of Kenya, in a settler colony that had prospered during World War II and had shown both white settlers and Kikuyu farmers the potential for export agriculture. There, as elsewhere in Africa, the late colonial period was marked by developmentalist initiatives that among other things could justify colonial rule. These came with arduous physical demands, particularly on rural peoples, yet simultaneously raised expectations for change and prosperity. In Kenya, for example, rural development projects to combat soil erosion contributed to the frustrations that boiled over in association with Mau Mau.

Yet decolonization in Kenya and in the rest of Africa had little impact on state structures. In his contribution to this collection Donald Donham summarizes an argument about the nature of African polities as "gatekeeper states" that was first articulated by Fred Cooper (2002). Created by colonialism, the gatekeeper state left local systems of governance and authority mainly intact, allowing the colonial monopoly on power to assert itself in the crucial areas of state economic interest, in the processes that moved primary products toward the metropole and returned manufactured goods. The revenue bases of gatekeeper states were related in the main to external commerce:

import and export duties, licensing fees, and controls over cross-border travel. State revenues could support the relatively limited expenses of colonial governance. However, the post–World War II emphases on development initiatives changed the economic calculus, requiring massive investment in physical and human infrastructure. In the face of nationalist movements, the price of maintaining control combined with imperatives for development moved colonial authorities to a cold calculation of costs. Independence rapidly followed.

Faced with the difficulties of governance, postcolonial rulers opted to continue the form of the gatekeeper state, which, "lacking the external coercive capacity of its predecessor, was a vulnerable state, not a strong one. The stakes of controlling the gate were so high that various groups tried to grab it—officers or noncommissioned officers in the army, regional power brokers" (Cooper 2002, 5). In effect, those who came to power had no incentive to share or relinquish it, and patronage systems became the vehicle for the distribution of state resources downward to clients who worked to keep their leaders in control. At the same time, postcolonial states inherited administrative structures expanded in the wave of the late colonial developmentalist energy. Social services such as education and health care, which had been severely limited until late in the colonial period, were dramatically expanded and became baseline expectations of new citizens. These dual demands on state resources—developmentalist efforts and the maintenance of patronage systems—in the long run could not be sustained.

Nevertheless, the fragile economies and inelastic revenue streams of gatekeeper states sustained moderate growth until the oil crises of the 1970s. Then a downward spiral of economic decline became coupled with diminishing resources for state initiatives and increasing authoritarianism. By the mid-1980s interventions by international financial institutions were putting an official end to developmentalist efforts. Structural adjustment programs became the price for continued international support. They reduced patronage excesses but also dashed the hopes of many for adequate health care, educational opportunity, and salaried employment. With patronage channels blocked, or at least much reduced, many discredited rulers of effectively bankrupt polities were driven from office in a wave of democratization in the early 1990s. Others presided over states' collapse and their decline into warfare.

The first half of the decade of the 1990s suggests the range of responses to economic decline and political paralysis over much of Africa. They spanned a spectrum from hope to despair: constitutionalism and functioning democracy in Benin, Botswana, and Senegal; the collapse of the apartheid state in South Africa; failed attempts at electoral reform in Nigeria and Togo; government structures replaced by warlord rivalries in Somalia and Liberia; and liberal political reforms followed by genocide in Rwanda. Against this backdrop of inherited colonial state structures and a variety of outcomes to economic decline, some devastatingly violent and others peaceful, the papers of this collection offer glimpses into ways in which peoples in Africa have measured their levels of intimate unease, debated through words and actions the nature of their relationship to state structures, argued about the nature of the state and accountability, and made demands of those who would claim to govern.

Abdullahi an-Na'im has spoken of the paradox of sovereignty in postcolonial Africa. With independence, new states entered normative international communities that recognized their full authority in external affairs. At the same time, African states have often been incapable or unwilling to establish and maintain sovereignty within their national boundaries. The recent inability of the Sudanese state to restrain violence and maintain control in the province of Darfur, for example, was related not only to the actions of out-of-control militias and possible state collusion but also to the near-complete absence of state activity in the region, the lack of infrastructure, and the preoccupation of officials with the north-south settlement of civil war (An-Na'im 2004).

Endemic poverty, decaying infrastructure, debt, and health crises have made the establishment of internal sovereignty in much of Africa that much more difficult. And the problem of internal sovereignty is compounded by the easy flow of inexpensive weapons, particularly in the wake of the ending of the cold war, which make violent protest easy and lethal. External sovereignty, as Will Reno points out in the case of Sierra Leone, permits rulers to "make deals with outsiders to exploit resources," a phenomenon that applies to other resource-rich states such as Nigeria, the Democratic Republic of Congo, Liberia, or Angola. Meanwhile, local practices such as vigilantism, the subject of Daniel Jordan Smith's essay, have been tolerated in Nigeria, Cameroon, and South Africa, among other sites, on the grounds that the state was unable to protect its citizenry. Similarly, the gang warfare in urban South Africa that is the subject of Elaine Salo's essay reflects a degree of state weakness and a continuation of an apartheid state's strategy of encouraging informal local control over segregated districts.

The relationship of the state to violence is more complicated than a simple restatement of the Weberian model of the state and its right to monopolize coercive power. Indeed, separating state violence from nonstate violence and legitimating one or the other has been contested since the opening of the colonial period. Not only was colonialism established through violence, but African colonial states used excesses of violence in efforts to maintain control: forced labor and the collective punishment of communities, for example.

Nationalist movements and anticolonial critics such as Frantz Fanon argued that antigovernment violence was a legitimate response. Both state aggression and antistate violence have continued in the postcolonial period. And in the past fifteen years rebellions against African states have been legitimized by an international community that has insisted that state authorities negotiate to share power with rebel groups—in Mozambique, Liberia, Sierra Leone, and the Democratic Republic of Congo, to name a few examples.

William Reno's study of state collapse in Sierra Leone and Joanna Davidson's analysis of the relationship of a local dispute to state action show how lines of patronage and control can be involved in the complex working out of violent or potentially violent conflict. Reno argues that the predatory behavior characteristic of the Sierra Leone war can be traced back to the 1950s and attempts to manipulate access to economic opportunities associated with the mining of alluvial diamonds. Over the second half of the twentieth century Sierra Leone's rulers found that their interests lay in undermining the formal institutions of the state as they politicized and personalized control over the licensing of miners. Reno delineates two different patterns of response to the coming of war. In one, local strongmen were closely integrated into centralized political networks prior to the war, and predation was intense. In the other, local systems of authority remained relatively distant from the web of vertical links to national rulers, and chiefs were able to maintain greater order and protect their communities. Reno notes that predation was greatest in areas where rulers were from outside the area and there were no social consequences to their behavior. International intervention stopped the war, but no changes were made in the political networks that brought about state collapse in the first place. The dilemma remains: how to establish a state that provides services and uses resources for the benefit of the population as a whole.

At the heart of Reno's article lies the question of illegal diamond mining, frequently carried out by "stranger" youth from outside the diamond region and even from outside the country. Davidson similarly focuses on the problem of integrating "strangers" into a community in Guinea-Bissau. The proximate cause of the incident analyzed by her was the destruction in 2000 of a mosque built by Fula "strangers" in a Diola village, in which Muslims were in the minority. In fact, Fula had been resident in the town since the 1960s and had intermarried with Diola women, which would seem to follow well-known West African practices for the integration of outsiders (Brooks 1993). In this case, absorption of strangers proved transitory as state intervention failed to resolve the conflict over the mosque, and the resident Fula ended up elsewhere as refugees. Davidson notes that the dispute as viewed from outside stressed national concerns—ethnic conflict, religious strife, and the machinations of political patronage networks—while local people insisted that the proximate causes were associated only with land usage and violations of community norms. Her analysis resonates with Belinda Bozzoli's study of the changing constructions of a South African township rebellion when viewed from a national level, which also found that local complexities disappeared when causes of violence were assigned by outsiders.

Conference participants struggled with the relationship of ethnicity and religion to violence in other areas of Africa, most notably Sudan and Nigeria. While acknowledging that religious institutions, like other powerful bodies, can bring order or sponsor disorder, Timothy Longman stressed the ambivalent nature of religion, suggesting that people too easily accept the idea that religion alone promotes conflict. On the other hand, religious ideas may provide a template allowing violence to be cast in terms of cosmic conflict between right and wrong, good and evil. Several participants noted a popular perception in Nigeria that religion as a source of violent conflict is simply a smokescreen for ethnicity or regionalism. Speaking from the perspective of southeastern Nigeria, Daniel Jordan Smith noted that while southerners talk about northern adoption of shari'a as a kind of cover for a "Hausa" agenda, evangelical Protestantism is taking hold in ways that conflate religion and ethnicity among the Igbo. Fundamentalism, whether Christian or Islamic, with its clear moral standards and its sense of order, community, and security, was noted by conference participants as an attraction for youth, an observation that will be pursued shortly.

Davidson's careful look at how the local came to be interpreted in terms of "global" identity suggests other patterns with parallels elsewhere in African settings. As Donham observes, violence can "primordialize" identity, changing locally based disputes into morals about behaviors associated with ethnicity or religion, or regional and national origin. And, in a situation of limited resources, identity politics is often associated with powerful currents of zero-sum popular thinking. The expulsion of foreign, or "stranger," nationals has been carried out by African states—Ghana, Nigeria, and Côte d'Ivoire, for example—since early in the postcolonial period, on the grounds that they were a threat to national resources. Nigeria's religious and ethnic tensions can be read as conflicts over control of a finite resource base, the distribution of oil revenues. Dan Smith, in analyzing Igbo support of vigilantes, highlights the competing images of the state and its obligations. He describes contradictory popular ideas about accountability in governance: the belief in principles of fairness for all contrasting with the obligation of patron-rulers to support their clients. John Anene spoke in our discussions of the moral imperative that leaders use whatever means necessary to bring resources into ethnic spheres. On a popular level, and in states conceived as responsible only for processes that cross boundaries, including the exploitation of limited primary resources, zero-sum thinking means that one's allegiance and identity determine one's sole access to crucial resources.

Youth

The discourses that surrounded decolonization stressed youth. The young nations of Africa would emerge into modernity on the shoulders of youthful populations benefiting from the rapid expansion of Western schooling. The national leaders who took power with independence were relatively young, and developmentalist youth brigades were mobilized across the continent to serve communities and lead the less well educated into a future of prosperity. Youth at the time of independence was equated with modernity and hope.

The African renewals of the 1990s similarly focused on youth, but this time with youth constructed as danger and threat. The proportion of the African population within the fluctuating category called "youth" was variously estimated at 40 percent or more. Poorly educated and with few opportunities for salaried employment, youth were a smoldering fire ready to burn African urban areas. Muslim youth were being drawn to militant fundamentalist action, while children in the form of child soldiers weaned on drugs and violence or homeless street urchins learning criminal behavior were a volatile commodity.

Several points are relevant here. First, over the course of the twentieth century recurrent patterns of tension between generations and genders are discernible virtually everywhere in Africa. Indeed, African cultures struggle with the classic human problem of the generations, that fathers must get their sons to fight their battles and still remain subservient. If fathers' sense of self is related to control over daughters and sons, sons' coming of age arrives with wives to control. The jury is still out on the question of companionate marriage in Africa, but women there have shown a remarkable capacity to create autonomous lives while acquiescing in marital inequalities.

Early in the century the first generation of wage-earning African youth upset ideas about readiness for adulthood when they independently acquired cash for bridewealth. Western-educated youth proved able to interact with colonial authorities in ways that challenged their elders' authority. Yet the cure for youth is time. Once secure in power, the youthful leadership of decolonized African nations discovered the "traditional" importance of the wisdom of age. Elders in the 1920s and 1930s worked with colonial authorities to codify a "customary" law that would enshrine the authority of older men over women and younger men. Women found it in their interest to look forward to postmenopausal prerogatives.

Beneath and behind these struggles were genuine changes in cultures, carried on simultaneously at the levels of household and society, yet ideas about proper order remained. Responsible elders, both male and female, should accept authority and wield power responsibly. Youth will press against envelopes of control but ultimately need to yield to the responsibilities of age. But what if elders fail to preserve community resources? What are youth to do when they realize that there are no opportunities for a rewarding adulthood? The intimate unease of the 1950s forest fighters of Mau Mau is a close relative of the frustration of unemployed urban youth in the 1990s.

The essays by Martha Carey, Daniel Jordan Smith, and Elaine Salo explore the relationship of youth to violence in Sierra Leone, southeastern Nigeria, and South Africa, respectively. All three find patterns of behavior that reflect popular distrust of state authority and those who benefit from it. Paul Richards (1996) has argued that educated Sierra Leonean youth disillusioned with political leaders used violence as a form of discourse to force patrons in towns to respond to their needs. Carey goes beyond Richards in her analysis of what many might argue is an ultimate form of senseless atrocity, the meaning of the amputation of hands and arms during the Sierra Leonean wars of the 1990s. For Carey, generational conflict in the lessons of the myth of Musa Wo, an incarnation of the Mande culture hero Sundiata, lies behind youths' willingness to amputate. Understood in Sierra Leone as an unwanted son, but heir to a chief, Musa Wo revolts against his father, indulging in horrible acts of violence in order to restore his mother's good name and return order and social continuity to the community. In amputating innocents, youth perform the anarchic destructiveness of Musa Wo, warning the international community and their own leaders of the price of elders' irresponsibility.

Salo explores gang violence among youth in a changing South Africa. In the Cape Flats of the apartheid era, where race hierarchy reserved low-paying employment for colored women, responsible adulthood was associated with being female. Men and masculinity were defined spatially in the gang-controlled neighborhoods, where age hierarchies of male identity were associated with resistance to the state. In the postapartheid dominant ideology, men are breadwinners and women no longer have privileged access to housing or jobs. Without the restraints of women's authority, ganging occurs at younger ages and is tied into the international drug trade through advanced technology. In short, political liberalization has proved an invitation to the expansion of violence threatening the local community.

Youth violence is often condemned, or excused, as an excess of the age.

William Murphy points out that when the Revolutionary United Front (RUF) in Sierra Leone apologized for amputations, it blamed them on youth, the "young disenfranchised" (Murphy 2004).[1] Belinda Bozzoli shows that in the aftermath of the Alexandra Rebellion of 1986 in South Africa, youthful excesses were similarly blamed for violence. Yet Bozzoli also makes the point of youthful idealism, that youth had designed and were trying to implement a utopian response to state violence. Even the amputating youth of Sierra Leone, if one accepts Carey's argument, were trying to restore order, acting in a way meant to attract the attention of elders who had neglected their moral obligations. The Bakassi Boys of southeastern Nigeria were seen for a time as youth forced to intervene where elders had failed. Welcomed as impeccably honest and blessed with supernatural approval, these youths were expected to transform local law enforcement by their incorruptibility and their magical ability to expose criminals and mete out punishment. Sadly, their vigilantism channeled anger at wrongdoing toward local petty criminals rather than the elite political establishment guilty of massive misuse of state resources. The Bakassi Boys' fall came when they were perceived as associated with politicians, the failed elders whose example they had been expected to avoid.

Smith, in commenting on his work on the Bakassi Boys, reminded conference participants that generational conflict has limits as a category of analysis, for vast differences obtain within the categories of youth and elder. It is only a small elite who reap benefits from their positions of control at the top of the patrimonial pyramid of Nigeria, for example. Carey concurs in her description of the complex hierarchies of rank within Sierra Leone's initiation regime of Poro. And what is youth when the category is constantly shifting, an elastic grouping grown difficult because the young often cannot acquire the resources to move into a socially defined adulthood. At various times and places in twentieth-century Africa, literacy or Western education became a marker that placed the physically young above their chronological elders. In short, youth and elders, women and men, are categories of relationality that are tempered by education and class. Nevertheless, they represent deeply felt principles of moral order.

Memory

Problems of the study of violence extend also to memories of violence. What can we do with an overdose of memory, queried Fred Cooper during conference discussions. How can we deal with memories that are divergent, yet based on the undeniable experience of physical hurt, bodily violation, intense pain? Madeleine Fullard, who worked closely with South Africa's Truth and

Reconciliation Commission (TRC), observed that in the end she had left the TRC with a sense of disbelief, a profoundly unsettling recognition of the gap between the experiential and interpretive levels of violence. What is owed to victims of violence, and who should pay? Indeed, to what extent do terms like *violence* and *genocide* set conflict into inflexible dichotomies of victim and perpetrator, innocence and guilt, right and wrong? The TRC in its public hearings proved unable to acknowledge that those who ultimately suffered most might also have used violence in the course of struggle. Finally, how do neighbors, citizens of a single state, who must continue to interact with each other after violence ends, reconcile the past to the present?

The three essays that conclude this volume draw on recent constructions of memory, and focus exclusively on national memory and its association with violence. The essays by Belinda Bozzoli, Timothy Longman and Théoneste Rutagengwa, and Jocelyn Alexander and JoAnn McGregor all show the state through its organs, or through the ruling party, to be intent on shaping memory to its own vision and interests. They demonstrate as few examples can that memory and history are not synonymous. Cooper was perhaps strongest in his response to these three cases, arguing that the actions of states in all three represented travesties of history, political constructions that were not only inaccurate but alienating to the people whose history they were meant to represent. A close look at these cases suggests that the provision of an accurate historical account is at best secondary to the transformative goals of the politics of state as memory plays out over time in a political context.

In perhaps the most detailed elaboration of a historical event and its transformation through the rhetoric of politics, Bozzoli meticulously chronicles the shaping of the memory of the Alexandra township rebellion of 1986, which was in part a utopian youth rebellion against both the state and the older generation and in part a movement led by adult activists to create viable institutions for township self-government. In the South African national memory shaped by the TRC, the rebellion was transformed into a united community effort with nationalist objectives congruent with those of the African National Congress.

Longman and Rutagengwa describe efforts by the Rwandan government in the wake of the 1994 genocide to build national memory in such a way that the Tutsi minority would never again be subject to persecution. This new history argued that ethnic consciousness was virtually unknown in the precolonial past and that the divisions of Hutu, Tutsi, and Twa referred mainly to occupational categories. Ethnic tensions were systematically created in the colonial period and were used to set Hutu against Tutsi at the dawn of the postcolonial era. The goal of national reconciliation thus was to return to a precolonial "national" unity. In setting such a goal, the authors charge, the Tutsi-dominated state refused to confront its own recent history of abuses and established a double standard in human-rights enforcement that worked against reconciliation.

Alexander and McGregor, in their history of twenty-some years of changing memories of the war of liberation in Zimbabwean politics, trace complex state redrawings of the boundaries of nation that in the 1980s included elites and excluded the Ndebele, and then in the 1990s were reworked to include all rural Africans but to exclude the urban and educated, whites, Asians, and others associated with political opposition. The authors follow a group of former Zimbabwe People's Revolutionary Army (Zipra) guerrillas who found themselves able to forget the rivalries of the liberation struggle and their state-sponsored persecution in the 1980s as they embraced state patronage and state-sponsored violence in the interest of their own economic advancement.

The state, these essays suggest, at times tries to rework a violent past to demand silence and acquiescence even by those most impacted by violence. Interestingly, Longman and Rutagengwa observe that Rwandans, like the villagers in Davidson's story of conflict in Guinea-Bissau, blamed the genocide on bad politicians and greed, not on sweeping historical forces. In Rwanda as in South Africa, the survivors of violence longed for admissions of wrongdoing by those who had committed violent acts. They could conceive of moving forward if perpetrators could conceive of asking forgiveness. The rooting of the present in the particulars of neighborhood and the practicalities of gaining access to resources returns us to the level of intimate unease, to people's efforts to make a life for themselves, to find and use resources, and to live a moral, if not exemplary, life.

It is a truism that history is written by the victors. In these explorations of the drafting of memory by state initiative, the state appears triumphant in bending and forming nationalist sentiment to its vision. Yet the lessons of Mau Mau perhaps suggest something else, that in the longer term the right to rework and invoke memories of violence may and will be appropriated by people other than those who represent the state. In the years since Mau Mau, Kenyans have repeatedly invoked the movement in hundreds of settings and causes. Indeed, Mau Mau in Kenya has become a way to talk about the nature of the state and ideology, about what government should and can do. In the 1990s, when Kenya was immersed in a struggle about the nature of the state and the need for more democratic governance, Mau Mau became a multivalent metaphor for debates about the abuse of power, inequality, and the continued desire of people for land and freedom, for opportunities for self-actualization (Sabar-Friedman 1995). In assessing the meanings of Mau Mau,

John Lonsdale suggests the continuing salience of vertical relationships, of those links from individual Kenyans, and Africans, to national and international constraints and potentials (2003). Violence may not be inevitable, but its occurrence is not unrelated to inequalities of education and to inequalities of opportunity for the educated. The continuing failures of African states to widen forms of distribution of state wealth, and their inability to encourage institutional changes that would create wealth rather than simply exploit it, suggest that violence will remain a too-common response to local frustrations. Africans, young and old, need to be able to imagine a future that will be at least as good as the past of their parents.

Note

1. In a presentation made at the 2004 annual meeting of the African Studies Association, Murphy noted that all evidence indicated that the amputations had been organized. He argued that the meaning of amputation has to do with punishment, that ingratitude is unacceptable in a patrimonial system.

References

An Na'im, Abdullahi. 2004. Darfur Crisis: The World Responds. Lecture given at Emory University, Atlanta, 16 October.

Brooks, George. 1993. *Landlords and Strangers: Ecology, Society, and Trade in Western Africa, 1000–1630.* Boulder, CO: Westview.

Cooper, Frederick. 2002. *Africa since 1940: The Past of the Present.* Cambridge: Cambridge University Press.

Kaplan, Robert D. 1994. The Coming Anarchy: How Scarcity, Crime, Overpopulation, and Disease Are Rapidly Destroying the Social Fabric of Our Planet. *Atlantic Monthly,* February, 44–76.

Lonsdale, John. 2003. Authority, Gender, and Violence: The War within Mau Mau's Fight for Land and Freedom. In *Mau Mau and Nationhood: Arms, Authority, and Narration,* edited by E. S. Atieno Odhiambo and John Lonsdale, 46–75. Athens: Ohio University Press.

Murphy, William. 2004. Constructing the Meaning of Child Solders' Violence in the Accountability Practices of Liberian and Sierra Leonian Reconstruction. Paper presented at the annual meeting of the African Studies Association, New Orleans.

Richards, Paul. 1996. *Fighting for the Rain Forest: War, Youth, and Resources in Sierra Leone.* Oxford: James Currey.

Sabar-Friedman, Galia. 1995. The Mau Mau Myth. *Cahiers d'études africaines* 35 (1): 101–31.

White, Luise. 1990. Separating the Men from the Boys: Constructions of Gender, Sexuality, and Terrorism in Central Kenya, 1939–1959. *International Journal of African Historical Studies* 23 (1): 1–25.

Staring at Suffering
Violence as a Subject

DONALD L. DONHAM

> The trouble with Eichmann was precisely that so many were like him, and that the many were neither perverted nor sadistic, that they were, and still are, terribly and terrifying normal.
>
> —Hannah Arendt, *Eichmann in Jerusalem*

OVER the past two decades or so violence has become a subject in the cultural sciences in perhaps a new way.[1] Before, violent action was a potential within any number of fields, such as politics, ethnicity, or the family. With the exception of a literature on warfare and evolutionary theories of aggression, however, there was not much thought about violence in itself.

This situation has begun to change, and in retrospect the literary theorist Elaine Scarry's controversial book *The Body in Pain: The Making and Unmaking of the World* (1985) can perhaps be taken as a point of departure. Within anthropology, a number of ethnographies of violence have followed, perhaps the most successful of which has been Allen Feldman's *Formations of Violence: The Narrative of the Body and Political Terror in Northern Ireland* (1991). And these two strands of work, literary and anthropological, have begun to interact with a burgeoning historical literature on horrific events, for example, Christopher Browning's remarkable study of the Nazi murders of European Jews in *Ordinary Men: Reserve Police Battalion 101 and the Final Solution in Poland* (1998).

These individual studies and others have made their mark. But perhaps the surest indication that we have a new "subject" in the human sciences is the recent spate of collections and readers on violence.[2] In one of the best of these the anthropologists Nancy Scheper-Hughes and Philippe Bourgois introduce their subject as follows:

Violence is a slippery concept—nonlinear, productive, destructive, *and* reproductive. It is mimetic, like imitative magic or homeopathy. "Like produces like," that much we know. Violence gives birth to itself. So we can rightly speak of chains, spirals, and mirrors of violence—or, as we prefer—a continuum of violence. We all know, as though by rote, that wife beaters and sexual abusers were themselves usually beaten and abused. Repressive political regimes resting on terror/fear/torture are often mimetically reproduced by the same revolutionary militants determined to overthrow them. . . . Structural violence—the violence of poverty, hunger, social exclusion and humiliation—inevitably translates into intimate and domestic violence. (Scheper-Hughes and Bourgois 2004, 1)

This line of argument, which has become widespread of late, is perhaps most arrestingly presented in Pierre Bourdieu's assertion that there exists "a law of conservation of violence" (2000, 233). What goes around comes around.

When one turns from this way of approaching violence to the African continent, an immediate uneasiness sets in. Africa has long functioned in the European imagination as an essentially violent "darkness" that serves to define and to emphasize a rational "light," an enlightenment. European philosophers such as Kant and Hegel grounded the opposition between Africa and Europe in the belief that Africans lacked the same capacity to reason and thus to reach the universal. While such explicitly racist discourses are no longer so openly expressed, a series of horrendous post–cold war conflicts in Africa have been reported upon in a way that continues to construct Africa as an exception: Africa remains a space in which universal reason somehow does not operate and therefore in which "senseless" violence erupts. (I shall return to the connections between the notions of violence and rationality below.)

It would be easy, then, to line up new work on violence with a very old way of typifying Africa, as a space in which like produces like, in which structural violence produces physical violence, in which opposition to violence mimetically becomes violent itself, in short, in which Bourdieu's Law operates with a vengeance. But of course the very ease of making this connection immediately creates a dis-ease.

When we look more closely at Scheper-Hughes and Bourgois's formulation above, a curious mixture of confidence and conditionality appears: "We all know, as though by rote, that wife beaters and sexual abusers were themselves *usually* beaten and abused. Repressive political regimes resting on terror/fear/torture are *often* mimetically reproduced by the same revolutionary militants determined to overthrow them." And then more categorically: "Structural violence . . . *inevitably* translates into intimate and domestic violence."

The slipperiness that results is not unusual. In fact, it may be required to create violence as a subject in itself. Certainly it is required for Bourdieu's Law to be seen to hold (tautologically): Have an example of physical violence to analyze? Look for its roots in structural violence, since, as we all know, violence produces violence.

There is no doubt that the notion of structural violence has its uses. It reminds us of all the silent and unremarked-upon factors that, just as surely as the blow of a machete, snuff out life. And it is clear that factors such as exploitation can contribute to patterns of physical violence, though it is also clear that they do not always do so. And if we see that they do not always do so, then we, as analysts, are pushed toward finer understandings. An ambiguous and expansive notion of violence, combined with Bourdieu's Law, threatens to short-circuit and shortchange this complexity.

The present volume attempts, then, to dissolve violence into its contexts rather than to create it as an academic subject to be theorized (for an example of the latter, see Girard 1977). Accordingly, our approach begins with a relatively narrow definition: violence is force that directly threatens bodies and the bare life of bodies. Such force is variably culturally defined, employed differently in diverse political contexts, and depends in various ways upon economic conditions. However the cultural, the political, and the economic come together, we might say that violence is red:

The violent act, the violent event, is a bodily occurrence. It is the sharp flash against flesh, and it is the blood-colored response. The red act is a rape, the tearing of genitals and the bruising of forced arms and choked neck. The red event is a head aflame in a state-sanctioned execution. The spilling of human blood is the fact of violence, and in those instances where it is not spilled, it nevertheless remains as the flow of life barely kept from the blows or beating by the thinness of human skin. Because our lives are metered in the flow of blood at every moment, its appearance, its color, accompany attacks on our lives. Violence, act and event, is red. (Alfred Arteaga in Aldama 2003, vii)

Whatever the drawbacks of this characterization, its immediacy encourages an understanding that stays close to people's bodies and lives, that explores threat in its many instantiations, and that grapples with the stakes of remembering and forgetting forms of violence.

From this orientation, the following papers carry out a program of radical historicization in which incidents of violence are seen as the outcome of particular cultural, political, and economic struggles.[3] Contextualized, African violence can no longer be seen as an exception to universal reason. Whatever horrible events have occurred in postcolonial Africa, these, like those in Europe, such as the Holocaust, can be understood only as particular assemblages, as the result of cultural concepts put into action in political struggles that were themselves conditioned by economic realities.

Rationality and the State

A thought experiment will quickly illustrate just how entangled the category of violence is with other cultural assumptions. Can we imagine a current analyst in the human sciences (the case of creative writers may be different) who poses a problem as one of "violence," while adopting a positive attitude toward it? Does not speaking of "violence" always already contain a condemnation,[4] or at least the assumption of a historical counterfactual, an implied view that things could (and should) have turned out differently, that the violent outcome was not the only possible one?

David Riches, editor of one of the earliest anthropological collections on violence, noticed this embedding; he wrote that the very category of violence "strongly connotes behavior that is in some sense illegitimate or unacceptable." This means that *violence* "is very much a word of those who witness, or who are victims of certain acts, rather than of those who perform them" (1986, 1, 3).

We have, then, in the recent creation of violence as a subject, one different from, say, kinship or religion, in which analysts regularly take opposite stances toward their object of understanding. Religion can be seen as the opiate of the people, or it can be analyzed as the source of a society's deepest meanings. Simply posing a problem as one of "religion" does not determine the stance taken. The current subject of violence appears to be different. Earlier thinkers, like Georges Sorel, celebrated revolutionary violence, so it is possible to take a (limited) positive view, at least to the extent that violence is thought necessary to create a better (and ultimately nonviolent) society. Any number of cultural practices that involve risk to life, such as traditional initiation rites and modern forms of SM, or sadomasochism, are also thought to contribute to life in a fuller sense. What seems ipso facto impossible is a celebration of violence tout court, one that would negate all life.

What is the significance of this observation? It encourages us, I think, to take a next step and note, in reverse, that although great variation exists in this regard, there appears to be no human society that has uniformly condemned all forms of violence. Sociality itself seems to depend upon the threat of the application of some force in *some* circumstances. When legitimated, however, this violence becomes something else: the sanctioned and unmarked working out of a local form of what might be called (inexactly) "law." A child is punished. A criminal is imprisoned.

What is posed as violence is then always relative to the definitions of the legitimated sociality in which it occurs. In our time, that legitimated sociality is assumed to be the modern state. According to Max Weber's ideal type, the state has a monopoly over the uses of legitimate forms of coercion. And those forms of coercion are deployed in rational procedures, procedures designed to reach the truth, or to reach the closest possible approximation thereto. Truth-seeking legitimates forms of violence and turns them into "law." This means that our current notion of what counts as violence is fundamentally imbricated with ideals of the modern state. One cannot exist without the other. Violence is therefore always "senseless." It has to be, for violence is what falls outside the legitimated procedures of the modern state.

Increasingly over the last two decades, thinkers and activists have attempted to extend this notion of rationality beyond the boundaries of one state to encompass the notion of universal human rights. And here we may have come to the secret of the recent creation of violence as a subject. Just as in the modern state, so now across the globe, the category of violence is created by a notion of universal human reason. Violence is what transgresses reason and the reasonable procedures of truth-seeking and, lately, justifies the explosion worldwide of nongovernmental organizations, welfare, civic, and peacemaking groups, and so forth. In this vision, violence is always a problem even while it cannot be admitted that all forms of sociality require some form of violence (on the condition that it cannot be recognized as such).

Universal reason inevitably creates problems of understanding Africa, for of all world areas, Africa departs perhaps most fundamentally from the history of state-making in Europe (Herbst 2000). And of course it was the peculiar character of European state-making (Tilly 1985) that provided the conditions in which the notion of rationality, logically empty in and of itself, was filled in and given content. When that content is transferred to Africa, it creates a space of exception and lack in which senseless violence dominates all else. Nothing in the current European and North American imaginary sums up this tendency better than the icon of the twelve-year-old African boy soldier brandishing an AK-47, high on drugs, wearing designer sunglasses and a Tupac T-shirt.

While Weber's ideal type of the modern state has become hegemonic in the global system—when political elites speak, virtually everyone appears to assume, particularly after the end of the cold war, that Weber's kind of state is what the state *should* be—we have to realize that this ideal type describes political reality nowhere, not even in the developed "West." In operation, states, strong or weak, depend on various kinds of patronage systems, at times "private" security forces or underground mafias, "illegal" economic transactions, and so forth. As Fred Cooper pointed out in the discussions in the conference that led to this volume, it is considerably more revealing to compare the twentieth-century state in Africa with, say, city government in Chicago rather than with Weber's ideal typification.

If a category of violence, which varies, can be posited only in relation to a particular legitimated form of sociality, then in order to understand patterns of violence, we must also understand something of the relevant structures of sociality. Before colonial rule, African modes of sociality varied widely and waxed and waned over time. The social body—the group within which violence was suppressed through the threat of socially sanctioned violence (which was not seen as such)—ranged from a few hundred individuals, sometimes of the same "lineage," sometimes of the same "town," to many millions of people gathered in empires with allegiance to emperors. Even if, in the latter cases, emperors typically claimed the right over subjects' very lives—for Foucault (1978) and Agamben (1998) such power constitutes "sovereignty"—this claim was often more a fiction than an institutionalized practice. "Smaller," local forms of sovereignty continued to define rights and wrongs as long as certain minimal conditions were met, typically the flow of tribute to the center.

After the Berlin Conference of 1885, almost all of Africa was put under forms of formal colonial sovereignty. But as scholars such as Berry (1992), Cooper (2002), and Herbst (2000) have shown, colonial rulers, not unlike African kings, exercised power through a series of procedures that typically piggybacked onto older and "smaller" forms of sociality. Just how much change and how much continuity resulted in any particular community depended upon the exigencies of the historical process, but in Africa (unlike in Eurasia) it was always difficult to extend power over sparely concentrated cultivators linked by poor systems of communication.

This, then, was the kind of state—with power concentrated in a few centers but rapidly diminishing outside them, with the principal resources to be mobilized through what Cooper (2002, 156–90) has called gatekeeping—that African elites inherited when the process of decolonization began in the late 1950s. It is important to note that these new states entered into an international system that assumed the norms of modern statecraft, for example, that boundaries were precisely declared, that state institutions controlled legitimate force, and so forth. This was the facade that African states had to present to the outside world. Internally, however, such states functioned quite differently, and given these contradictions, they were inherently unstable:

> The gatekeeper state was vulnerable: it made the stakes of control at a single point too high. Politics was an either/or phenomenon at the national level; local government was almost everywhere given little autonomy. Leaders often saw opposition as "tribal," which could encourage regional leaders to accuse the "national" elite of being tribalist itself. Gatekeeper states' insistence on the unity of the people and the need for national discipline revealed the fragility of their all-or-nothing control. (Cooper 2002, 159)

Patterns of violence developed not only as national elites played games of winner take all but also as the forms of actually existing sovereignty came into collision. Violence according to one frame was not necessarily so according to another. As structural adjustment programs insisted upon by the International Monetary Fund undermined systems of patronage in some states and as the end of the cold war reoriented external relations in others, even the facade of the modern state crumbled in places like Somalia and Liberia.

In other words, to understand violence in Africa requires not just contextualization in time. It requires as well contextualization in space, for the national space in Africa was and is remarkably heterogeneous. Forms of sociality, or what I have called local sovereignties, stacked one upon another, and often the most effective of these were far smaller in scale than a nation. The insight to be gained from understanding forms of violence against the backdrop of these scales emerges in a number of the papers that follow.

Representation of Violence and the Problem of Excess

So far I have concentrated on the peculiar problems of analyzing violence in Africa. Let me turn now to two wider issues. The first is the problem of representing violence, any violence, and the second involves what I argue are the peculiar methodological challenges presented by an attempt to reconstruct and to explain violent events.

At the beginning of *Charred Lullabies,* an account of violence in Sri Lanka, E. Valentine Daniel asks, "How does an anthropologist write an ethnography of violence . . . without its becoming a pornography of violence?" (1996, 4). It is useful to pause and consider just how striking this question is. Had the subject been labor or politics, it is doubtful that an anxiety about appealing to so-called prurient interests would have occupied a beginning page. What are we to make of this comparison between writing about violence and writing about sex (see Harvey and Gow 1994)?

The answer appears to be that not all objects of representations are equal. Some by their very nature, by being so close to the flesh, incite greater intensity and complexity in reception, so much so that controlling signs becomes more than usually difficult for the writer. If, for example, the stated or implied aim of representing violence is somehow to oppose it, it is often asserted that certain kinds of representation can have the opposite effect—either to indulge readers' fascination and vicarious participation in violence or, after repeated consumption of images of human suffering, to dull all response.

As often as such claims are made, few writers in the humanities or social sciences have offered much evidence to back up their assertions. Unlike in other areas of contention, however, such a lack does not discourage the formation of strong opinion. For example, Arthur Kleinman has recently claimed that "the mediatization of violence and suffering [in the form of fundraising advertisements by humanitarian agencies in the United States] creates a form of inauthentic social experience: witnessing at a distance, a kind of voyeurism in which nothing is acutely at stake for the observer" (in Das et al 1997, 232).[5]

In the absence of much evidence, one point may perhaps be safely made, namely, that analysts of violence (not just Daniel) are often anxious about how their stories and pictures will be received, so much so that invocations of the dangers of "pornography" seem to be designed, as much as anything else, to undercut anticipated criticism. But the use of the label "pornography" may be misleading.[6] That the issue before us is actually different was brought home to me at a recent seminar when a senior anthropologist long involved with studies of violence commented that the work of another was interesting—"at least if you can believe him." The line drew immediate laughter, as if more than one person in the audience had had the same feeling.

The work being commented upon involved harrowing descriptions of the effects of violence upon the lives of poor peoples. It is perhaps important to note that it is extremely rare that anthropologists question the veracity of others' data. Unlike historians' archives, anthropologists' materials are so personal to begin with that typically they offer little basis for disagreement. But in this off-the-cuff remark the truth value of some of the most morally charged writing in the discipline was being questioned. What was going on here? Arguably, it was not that the writing in question appealed to readers' prurient interests. Rather, the stakes were if anything higher: whether or not the writing could be believed.

I would suggest that by associating himself so closely to the topic, by adopting such direct language, such an unflinching gaze, the author had caused the excess of the representational process to settle upon himself. In other words, readers had begun to ask themselves why the author had sought out such a topic. We all know that the world suffers. What personal drama was being played out here? Once such conjectures about the author are raised, they deconstruct representational processes much more efficiently than, say, internal contradiction. They demolish trust, and once such a shift has occurred, the object of representation is difficult to retrieve.

Anthropologists who rely upon participant observation in situations of violence face this issue with a peculiar intensity. At the beginning of *A Different Kind of War Story,* the anthropologist Carolyn Nordstrom complains:

One question I encounter from western audiences I find particularly offensive. Phrased both delicately and not so delicately, people want to know why I do this research. Do I get some kind of thrill from it? Is there some kind of adrenaline rush to studying violence? Have I become addicted to the excitement of the frontlines? Is there some kind of inescapable perverse fascination in horror? . . . I respond: Do you get some kind of thrill from studying market systems? Is there some kind of rush to investigating kinship? Is there an inescapable albeit perverse fascination in narrative? (1997, 19)

But this response ignores too much evidence that violence *is* a different kind of representational object than market systems or kinship. Violence is red. There is a kind of excess, an ambivalence of both attraction and repulsion, that does not affect other subjects. If this is so, then it may be that a self-conscious adaptation of representational strategies is called for.

Artists have long known, of course, that some presences are more compellingly portrayed by an absence presented in the right way. In Daniel's *Charred Lullabies* he returns to his native Sri Lanka to study folk songs but instead becomes caught up in the violence between Sinhala and Tamil. Notice how this particular "arrival" story accomplishes its rhetorical work in this ethnographic instance. It announces something like the following: I did not seek out this topic. It sought me out. I have tried not to write about this. But in the end, I could not *not* write. You (the reader) have not had such experiences, but in order to claim a common humanity with the rest of the world, it is important for you to understand something about what I am reluctantly going to tell you.

In this book about violence Daniel hardly ever describes actual instances. Had his subject been a market system or kinship, this lack would immediately have raised doubts: Did he do "enough" fieldwork? Did he understand what was going on? But in respect to violence, such thinness gathers about itself an all-too-believable thickness. In the few cases in which Daniel directly addresses violence, he quickly averts his eyes, changes the subject. Note how successfully the following description connects the reader to the event:

Piyadasa (a pseudonym) is a Sinhala in his twenties. I knew him as a young boy who played soccer in the town of Nawalapitiya, where I grew up. He lived in a village near Kotmale and used to ride the bus back and forth to his school with Tamil schoolchildren who came to Nawalapitiya from the tea estates. At times, after a game of soccer, he and his bus-mates would feel so famished that they would pool all their small change, including their bus fares, to buy buns and plantains from the local tea shop. Having eaten, they would start walking up the hill to Kotmale, all of six miles. His village now lies buried under the still waters of a reservoir built by the Swedes as part of the Mahhawali River damming project.

In 1983, the pantaram (the boy who makes garlands) of the local Hindu temple was killed. I was informed by another Sinhala man, a close friend of one of my brothers, that Piyadasa was among those who had killed the pantaram and he too had wielded a knife. I visited Piyadasa, who has been resettled in the North-Central Province, and asked him to describe to me what had happened. He denied that he had directly participated in the violence but was able to give me a detailed account of the event. The following are a few excerpts:

> He was hiding in the temple when we got there. The priest, he had run away. So they started breaking the gods. This boy, he was hiding behind some god. We caught him. Pulled him out. So he started begging, "Sami, don't hit. Sami, don't hit." He had urinated. He pleaded. "O gods that you are, why are you breaking the samis?" They pulled him out to the street. The nurses and orderlies were shouting from the hospital balcony. "Kill the Tamils! Kill the Tamils!" No one did anything. They all had these long knives and sticks. This boy was in the middle of the road. We were all going round and round him. For a long time. No one said anything. Then someone flung at him with a sword. Blood started gushing. . . . Then everyone started to cut him with their knives and beat him with their sticks. Someone brought a tire from the Brown and Company garage. There was petrol. We thought he was finished. So they piled him on the tire and set it aflame. And can you imagine, this fellow stood up with cut-up arms and all and stood like that, for a little while, then fell back into the fire.

The constant shifting from the including "we" to the excluding "they" is noteworthy. This was in the early days of my horror-story collecting, and I did not know what to say. So I asked him a question of absolutely irrelevance to the issue at hand. Heaven knows why I asked it; I must have desperately wanted to change the subject or pretend that we had been talking about something else all along. "What is your goal in life" I asked. The reply shot right back: "I want a video [VCR]." (Daniel 1996, 208–9)

But what is the underlying rationale of representation successfully carried out? Given the unusual moral valences involved in looking at violence, the impossibility of accepting violence as an unalloyed good, the answer has to be explanation, explanation that contains within it some depiction of the conjunction of factors that one hopes can be avoided in the future. On this point, Daniel's tendency to "turn away" is far from successful. It is, in fact, deadly: "Anyone who reads this book to find causes and their corollary, solutions, to what has come to be called the ethnic conflict, reads in vain. If there be solutions, they may well rest in forgetting the causes and remembering the carnage in 'paradise'" (Daniel 1996, 9). Unfortunately, not all causes have one-to-one corollaries in solutions. Would that the world were so simple. And forgetting or working through horror—not causes—is what is necessary for victims. But for those of us not involved as victims, who look at events like the Rwandan genocide, how can we *not* ask about its causes? What other justification is there for staring at suffering?

Without engaging questions of causality, Daniel's analysis, while successful in a strictly representational sense, lacks a certain sense of "seriousness." Without explanation, "looking" becomes only an intrusion and a further violation of other people's lives. The typical reader responds: How dare Daniels make a career out of other people's sufferings?

The Methodology of Explanation in Extraordinary Situations

If violence as a topic sets up peculiar pressures for explanation, it also creates unusual barriers to realizing it. Unlike the vicissitudes of representation, however, almost no one discusses methodology—how one collects information critically and connects it with propositions. Here, too, at least for anthropologists and political scientists (but not perhaps for historians), investigating violence presents far greater challenges than does studying topics like kinship or elections.

After all, one can calmly construct a plan to observe, to interview, and to collect "data" on patterns of kinship or electoral processes as they transpire across time. Methods can be devised to minimize potential biases and to avoid possible pitfalls. But episodes of violence hardly submit to such controls. Rather, a riot or pogrom or a murder occurs and then policemen and reporters arrive, only to be followed, at several removes, by an anthropologist, a political scientist, or, after yet more time has passed, a historian. The perpetrators of violence and those they can intimidate inevitably have every reason to obfuscate, to cover up, and to change the subject.

This means that almost no analyst of violence has actually observed the *process* of the creation of violence. (An examination of the exceptions suggests that firsthand observation under intense threat of danger does not help that much. In such situations the vision of a participant observer constricts and closes down rather than broadens and opens up (see, e.g., Philippe Bourgois in Scheper-Hughes and Bourgois 2004, 425–34). This means that "what happened" in any particular case of violence typically is established by after-the-fact narratives, most often by a combination of those affected by the violence who are either willing or chosen to speak; by members of the public sphere, such as reporters and newscasters, who may or may not gather information from as many different viewpoints as possible; and by agents of the state, such as policemen and judges, who may or may not have agendas of their own. Anthropologists or political scientists who arrive later can conduct their own interviews, of course, but these necessarily take place in relation to an always already narrated event.

This "after-the-factness" about narratives of violence is not sufficiently problematized. That is, the "data" of violence are produced by a local cultural and political process quite different from the protocols of social science. Historians, of course, are well aware of the problems of reconstructing events on the basis of "found" data, but many anthropologists and political scientists are not (and for most topics they do not need to be). For example, in *The Deadly Ethnic Riot,* a book of almost six hundred pages, the political scientist Donald L. Horowitz devotes approximately six pages to a consideration of the materials on which he will generalize in the rest of the book. He writes with a kind of matter-of-fact confidence:

Adequate reports exist for approximately 150 riots in 50 countries. All but a few of these episodes took place in the post–World War II period, and the majority are from the period from 1965 to 2000. There is, of course, some unevenness of detail in the data sources. For many incidents, there are complete accounts covering all the questions to be pursued, in multiple sources that lend themselves to factual cross-checking; for others, there is useful material on only some of the issues. The immediate precipitants of riots, for example, are almost universally described at some length, whereas the planning of violence, where planning is present, tends to be clandestine and thus less frequently reported in detail. In virtually every case, there is more than one source, and in all there is some good assurance of reliability. The data on each episode are far more extensive and much higher in quality than the usual events— data sources, which tend to rely on the international press and events—data banks. (2001, 29–30)

The adequacy of materials can of course only be assessed in relation to the types of questions being posed. In any case, Horowitz appears to assume that what might be called the epistemology of everyday life—how one knows what one knows about routine and repetitive social interactions—can be transferred to the epistemology of the extraordinary.

I would suggest that it cannot. Violence is red. It overtakes and over-whelms. It disorients and disrupts. Under threat, with palm sweating, mouth dry, the throat so tight that it cannot scream, the body no longer calmly observes. "Being there" no longer provides the usual guarantees of narrative reliability. What happened? Is this the man who raped you? We know that victims can be both absolutely certain in their identifications of attackers and wrong. In the end, we must accept this as one of the crucial properties of violence: it has the inherent potential to "unmake" the social world, to create murk and uncertainty (see Scarry 1985; and Taussig 1984). Sometimes analysts will not be able to rise above this murkiness, and pretending to do so may be one of the most serious kinds of misrepresentations of violence.

If this presents an uncomfortable situation for analysts—we do not like to emphasize what we do not know—it is often exquisitely so for persons caught up in a violent episode. What happened? With so much more at stake than "analysis," participants often have to assign meanings. They have to narrate (see Jackson 2002; and LaCapra 2001). And in such situations it is not un-common for simplified yet widely shared stories to make sense to people. The Zulus attacked the Xhosa. In such a situation, simple cross-checking across sources will not provide methodological guarantees.

The point is this: violence, because it creates uncertainty, also establishes the seedbed in which people can change their attitudes, commitments, and identities. In this sense, it can "speed up" history. This means that narratives created *after* violence, particularly by victims, can unconsciously project back upon the past attitudes and identities in fact created by the experience of violence (Malkki 1995; Rosaldo 1989). In such narratives the "projected" past marches toward the present as what are arguably outcomes are understood as preexisting causes.

This tendency to read the present (after violence) into the past necessarily overemphasizes and overplays the role of hatred of the other as an explana-tion of violence. Nothing "primordializes" identity more efficiently than the personal experience of violence, especially violence that appears to be directed at one's group *as* a group. After that part of one's identity suddenly becomes literally a matter of life and death, what was previously lightly worn—"I am a Zulu," "I am a Jew"—can become far more determinative. And as it does, the transformation of the present requires for most people a reorganization of the past as events and incidences are renarrated and fit into new narrative constructions.

The analyst of violence, consciously or not, steps into this fast-moving stream, with all of its undertows and crosscurrents. And analysis itself—after all, only another narrative in a world of narratives—can "join" a conflict, and the analyst can become virtually indistinguishable from a participant.[7] I do not mean to suggest that political "neutrality" is possible or even desirable. Rather, what I have argued in this section is that analysts distinguish themselves from participants to the degree that they deal critically and self-consciously with the demands posed by the epistemology of extraordinary situations. That means retrieving the complexities of a situation that the experience of violence nearly always simplifies.

Conclusion

In many ways violent acts are "limit" events, both for social actors and for cultural analysts. Precisely for that reason, they put the understanding of repetitive, unmarked, and everyday life in a different light.

Charlotte Delbo, a Frenchwoman who survived Auschwitz, described the following scene:

A woman dragged by two others, holding on to her arms. A Jewish woman. She does not want to be taken to Block 25. [Block 25 was the holding barrack for women condemned to the gas.] She resists. Her knees scrape the ground. Her clothing, pulled up by the tug of her sleeves, is wound out behind her, fastened to her ankles. A flayed frog. Her loins are exposed, her emaciated buttocks, soiled by blood and pus, are dotted with hollows.

> *She is howling. Her knees are lacerated by the gravel.*
> *Try to look. Just try and see. (Quoted in Clendinnen 1999, 54)*

After repeating this passage, Inga Clendinnen responds rhetorically, "But why should we look, how dare we look, at such degradation? What are we meant to learn from this viewing of a fellow human *in extremis*?" Clendinnen goes on:

There are a number of answers to that question. One is prudential: this knowledge is not useless but essential. Two women are dragging the one we have been made to see. Who are they? Why do they do what they are doing? Such things were done because men and women willed them and were able to implement their will. We would be fools not to try to understand as precisely as we are able how that situation came about.

There is also . . . a deeper moral imperative. These things were done—some survived to tell what had been done. We, to whom such things have not been done, have an obligation to be attentive. In another context the English critic Michael Wood has written of the "unusual but not impossible demands" the dead make upon the living. This is one of those demands—unusual, close to unendurable, but surely, not impossible? (54–55)

Clendinnen wrote these words while she herself was slowly dying from cancer. Her own situation, rather than narrowing her view, seems only to have widened and deepened it. Her questions about causes, almost unendurable but not impossible to answer, are the ones we need to attempt to answer in studies of violence.

Notes

While writing this essay, I learned of the death of one of my first PhD students, Alexander Naty. In his mid-forties, an Eritrean teaching at the University of Asmara, Alex had been dismissed from his university post after attending an Ethiopian studies conference in Germany. Even if cerebral malaria was the "final" cause of his death, the stress and humiliation of his dismissal must have contributed to it. Alex was a cosmopolitan with a sly humor, a polyglot with a remarkable ability to adapt to different cultural contexts. Even though he got along with everyone, his skills did not, in the end, protect him in postwar Eritrea.

"Eritrea," of course, did not exist as such in the nineteenth century. It was only a part of the cultural core of the Abyssinian Empire. Yet in 1998 people who saw themselves as Eritreans and Ethiopians began a war that would kill an estimated one hundred thousand people, waste millions of dollars, and entrain a series of continuing tensions.

Alex's death was a part of the wake created by that war, and it has reminded me yet again of the stakes of understanding violent events. As Inga Clendinnen wrote of the Holocaust, "We need to know both ourselves and the world we are capable of making if we can hope to change any part of either" (1999, 16).

1. In another sense, of course, violence is an old topic, one that seems to recur after particularly troubling historical experiences. In this connection, one thinks of Walter Benjamin writing after World War I and Hannah Arendt writing after World War II (Benjamin 1920–21/1978; Arendt 1965, 1970).

2. An incomplete list would include Aldama 2003; Besteman 2001; Das 1990; Das et al. 1997; Das et al. 2001; Hinton 2002a, 2002b; Kleinman, Das, and Lock 1997; Peluso and Watts 2001; Riches 1986; Robben and Suárez-Orozco 2000; Scheper-Hughes and Bourgois 2004; and Schmidt and Schröder 2001.

3. For examples of analyses that attempt to carry out such a program, see, among others, Brass 1997; Des Forges 1999; Ferme 2001; Hansen 2001; Kapferer 1988; Mamdani 2001; Stewart and Strathern 2002; Tambiah 1996; Taylor 1999; and Uvin 1998.

4. This moral content seems to provide the basis for the real attraction of the idea of structural violence. If class exploitation, for example, is accepted as a form of violence, then surely its negative aspects can be appreciated.

5. In a fascinating ethnographic examination of images of violent death in Thailand, Alan Klima (2002) shows exactly the reverse: how such images connected and mobilized Thais in struggles against military dictators.

6. Lynn Hunt argues that the concept of pornography arose in Europe at the end of the eighteenth century and at the beginning of the nineteenth and that it highlighted an anxiety not only that representation could sexually arouse but also, more crucially, that such arousal could be extended, inappropriately, to the poor and to women. In this sense, the notion of pornography was "a response to the perceived menace of the democratization of culture" (1996, 13).

7. Has, for example, the all-too-easy popularity of Holocaust museums in the United States contributed to an uncritical American support of Israeli policies, policies that sometimes spawn yet more violence? And do they contribute to a defense and deflection from dealing with forms of violence far closer to home, to racial slavery and to the near extermination of native North Americans? These are Peter Novick's questions (1999), and they make the politics of, for example, labor history wistfully and attractively simple by comparison.

References

Agamben, Giorgio. 1998. *Homo Sacer: Sovereign Power and Bare Life.* Translated by Daniel Heller-Roazen. Stanford: Stanford University Press.

Aldama, Arturo J., ed. 2003. *Violence and the Body: Race, Gender, and the State.* Bloomington: Indiana University Press.

Arendt, Hannah. 1965. *Eichmann in Jerusalem: A Report on the Banality of Evil.* Revised ed. New York: Penguin.

———. 1970. *On Violence.* New York: Harcourt Brace.

Benjamin, Walter. 1920–21. Critique of Violence. In *Reflections: Essays, Aphorisms, Autobiographical Writings,* edited by Peter Demetz, translated by Edmund Jephcott, 277–300. New York: Schocken Books, 1978.

Berry, Sara. 1992. Hegemony on a Shoestring: Indirect Rule and Access to Agricultural Land. *Africa* 62:327–55.

Besteman, Catherine, ed. 2001. *Violence: A Reader.* New York: New York University Press.

Bourdieu, Pierre. 2000. *Pascalian Meditations.* Translated by Richard Nice. Stanford: Stanford University Press.

Brass, Paul R. 1997. *Theft of an Idol: Text and Context in the Representation of Collective Violence.* Princeton, NJ: Princeton University Press.

Browning, Christopher R. 1998. *Ordinary Men: Reserve Police Battalion 101 and the Final Solution in Poland.* 2nd ed. New York: Harper.

Clendinnen, Inga. 1999. *Reading the Holocaust.* Cambridge: Cambridge University Press.

Cooper, Frederick. 2002. *Africa since 1940: The Past of the Present.* Cambridge: Cambridge University Press.

Daniel, E. Valentine. 1996. *Charred Lullabies: Chapters in an Anthropography of Violence.* Princeton, NJ: Princeton University Press.

Das, Veena, ed. 1990. *Mirrors of Violence: Communities, Riots, and Survivors in South Asia.* New Delhi: Oxford University Press.

Das, Veena, Arthur Kleinman, Margaret Lock, Mamphela Ramphele, and Pamela Reynolds, eds. 2001. *Remaking a World: Violence, Social Suffering, and Recovery.* Berkeley and Los Angeles: University of California Press.

Das, Veena, Arthur Kleinman, Mamphela Ramphele, and Pamela Reynolds, eds. 1997. *Violence and Subjectivity.* Berkeley and Los Angeles: University of California Press.

Des Forges, Alison. 1999. *"Leave None to Tell the Story": Genocide in Rwanda.* New York: Human Rights Watch.

De Vries, Hent, and Samuel Weber, eds. 1997. *Violence, Identity, and Self-Determination.* Stanford: Stanford University Press.

Feldman, Allen. 1991. *Formations of Violence: The Narrative of the Body and Political Terror in Northern Ireland.* Chicago: University of Chicago Press.

Ferme, Mariane C. 2001. *The Underneath of Things: Violence, History, and the Everyday in Sierra Leone.* Berkeley and Los Angeles: University of California Press.

Foucault, Michel. 1978. *The History of Sexuality: An Introduction.* Translated by Robert Hurley. New York: Vintage Books.

Girard, René. 1977. *Violence and the Sacred.* Translated by Patrick Gregory. Baltimore: Johns Hopkins University Press.

Hansen, Thomas Blom. 2001. *Wages of Violence: Naming and Identity in Postcolonial Bombay.* Princeton, NJ: Princeton University Press.

Harvey, Penelope, and Peter Gow, eds. 1994. *Sex and Violence: Issues in Representation and Experience.* London: Routledge.

Herbst, Jeffrey. 2000. *States and Power in Africa: Comparative Lessons in Authority and Control.* Princeton, NJ: Princeton University Press.

Hinton, Alexander Laban, ed. 2002a. *Annihilating Difference: The Anthropology of Genocide.* Berkeley and Los Angeles: University of California Press.

———. 2002b. *Genocide: An Anthropological Reader.* Oxford: Blackwell.

Horowitz, Donald L. 2001. *The Deadly Ethnic Riot.* Berkeley and Los Angeles: University of California Press.

Hunt, Lynn, ed. 1996. *The Invention of Pornography: Obscenity and the Origins of Modernity, 1500–1800.* New York: Zone Books.

Jackson, Michael. 2002. *The Politics of Storytelling: Violence, Transgression, and Intersubjectivity.* Copenhagen: Museum Tusculanum Press.

Kapferer, Bruce. 1988. *Legends of People, Myths of State: Violence, Intolerance, and Political Culture in Sri Lanka and Australia.* Washington, DC: Smithsonian Institution Press.

Kleinman, Arthur, Veena Das, and Margaret Lock, eds. 1997. *Social Suffering.* Berkeley and Los Angeles: University of California Press.

Klima, Alan. 2002. *The Funeral Casino: Meditation, Massacre, and Exchange with the Dead in Thailand.* Princeton, NJ: Princeton University Press.

LaCapra, Dominick. 2001. *Writing History, Writing Trauma.* Baltimore: Johns Hopkins University Press.

Malkki, Liisa. 1995. *Purity and Exile: Violence, Memory, and National Cosmology among Hutu Refugees in Tanzania.* Chicago: University of Chicago Press.

Mamdani, Mahmood. 2001. *When Victims Become Killers: Colonialism, Nativism, and the Genocide in Rwanda.* Princeton, NJ: Princeton University Press.

Nordstrom, Carolyn. 1997. *A Different Kind of War Story.* Philadelphia: University of Pennsylvania Press.

Nordstrom, Carolyn, and JoAnn Martin, eds. 1992. *The Paths to Domination, Resistance, and Terror.* Berkeley and Los Angeles: University of California Press.

Novick, Peter. 1999. *The Holocaust in American Life.* Boston: Houghton Mifflin.

Peluso, Nancy Lee, and Michael Watts, eds. 2001. *Violent Environments.* Ithaca, NY: Cornell University Press.

Riches, David, ed. 1986. *The Anthropology of Violence.* Oxford: Blackwell.

Robben, Antonius C. G. M., and Marcela M. Suárez-Orozco, eds. 2000. *Cultures under Siege: Collective Violence and Trauma.* Cambridge: Cambridge University Press.

Rosaldo, Renato. 1989. Grief and a Headhunter's Rage. In *Culture and Truth: The Remaking of Social Analysis,* 1–21. Boston: Beacon.

Scarry, Elaine. 1985. *The Body in Pain: The Making and Unmaking of the World.* New York: Oxford University Press.

Scheper-Hughes, Nancy, and Philippe Bourgois, eds. 2004. *Violence in War and Peace: An Anthology.* Oxford: Blackwell.

Schmidt, Bettina E., and Ingo W. Schröder, eds. 2001. *Anthropology of Violence and Conflict.* London: Routledge.

Stewart, Pamela J., and Andrew Strathern. 2002. *Violence and Ethnography.* London: Continuum.

Tambiah, Stanley J. 1996. *Leveling Crowds: Ethnonationalist Conflicts and Collective Violence in South Asia.* Berkeley and Los Angeles: University of California Press.

Taussig, Michael. 1984. Culture of Terror, Space of Death: Roger Casement's Putumayo Report and the Explanation of Torture. *Comparative Studies in Society and History* 26:467–97.

Taylor, Christopher S. 1999. *Sacrifice as Terror: The Rwandan Genocide of 1994.* Oxford: Berg.

Tilly, Charles. 1985. War Making and State Making as Crime. In *Bringing the State Back In,* edited by Peter Evans, D. Rueschemeyer, and Theda Skocpol, 169–91. Cambridge: Cambridge University Press.

Uvin, Peter. 1998. *Aiding Violence: The Development Enterprise in Rwanda.* West Hartford, CT: Kumarian.

Modern States and the
Local Definition of Insiders/Outsiders

The Political Economy of Order amidst Predation in Sierra Leone

WILLIAM RENO

THE January 2002 agreement between Sierra Leone's army, the Revolutionary United Front (RUF), the quasi-official Civil Defense Forces (CDF), and others ended an eleven-year war that exemplified recent violent internal conflicts afflicting some of the world's poorest states. One set of analyses finds causes of these wars in demographic trends and failures of local cultures to adapt to the complexities of modern global society. The journalist Robert Kaplan wrote: "In cities in six West African countries I saw similar young men everywhere—hordes of them. They were like loose molecules in a very unstable social fluid, a fluid that was clearly on the verge of igniting." He complained that "young men with restless, scanning eyes surrounded my taxi, putting their hands all over the windows" (1994, 44). Samuel Huntington echoed his pessimism, noting "an immense youth bulge in most Muslim countries, where the proportion of the population between the ages of fifteen and twenty-five exceeds 20 percent of the total. And when that happens . . . there's usually trouble of some sort" (1997).

Concerns about idle youth are old. "The problem of unemployment among youths has been a matter of urgency for many years in Africa, Asia, and Latin America," wrote Peter Hodge (1964, 113). Lord Baden-Powell, the founder of the Boy Scouts, wrote: "With the introduction of European rule the tribal system was largely broken down. . . . If you take former hunters and warriors away from their kraals and traditional discipline and place them as workers in mines and cities, with freedom from moral constraints, you thrust upon them the temptations and vices of the underworld of civilisation without having given them any education in character for facing these" (1936, 369).

An alternative explanation for violence in the poorest countries focuses on the economic interests of fighters and finds causes of warfare in competition between armed groups for resources and opportunities to prey upon noncombatants (Collier 2000; Collier and Hoeffler 2002). The disappearance of effective state authority means that combatants often come under the control of small groups of well-armed thugs, "often drunken criminal and hooligan elements" who overwhelm people fighting for other reasons (Mueller 2000, 43). Sierra Leone's diamond trade, which generated an estimated illicit income of $150 million to $250 million in a country with an official gross domestic product of only $636 million in 2000, thus attracted predators. Unlike Kaplan's "loose molecules," this approach focuses on rational motivations among fighters that included trading diamonds for weapons with Charles Taylor, president of neighboring Liberia, and various overseas criminal groups (*Economist Intelligence Unit* 2001, 32; Smillie, Gberie, and Hazleton 2000; United Nations 2000, 4).

The social impact of this fighting was severe. During a peak in fighting in 1999 about six hundred thousand of Sierra Leone's 5 million people fled to neighboring countries. Two-thirds of those who remained were displaced inside Sierra Leone (ICG 2001, 2). State administration nearly collapsed as official internal revenues fell to about $10 million in 2000, 4 percent of revenues twenty-five years earlier (African Development Bank 2003, 292; Government of Sierra Leone 2001, 12; IMF 1990, 243). Sierra Leone's experience mirrors conflicts in countries such as Congo, Guinea-Bissau, Liberia, and Côte d'Ivoire, where armed groups overwhelm what is left of state administration. Both approaches, however, pay little particular attention to underlying social structures that shape patterns of violence. In particular, neither explains why some people do not loot in situations when others do, nor why widespread violent predation appeared when it did and not at other times when ample opportunities existed.

The Argument

Violent competition during the 1990s to control natural resources played a key role in provoking mass flight and in breaking down state administration. I stress in the historical analysis below, however, that predation in fact emerged in distinctive patterns as a consequence of particular political strategies that predate Sierra Leone's war. Violent political networks, many dating to the 1950s, created a social context in which key officials supported militarized clandestine commerce in natural resources. This politics, from the late colonial era, then more so after the establishment of a single-party state in 1978, relied upon a network of personal rule. After independence in 1961 this network developed behind the facade of sovereign statehood. It was not based upon conventional concepts of legitimacy or on supporting formal bureaucratic institutions. Instead, Sierra Leone's leaders controlled commerce, especially in diamonds, and manipulated citizens' access to economic opportunities to enhance their power during the long prewar period of relative stability.

The fact that high officials found it in their interests to undermine the institutions of their own state shaped this patronage-based political strategy. Since global recognition of their sovereignty provided these officials with the means to make deals with outsiders to exploit resources, they did not need to build an efficient army or civil ministries that could challenge their personal economic and political power. In any event, Sierra Leone's rulers found that they could weather the collapse of their own state. They recruited armed gangs to maintain coercive control over markets that sustained patronage networks while choking off the autonomous social space for political organizing that truly free markets would provide. Like the predatory armed groups that arose in the 1990s, this political organization was deeply rooted in exploiting diamonds. As before the war, most violent groups exercised political power in their own right through controlling markets, not through building administrations or mobilizing citizens. They became more violent, however, as the centralized patronage network fragmented, removing a disciplining force and unleashing competition among former presidential associates and newcomers.

Historical roots of violence in Sierra Leone (and in other collapsed states) raise broader issues. Not until the twentieth century did European-style sovereign states cover the entire globe. Is this historically unusual situation coming to an end, a symptom of which is state failure? Is associated conflict distinctive, especially in the nature of violence it directed toward civilian communities? Have armed groups in these wars lost the capacity to regulate violence, control predations of their members, and provide public goods to communities, or does the availability of "conflict diamonds" and other connections to global economic opportunities preclude these strategies? If so, future state-building efforts in less regulated arenas of the world economy will be difficult and halting.

Yet despite the weakness of many states in Africa, some accounts of violence, not just in Sierra Leone but also in Guinea-Bissau, Côte d'Ivoire,

Liberia, Congo, Somalia, Sudan, Afghanistan, parts of the Caucasus, and elsewhere, reveal that some armed groups actively promote the productivity of their "victims" under certain social structural contexts, even amidst pervasive disorder. Charles Tilly explained how creating political order was not a uniform process. If some people could withhold resources from their "oppressors," warlords recognized rights and granted other compromises that limited their personal opportunities for predation (Tilly 1992). Order emerged when self-seeking violent entrepreneurs traded freedom to loot for the long-term prospect of protecting their most productive victims in return for payments, a much larger absolute gain for both (Olson 1993).

It is easier to understand why Sierra Leone's army and the RUF ultimately failed to protect local people who shared members' disdain for the country's corrupt politicians. But why did some Sierra Leone fighters who found themselves in very similar circumstances protect their communities? Those groups' exploitation of natural resources and close ties to criminal rackets show that such activities do not automatically lead to predation. Likewise, Somalia suffers a legacy of patronage-based rule and destruction of state institutions. Even so, Somalia's better-endowed north saw the emergence of a local administration, while Mogadishu remains a city where warlords clash frequently and maintain tenuous control over the militias of allied subclans (United Nations 2003, par. 27). Economic incentives fail to explain why Afghanistan's Taliban cut opium production by 96 percent between 2000 and 2001, giving up about $100 million as they faced well-armed warlord rivals (UNDCP 2001, iii, 11). These and many other cases show the limits of generalizing from the behavior of those armed groups that do grab resources and prey upon local communities.

These diverse outcomes are compatible with an analysis that attributes predatory behavior to specific elements of political authority and state collapse prior to conflicts rather than mainly to the economic character of natural resources or to the frustrations of alienated youth trapped in a spiral of official corruption. They suggest that conflicts following state collapse illustrate multiple social uses of violence and predation. In the following sections I examine this social development in Sierra Leone's war and explain why some groups preyed on their communities, while groups in adjacent diamond-mining areas showed a greater tendency to use violence in ways that provided public goods—especially security—to home areas. Variation in wartime behavior is linked to actors' situations in the prewar political economy of state collapse. Thus, state collapse can generate predatory violence, but it does not preclude other political uses of wartime violence. Regions where local strongmen were more closely integrated into centralized prewar political networks experience more predatory uses of violence in wartime. Strongmen who occupied more marginal positions in prewar political networks employ different social capital during wartime, resulting in less predatory uses of violence (even if they engage in widespread abuses of human rights). The origins and length of incumbency of local strongmen is important too. Those from outside local communities and more recent arrivals to politics tend to adopt more predatory strategies in wartime.

These developments raise important questions about contemporary global norms, especially those human-rights norms that fail to acknowledge differential uses of violence among combatant groups in wars that follow state collapse. It is possible that some groups may use violence to forge new social bonds in a manner more reminiscent of early modern Europe's successful state builders than of the socially destructive predators that feature in most accounts of contemporary wars.

In the analysis that follows I point out that what might appear to be predatory violence may exhibit an organization that reflects underlying social structures of order. In this, recent developments that shock the conscience of the world community are not especially novel (Kalyvas 2001). This shock may reflect more freely available information and evaluations in the context of norms that are fairly new. A deeper analysis is needed to understand what happens in places like Sierra Leone and for guiding international reactions to it. For example, if violence in Sierra Leone's war really was a consequence of unrestrained predation and if order could not be restored through indigenous means, long-term international intervention is essential. This situation more generally may call for the establishment of protectorates over collapsing states (Fearon and Laitin 2004). But if at least some of this violence emerges from a varied set of emerging social relationships, it may be that societies in subordinate positions in the world political economy are capable of establishing stable and at least passably legitimate political authorities able to manage the challenges of regulating political competition and economic transactions.

Patronage, Resources, and the Uses of Violence

Income from Sierra Leone's alluvial diamonds, discovered in 1930, generated revenue for state services and investment. This occurred even though these diamonds were accessible to people equipped with hand tools, and thus easily smuggled. The diamonds soon attracted armed groups, less because of an innate character of diamonds than because of state policies. Even so, as late as the 1970s few would single out Sierra Leone as a candidate for state failure, in part because of its steady income from diamonds. In 1959, for example, the royal commissioner for Sierra Leone reported that "by the end of the war in 1945–46, the revenue of Sierra Leone was £3 million, but due to the diamond boom of 1955–57 the revenue rose to about £10 to £11 million" (Cotay 1959, 213).

But, by the 1980s, a study reported that "most of the services provided by the government have deteriorated sharply." Electrical blackouts were common. "The level of repair of roads has grown extremely bad. . . . Salaries and wages have declined dramatically in real terms and have remained unpaid for months at a time" (Fyle 1993, 17). And with the start of the war in 1991, conditions grew even worse. By 1995 the fight against the RUF absorbed 75 percent of official spending (Karimu 1995, 10).

This prewar recession of state capabilities highlights the centrality of local struggles to control natural resources to the capacity of a remote central government to impose its political order, a dilemma that points as much to distinctive features of the state as to the character of the resources. The primary difficulty facing development-minded officials in the capital was that the commercialization of alluvial diamonds occurred in a colonial legal context that preserved and reshaped social distinctions between migrants and original inhabitants. This meant that colonial statutes accentuated the precarious elements of the customary social standing of newcomers, forcing them into a vulnerable and permanent "stranger" category, which reinforced their need to seek protection from local strongmen. Previously, local chiefs and headmen had regularly reviewed land-use rights, but strangers had customarily married into local lineages, reducing their patrons' power over them (Conteh 1979, 59–69). More broadly, this legal regime gave local chiefs economic power, which they translated into a role in postcolonial administration.

Soon after the discovery of diamonds, clandestine mining, known officially as illicit diamond mining (IDM), began in Kono and Kenema districts. IDM attracted young men from all over Sierra Leone and from neighboring West African territories. Their arrival alarmed colonial officials, who feared the political and social consequence of mobile job-seekers, echoing contemporary concerns about idle, economically expectant urban youth and their roles in the proliferation of informal commercial rackets. These newcomers helped create clandestine cross-border trade networks that would play an important role in supplying arms and military support to RUF fighters in the 1990s. The governor of Sierra Leone, Sir Maurice Dorman, observed in December 1958 that "chiefs have not controlled entry of strangers as effectively as was hoped. Stories are frequently repeated of large sums being paid to Chiefs for a permit. As much as £300 is quoted. As a result, there are something like 20,000 Sierra Leone people and 5,000 foreigners in Kono" (Dorman 1958c). Others estimated as many as 35,000 outsiders and Kono people mined diamonds during the 1950s and 1960s, while the colonial government claimed that in the whole country 75,000 people engaged in mining in 1956, the majority of them illegally (Sierra Leone, Department of Mines 1957, 4; van der Laan 1965, 10–11).

These newcomers had to appeal to local chiefs, not only to gain access to diamonds, but now for protection from Freetown officials. Their arrival also had a dramatic demographic impact on Kono, where they were 43 percent of inhabitants in 1963, and 48 percent by 1970 (King 1975, 62). In addition to extracting informal "license fees" and "fines" from young men in return for protection for their IDM activities, politically savvy chiefs manipulated the widespread local sentiment that diamonds really belonged to Kono people, keeping their "stranger" clients in a permanently vulnerable position. A foreign mining company reported that "the vast majority if not all of the employees have an exaggerated impression of the value of the diamonds mined by the company. These factors loom vary large and give rise to widespread discontent" (Perry 1959), an attitude that undermined control of even those employed to protect this important source of official revenue.

Even so, the colonial government preferred to have a large foreign firm mine diamonds, ensuring regular payments of royalties and taxes, rather than rely on its own officials to regulate this vital economic sector. Anglo-Americans started working a large concession in the mid-1930s, employing armed security guards to confront IDM poachers. After 1956, Freetown officials tried to co-opt local IDM activities into a licensing system to entice clandestine operators into state-regulated channels. Sierra Leone's foreign creditors preferred this strategy prior to the war's start in 1991, and it resurfaced in recent prescriptions to rebuild government revenue capacity where corruption hinders official efforts to monitor small-scale enterprises (IMF, African Department 2004, 16).

But foreign investment aggravated conflicts between IDM miners, chiefs, and national authorities. Chiefs had built up local political power by controlling their IDM strangers and using them to marshal support for their preferred local headmen candidates and to intervene in disputes in neighboring areas. These strangers needed a chief's favor, since a chief could use the illegal nature of their activity to call upon Freetown officials to prosecute noncompliant guests. This arrangement cemented chiefs' informal social control over young men and diamond resources. It went against the interests and sanctions of the state, yet it was tolerated by many local people who resented government appropriation of "their" resources, and it was accepted by most strangers so long as chiefs controlled access to mining opportunities. It was when outsiders, such as the Freetown government or agents of foreign firms, interlopers in the view of strangers and indigenes alike, came to the diamond fields to do business that conflict worsened in the 1950s.

The government's 1956 decision to license small-scale miners initially grew from British fears that party politics in advance of independence would give voice to the demands of radical local and stranger youth for a share of the diamond resources. Many local people already favored "the continuous propaganda of the Kono Progressive Movement which is igniting Konos against the company," in the words of the then acting governor, Maurice Dorman (Dorman 1958a). In the wake of serious riots in 1955 and 1956, Freetown officials also feared that "with the diamond boom and other economic developments" local challenges to state authority were "not due to a noticeable increase in oppression but to a change in attitude from one of consent or tolerance to one of bitter resentment" (Government of Sierra Leone 1956, 7). More broadly, they feared that IDM "would bring much needed wealth to Guinea, and if there were any closer rapprochement with Communist countries, our diamonds could reach them through Guinea" (Dorman 1958b). While licensing required chiefs' cooperation, it was intended to weaken informal structures of chief control over IDM. But instead of its strengthening central administrative control, those who administered the policy shifted political resources to the new national parties and to powerful emerging politicians. The large, moderate Sierra Leone Peoples Party (SLPP), for example, used its tacit British support and its control over the state administration in the late 1950s to distribute diamond-mining licenses to party loyalists. Given British worries about communist influence, this behavior—which became a pattern in later decades—was tolerated (Sierra Leone Intelligence Committee 1959).

Despite the SLPP's roots in the IDM economy, in 1967 the All Peoples Congress (APC), under the leadership of Siaka Stevens, was elected. An army coup d'état blocked Stevens from taking office until a countercoup enforced the election's result in 1968. He then quickly shifted the legal right to grant mining licenses from chiefs to the Ministry of Mines in order to award licenses to loyal supporters more aggressively than the SLPP had done. Chiefs who supported the SLPP lost out as new licenses went to those who convincingly switched loyalties or were installed in office by the APC (Zack-Williams 1995, 164–66). Control of licensing gave Stevens a more certain tool to manage local associates than the unreliable army that earlier prevented him from taking office would offer. This strategy was vindicated in April 1971, when coup plotters entered his residence before bodyguards fought them off. Stevens thereafter limited the army to just fifteen hundred men. Tighter control over formal regulations and informal clandestine arrangements in the mining industry (now a central element in the strategies of key politicians) also gave Stevens greater influence over armed IDM gangs, to intimidate political opponents, so much so that some APC parliamentarians complained that thugs in the youth section of the APC intimidated constituents and extorted money, undermining the parliamentarians' own support among local people (Government of Sierra Leone 1969).

Chiefs in mining areas had to decide whether to side with Stevens. If they did, they had to give up their direct control over IDM and bear the political cost of suppressing opposition-party activity among their own people. But the circumstances of local authorities facing the new APC varied, even though IDM occurred both in Kono and in areas downstream from Kono, out to the sea. Though alluvial mining takes place in both regions, Kono also has hard-rock mining and buried alluvial deposits away from rivers. This distribution of resources meant that upstream deposits included diamonds that were more difficult to get without substantial capital investments and the involvement of outside firms, and therefore those resources were more easily managed by politicians from Freetown, who could use their official positions to attract large-scale private business partners. Downstream deposits are readily accessible by mining gangs with hand tools, an operation more amenable to local coordination of youth gangs and clandestine businessmen, though this type of deposit occurs upstream too. Conventional wisdom would consider this type of operation to be more susceptible to predation and attractive to armed gangs from outside the region and thus to pose a greater threat of social disruption. But this would assume that those who control the state also have an interest in limiting the private exercise of violence, a condition that did not pertain in Sierra Leone at that time.

In fact, in 1973 Stevens targeted upstream deposits for what he billed as an indigenization of foreign mining concessions. This move gave chiefs in that area positions in state-sanctioned joint ventures with businessmen and politicians dependent upon Stevens's favor and further concentrated distribution of the region's diamond wealth in the president's hands. The scheme also gave upriver political networks new opportunities to make a lot of money as partners in industrial-scale mining operations, though at the risk of hitching their political fortunes to politicians in the capital. Downstream chiefs and local officials were left to manage their IDM gangs, provided they showed sufficient loyalty to the ruling party. This difference in the approach of the APC regime was due in part to the relative absence downstream of large-scale opportunities that could be absorbed into Stevens's foreign business partnerships. Their marginalization also reflected the suspicion that Stevens harbored toward chiefs, who had tended to favor his rivals prior to his 1968 rise to power. Thus, from a prewar perspective, downstream chiefs faced uncertain prospects for getting rich through political ties to the president.

This prewar pattern of patronage shaped chiefs' social control over violence in the 1990s. IDM and youth gangs were more likely to collaborate with the RUF in places where prewar chiefs grew more dependent on the politically connected clandestine economy. In those same places, outside armed youth (including soldiers) also mined with more impunity. In downstream areas, during wartime some local authorities had the capacity to channel youth violence into home-guard units to defend communities. Although local strongmen downstream before the war appeared to follow self-interested agendas as vigorously as those in Kono, they used their social control to organize mining in ways that contributed to greater security for local people in wartime. Upstream chiefs and IDM gangs operated outside this context and thus behaved in a more predatory fashion vis-à-vis local communities before the war. The consequences of these different social relationships, especially with regard to the position of young men, grew more pronounced once war began.

Prewar clandestine businesses in individual chiefdoms reflected these differences. The chief of Kono's Nimikoro chiefdom, for example, moved into alluvial operations with associates of the president after 1968 and joined large-scale mining joint ventures (Rosen 1974). Stevens also interfered in the selection of new chiefs. A Kono chief who supported the SLPP was deposed in 1971 and replaced with a former mining company security guard who lacked strong local support. This chief was unpopular among IDM gangs in the early 1970s. "It was a case of this chief against the (illicit) miners," said the former provincial secretary of Eastern Province in 2001 (Interview 2001). The chief's unpopularity persisted through the 1980s as he joined Stevens's business partners at the expense of small-scale IDM gangs; and in 1992 RUF and IDM gangs chased him away and destroyed his house. This may explain the affinity of IDM gangs in this chiefdom for the RUF when rebel agents first appeared in this area in 1992. The RUF could tap into local grievances about chiefs who relied upon connections to Freetown to stay in power at the expense of local people's clandestine access to diamonds. This gave the RUF a tool to recruit local IDM miners who were disgruntled about their limited access to "their" diamonds and who condemned local chiefs who failed to behave as good patrons.

Prior to the war, however, Stevens was able to protect his client chiefs, which gave allied chiefs the political autonomy to defy the interests of local people. In 1982 a Kono chief shot a popular local critic of the president. The district officer recommended suspending the chief during the criminal investigation (District officer, Kono 1982). The president feared that his opponents might "capitalize on his fate and cause chaos and confusion in the chiefdom with a view toward disposing of him" (Government of Sierra Leone 1982) and later ordered that the case be dropped. But Stevens did remove a recalcitrant Kono chief in 1982 when an ethnic Lebanese business partner of the president set up his own large-scale mining operations in the chiefdom. Local miners rioted when they discovered that their former patron could no longer protect them from the business interests of Freetown officials who demanded that the new chief chase off the IDM gangs. Another Kono chief, installed in 1981, headed the newly nationalized diamond-mining corporation. Consequently, he had bad relations with IDM gangs and relied upon armed forces and APC youth gangs dispatched from the capital for his protection (*Africa Confidential* 1982).

Downriver, a government administrator complained that local chiefs and IDM gangs were "total SLPP," forcing Freetown officials to tread more carefully. This did not protect downriver communities from interference. Alpha Lavalie, a founder of the CDF in the early 1990s, wrote that the APC "condoned, perhaps even encouraged, chiefdom uprisings which entailed intimidation and coercion," mobilizing otherwise idle youths under the supervision of APC stalwarts to intimidate candidates who attempted to contest nominations for single-party elections (Lavalie 1983, 12). He noted that APC organizers brought youths from outside the area rather than make use of local idle youths. The APC's need to recruit outsiders reflected the success of local notables in "organizing an anti-APC campaign based on the use of Poro," a customary male initiation society through which "the SLPP was able to unify all its supporters in Mende land to drive out from their areas imported APC supporters" (Lavalie 1985, 80).

Lavalie's observations show the centrality of the positions of the local leadership in predatory state patronage networks for shaping the social context for the local exercise of violence. Though downriver communities were deeply involved in IDM, local chiefs generally kept greater political and social distance from the emerging APC-controlled elements of the clandestine economy than their Kono colleagues did. These chiefs did not necessarily dislike the president; rather, their former political associations made them suspect in presidential eyes, and they controlled resources that were less accessible to a centrally organized patronage network. Given a choice, some might have wished to enjoy presidential favor. Downriver chiefs also faced serious challenges from youth violence directed against them. In the long run, however, they maintained greater leverage over local youth through influence over long-established informal institutions such as an initiation society and patronage to local IDM operations rooted in their own stranger-landlord custom. This political distance from Freetown politicians gave local chiefs less income, but it enabled them to behave in a locally legitimate manner as patrons for IDM gangs since they did not have to heed directives from Freetown partners that would have forced IDM gangs off their land.

This connection between IDM and community interests became more significant in 1986, when local aspirants challenged externally imposed candidates in single-party elections. They rounded up local youths, including IDM miners, and armed them to defend local communities. Local militias emerged as these youths were recruited with help from religious authorities and organized as "traditional hunters" associated with initiation societies. This practice gave fighters a high level of commitment and a stake in obeying local social strictures regulating violence to protect local communities (Ferme 1999).

Urban society in Sierra Leone also showed how different configurations of social control over resources shaped the nature of youth violence. Armed APC youth and the Internal Security Unit (ISU), a presidential guard, attacked University of Sierra Leone students who protested in 1977 against the president and a precipitous economic decline. The ISU joined with local unemployed youth to repress students. The ISU and their local youth gang collaborators were accused even in the government-owned newspaper of "capitalizing on their position to harass innocent traders at night, attempting assault on women, and even going to the extent of store breaking" (*Daily Mail* 1977, 8).

This event showed the difficulties that an urban-based opposition to Stevens's rule faced in efforts to organize. Though some students tried to energize regime critics, their broad political ideas and strategies never emerged in the RUF. An observer of that era explains that the RUF later drew from "the largely unemployed and unemployable youths, mostly male, who live by their wits or who have one foot in what is generally referred to as the informal or underground economy" (Abdullah 1998, 207). The inability of the student movement to channel political protest or exert social control over this violence rendered it marginal to the war in the 1990s. Like youth in parts of the mining districts, urban youth had to calculate whether it was more advantageous to ally with politicians whom they considered to be odious for the sake of their own survival. Backing regime critics who did not control resources would leave followers vulnerable to politicians' militias and bereft of economic opportunities.

Stevens's control of new paramilitaries and youth gangs, though centralizing his patronage, gave him means to manipulate what was left of state institutions to loot the country's resources. He and an ethnic Lebanese partner, Jamil Said Mohammed, took over the state diamond-marketing monopoly in 1976 as a "private" operation. This left the two in control of up to $300 million (at 2001 prices) in diamond revenues. Stevens extended his personal control over state agencies for agricultural marketing, road transport, and oil refining.

The shift of resources to Stevens's personal control robbed state agencies of their ability to function as channels for patronage, making access to Stevens the primary vehicle for opportunity. Reflecting this shift, deficit spending jumped from about 50 percent of revenues in the mid-1970s to over 100 percent a decade later, which Stevens financed mainly through printing money, which spurred triple-digit inflation (IMF 1990, 173). The collapse of state services, accelerating inflation and mass impoverishment, reinforced the centrality of Stevens's control over clandestine markets that were important for people's survival strategies. Stevens retired in 1985, but not before handing power to Joseph Momoh, the commander of the weakened army. Stevens chose Momoh for his inability to threaten enterprises that presidential business partners had built in the clandestine economy. Momoh's lack of authority was reflected in the near-total collapse of official diamond exports by 1989 as Stevens's partners cemented their domination.

Momoh failed to build a political network capable of taking control over clandestine economic resources. Meanwhile, the government's accumulation of arrears led to a break between Freetown and the International Monetary Fund (IMF) in 1987 as some of Stevens's associates launched a coup attempt. Momoh had support in the army of about three thousand soldiers, many of whom existed only on paper so that commanders could collect additional salaries. He had little choice but to heed IMF pressure to address the government's growing arrears by reinstating corporate control over diamond-mining areas. Like colonial officials, IMF officials proposed that a large foreign firm could displace IDM and channel revenues to Freetown without building costly state institutions. A steady stream of revenues would pay Sierra Leone's debts and finance a smaller, more efficient bureaucracy. For Momoh, however, a large mining operation offered him the best chance to chase off Stevens's business partners, their local allies, and IDM gangs, and use those resources to ensure his own political survival. Finally, a U.S.-based firm promised to invest in a mining project in Kono on the condition that Sierra Leone's army remove IDM operators. In mid-1990 the army launched Operation Clean Sweep and Operation Clear All, forcing as many as thirty thousand IDM diggers out of the area. The vigor of the soldiers, many of whom did not receive a regular salary, reflected their eagerness to set up their own IDM operations or to go into business with the Freetown-based politician patrons on their own.

Stevens's political strategies and Momoh's troubles show how the mix of outside intervention and the organization of local patronage networks shaped how resources and violence were related once widespread conflict began.

Both the IMF and the president envisioned foreign firms contributing to a centralization of control over coercion and resources, though in different ways. IMF advisers wanted this to occur in a formal institutional framework, whereas the president preferred a reconstituted patronage network. In fact, outside intervention shifted control of resources to armed IDM gangs even more distant from central control. As young soldiers joined IDM gangs, they began to resemble even more strongly the groups that competed to control diamonds in the war that was to come.

Predation and Order

RUF fighters entered Sierra Leone from Liberia in March 1991 with help from Charles Taylor's fighters. To meet this threat, Momoh immediately increased his army to six thousand men, though his foreign minister admitted that most recruits were "drifters, rural and urban unemployed, a fair number of hooligans, drug addicts and thieves" (Gberie 1997, 153). Some frontline junior officers discovered that corrupt senior officers were diverting supplies meant for soldiers. Sergeant Valentine Strasser and other soldiers marched to Freetown in April 1992. Strasser's immediate concern was the absence of medical care; he allegedly had been injured in a battle with RUF fighters who had come upon his unit while they mined diamonds. Momoh's immediate reaction to demands from real soldiers was to flee to neighboring Guinea. Strasser and his associates set up a new regime and promised to defeat the RUF. By 1994, they had increased the army's numbers to fourteen thousand, recruiting more youths from armed gangs and criminal networks.

The expanded army, with help from Nigerian troops, managed to recapture the Kono mining district from RUF fighters in January 1993. But then many soldiers began to mine diamonds, sometimes in collaboration with RUF fighters, while the RUF developed a wider-ranging diamond business with its Liberian patron. "There developed," wrote a former National Provisional Ruling Council (NPRC) minister, "an extraordinary identity of interests between NPRC and RUF" in which "government soldiers by day become rebels by night" (Abraham 1997, 103). This simply reaffirmed for many Sierra Leoneans that the old connections between armed gangs and politicians persisted, especially in diamond mining. Most of the young officers who took power in the 1992 coup were among the marginalized youth who in other circumstances had sought the patronage of strongmen but now could act as their own bosses. As the RUF leader Foday Sankoh stated in his justification for the RUF's diamond mining, "They ask us why we mine diamonds. Why didn't they ask . . . Shaki [Siaka Stevens] that when the APC was in power?"

(Sankoh 2000). Thus, Sankoh criticized Freetown politicians as bad patrons, not because they appropriated resources, but because they did not take care of their "strangers." This was a potentially popular critique, but the predatory behavior of the RUF and Sankoh, echoing Stevens's strategy, left them unable to recruit a wide base of support.

The RUF's fortunes declined in April 1995 when Strasser's regime hired Executive Outcomes, a private South African security firm, to fight RUF rebels as they closed in on the capital. By December 1995, the firm had captured Kono's diamond mines from the RUF and was training fighters to keep downriver areas out of rebel hands. These anti-RUF fighters formed the core of the CDF as an official military force parallel to the army to help track rebels. These home-guard militias thus found a place in the strategies of Sierra Leone's presidents as they recognized that their army was almost as predatory and threatening as the RUF rebels were. The RUF faced defeat and accepted negotiations that led to the Abïdjan Agreement in November 1996 and a UN observer mission (United Nations 1996).

Domestic protests and international pressure had led to elections in February 1996, Sierra Leone's first multiparty presidential election since 1967, in which Ahmed Tejan Kabbah won. Immediately faced with IMF and donor pressure to stop spending the government's meager funds on Executive Outcomes, he told the firm to leave by early in 1997 (Hirsch 2001, 40). Then, on 25 May 1997 rebellious soldiers and RUF fighters conquered Freetown and created what many Sierra Leoneans called "the junta," with the army's Major Johnny Paul Kromah at its head and the RUF's Sankoh as his deputy. This regime forced civil servants to "donate" their efforts without payment, as fighters looted the city and human-rights abuses proliferated, and when civilians failed to comply, Armed Forces Revolutionary Council (AFRC) spokesmen announced that they would kill citizens and burn the city in Operation No Living Thing (U.S. Department of State 1998, 8). The civilian president returned only after Nigerian soldiers and CDF fighters defeated "the junta" in February 1998.

Those from the army who joined "the junta" behaved much like the RUF, looting and setting up roadblocks for the purpose of extortion. Many civilians saw little difference between soldiers, the RUF, and others who preyed upon civilians, but some CDF units used violence in different ways. During the December 1994 RUF attack on the downriver towns, the vigilantes that Lavalie and local chiefs organized under the rubric of religious authorities and initiation societies repelled the rebel invasion (Muana 1997). Though the CDF exploited ties of ethnic kinship in their home area, the survival of customs and the legitimacy of customary authorities who had regulated

IDM activities enabled them to integrate "stranger" youth into their organization. This denied RUF forces access to the social strata from which they commonly recruited members. It also ensured that local resources would be inaccessible to more predatory groups such as the RUF. This adaptation also continued to provide local chiefs with incentives to protect "their" strangers against politicians' predations. Local chiefs could make this choice only because they had been spared the degree of social disruption that the Freetown political and business elite's intrusion into commerce had caused in Kono's politics. Thus, prior political marginalization and then later pressures of war produced an armed group that mined diamonds while also maintaining order. This social context therefore limited the fragmentation and directed the self-interest of entrepreneurs that some scholars associate with war involving natural resources and the collapse of state institutions. Moreover, it showed that clandestine economies can contribute to order in some circumstances.

The CDF was not immune to predatory behavior. Once CDF units were deployed in areas removed from the social institutions that could impose penalties for misbehavior, more widespread CDF abuses of human rights occurred. This tendency showed the importance of a wide range of informal institutions, including chiefs' control of the clandestine regional economy for maintaining order where it did exist. As its absence shows, locally legitimate authority and its reciprocal social nature in the downriver communities was situated in the prewar positions of downriver communities in the wider prewar political network.

Outside intervention in Sierra Leone's war also influenced who would exercise social control over violence and how. As noted above, Liberia's president Charles Taylor had supported the RUF since the start of the war in 1991. This external support reinforced incentives for the RUF to simply loot communities in Sierra Leone to survive. Like chiefs in Kono in the 1970s under the APC, the RUF could rely on its distant patron to protect its access to diamond wealth and to provide military backing to chase off local people who opposed that arrangement (Hoffman 2003). As Stevens had done, the RUF and Taylor used foreign business connections to market diamonds and to supply weapons to fighters.

International recognition of Taylor's election as president of Liberia in 1997, after he warned that he would return to war if voters rejected him, reinforced his role as an external patron for diamond-mining rebels. Taylor saw that foreign recognition of his election and his access to Sierra Leone's diamonds could free him from any need to negotiate a social bargain with Liberia's citizens to rule. Even when military setbacks and international pressure forced the RUF to negotiate for peace, Taylor continued to aid the RUF. This arrangement ended in late 2001, when a British expeditionary force finally succeeded in backing UN peacekeeping troops and organizing CDF units to cut off RUF contracts with Taylor's forces and conquer the diamond-mining areas. Only then were rebels persuaded to hand over weapons to redeployed UN peacekeepers. British strategists also helped CDF units press the offensive against the RUF. By late 2001, 17,500 UN peacekeepers controlled most of the country, finally ending the war in January 2002.

Local Order versus Global Norms

Considerable expense characterizes international efforts to impose order in places like Sierra Leone. The UN deployment from 2000 to 2004 cost about $2.7 billion. The Special Court convened in 2003 under Security Council authorization is estimated to require a three-year budget of $60 million to prosecute war criminals, a multidonor trust fund called for contributions of $74 million to finance demobilization, and creditors in 2001 approved $950 million in debt service relief (United Nations 2002, 1, 3; cumulative peace-keeping expenses calculated from UN reports found at www.un.org/Docs/sc/index.html).

Aside from imposing order in Sierra Leone, intervention did little to change the distribution of resources that played a large role in shaping the country's war. This was owing in part to the recognition of foreign officials that the only way to limit the costs of intervention and bolster Sierra Leonean capabilities to pacify the country was to develop the government's revenue sources. Thus, intervenors support diamond-mining license schemes resembling the 1950s British effort to lure IDM operators into taxable channels. Like the earlier effort, current policy centralizes awards of licenses in Freetown. IDM gangs complain that politicians use this power to reward allies, as was the practice before the war. These gangs include ex-combatants who are eager to exploit one of the country's only sources of economic opportunity. Some of these miners join groups like the Movement of Concerned Kono Youth (MOCKY) and the Lower Bambara Youth Council (LBYC). These organizations mobilize youth from diamond-mining areas to resist the influx into the IDM sector of other young men who, like many MOCKY and LBYC members, are former combatants. MOCKY allegedly collaborated with local police units and CDF fighters to attack former RUF combatants and their families, and sought local political patrons, as opposed to predatory officials in the capital, to mine "their" diamonds (Human Rights Watch 2003), much as IDM miners and their protectors had in the 1950s.

Like British and prewar Sierra Leone officials, creditors advise that "capturing a substantial share of diamond mining rents in the form of taxes hinges mainly on attracting an international mining enterprise" (World Bank 2002, 9). Though large firms are interested in exploiting deep deposits, IDM gangs that I met fear that they will cordon off alluvial deposits and shift control of resources to the distant central government. A British-funded Anti-Corruption Commission also offers significant evidence that these resources continue to be distributed on a political basis determined in the capital. Since its establishment in 2000, the commission has reported corruption scandals involving several government ministers, all of whom have suffered mild reprimands and many of whom remain active in politics (Anti-Corruption Commission 2002).

Continued corruption leaves scant hope that government resources will be used to rebuild civil administration. Teachers in late 2001 waited for salary arrears of six to eight months. Rank-and-file civil servants earned about one dollar a day, equivalent to the UN definition of absolute poverty. In 2001 Sierra Leone had only eighteen judges to administer justice to five million citizens. Only one state employee dealt with local court matters outside of Freetown in 2002. The total judiciary payroll in 2001 amounted to only $215,000 (CHRI and Sierra Leone Bar Association 2002, 10, 12). Problems persisted in 2004, as a nongovernmental organization (NGO) reported that youths in mining areas resented "oppressive local cultures," especially chiefdom courts that levied arbitrary fines to extort cash (CARE 2004, 6).

This poor record of corruption and scarcity leaves reconstruction in the hands of local agents. Thus, local courts get rebuilt around existing social structures. The problem with this lies in the continued channeling of resources through old political networks. Though starved of formal revenues, politicians in the capital still find incentives to deal with local strongmen who will use their control over courts and law enforcement to favor business operators with connections in the capital at the expense of local miners. As ex-combatants, many of these miners evince little sympathy, especially from the international community, and often are defined as "thuggish youth" who threaten peace (United Nations 2002, 2).

Thus, at the cost of several billion dollars, international agencies have brought order to Sierra Leone by establishing a state (or UN) monopoly on violence. But this leaves political networks responsible for state collapse to control resources at the expense of local people's security and opportunity. The surest way to remove this threat is to build a real state administration that provides services to people and bases its claims on resources and control over economic opportunities in terms of their use for the benefit of the population as a whole. But this would be enormously expensive and would require intensive outside interference in administrative matters to reverse several decades of state decline. Foreign governments have already spent billions of dollars to bring fighting to an end in Sierra Leone. If they withdraw before a real state is established, war may resume. Sierra Leone may be a small and insignificant country, but its dilemma—whether to foster social revolution through direct foreign rule, intervene half-heartedly, or leave citizens to find their destinies on their own—provides lessons that are widely applicable elsewhere.

References

Abdullah, Ibrahim. 1998. Bush Path to Destruction: The Origin and Character of the Revolutionary United Front / Sierra Leone. *Journal of Modern African Studies* 36 (2): 203–35.

Abraham, Arthur. 1997. War and Transition to Peace: A Study of State Conspiracy in Perpetuating Armed Conflict. *Africa Development* 22 (3–4): 101–16.

Africa Confidential. 1982. 17 March.

African Development Bank. 2003. *African Development Report, 2003.* New York: Oxford University Press.

Anti-Corruption Commission. 2002. *Report Submitted to Parliament by the Anti-Corruption Commission.* Freetown.

Baden-Powell, Robert. 1936. A New Development in the Scout Movement in South Africa. *Journal of the Royal African Society* 35 (141): 368–71.

CARE. 2004. *No Rights, No Justice, More War.* Freetown.

Collier, Paul. 2000. Doing Well Out of War: An Economic Perspective. In *Greed and Grievance: Economic Agendas in Civil Wars,* 91–111. Boulder, CO: Lynne Rienner.

Collier, Paul, and Anke Hoeffler. 2002. On the Incidence of Civil Wars in Africa. *Journal of Conflict Resolution* 46 (1): 13–28.

Commonwealth Human Rights Initiative (CHRI) and Sierra Leone Bar Association. 2002. *In Pursuit of Justice: A Report on the Judiciary in Sierra Leone.* Freetown: CHRI.

Conteh, James Sorie. 1979. Diamond Mining and Kono Religious Institutions: A Study in Social Change. PhD diss., Indiana University.

Cotay, A. B. 1959. Sierra Leone in the Post-War World. *African Affairs* 58 (232): 210–20.

Daily Mail (Freetown). 1977. Halt Deteriorating Situation. 4 February.

District officer, Kono. 1982. Arrest of Paramount Chief of Gbense Chiefdom, Kono District. F/NA/405/1/2. 5 July.

Dorman, Maurice. 1958a. Telegram to secretary of state for colonies. Freetown. 6 October [PRO, CO 554/1508].

———. 1958b. Secret telegram to secretary of state for colonies. Freetown. 31 Dec. [PRO, CO 554/1508].

———. 1958c. Telegram to secretary of state for colonies. Freetown. 31 December [PRO, CO 554/1508].

Economist Intelligence Unit (Sierra Leone). 2001. September.

Fearon, James, and David Laitin. 2004. Neo-Trusteeship and the Problem of Weak States. *International Security* 28 (4): 5–43.

Ferme, Marianne. 1999. Studying *politisi:* The Dialogues of Publicity and Secrecy in Sierra Leone. In *Civil Society and Political Imagination in Africa,* edited by John Comaroff and Jean Comaroff, 160–91. Chicago: University of Chicago Press.

Fyle, C. Magbaily. 1993. The Political and Economic Scene in Three Decades of Independence, 1961–91. In *The State and the Provision of Social Services in Sierra Leone,* edited by Fyle, 1–19. Dakar: CODESRIA.

Gberie, Lansana. 1997. The May 25 Coup d'État in Sierra Leone: A Militariat Revolt? *Africa Development* 22 (3–4): 149–70.

Government of Sierra Leone. 1956. *Statement of the Sierra Leone Government on the Report of the Commission of Inquiry into the Disturbances in the Protectorate.* Freetown: Government Printing Department.

———. 1969. *Minute Paper.* Freetown. 14 January.

———. 1982. *Minute Paper.* Freetown. 14 July.

———. 2001. *Bulletin of Economic Trends.* Freetown: Government Printer.

Hirsch, John. 2001. *Sierra Leone: Diamonds and the Struggle for Democracy.* Boulder, CO: Lynne Rienner.

Hodge, Peter. 1964. The Ghana Workers Brigade: A Project for Unemployed Youth. *British Journal of Sociology* 15 (2): 113–28.

Hoffman, Danny. 2003. The Civilian Target in Sierra Leone and Liberia: Political Power, Military Strategy, and Humanitarian Intervention. Unpublished paper.

Human Rights Watch. 2003. Sierra Leone. *World Report, 2003.* New York.

Huntington, Samuel. 1997. Many World Orders. PBS Online NewsHour, 9 January. http://www.pbs.org/newshour/gergen/january97/order_1-10.html (accessed 3 December 2004).

International Crisis Group (ICG). 2001. *Sierra Leone: Time for a New Military and Political Strategy.* London.

International Monetary Fund (IMF). 1990. *Balance of Payments Statistics Yearbook.* Washington, DC.

International Monetary Fund (IMF). African Department. 2004. *Sierra Leone: Fourth Review under the Three-Year Arrangement under the Poverty Reduction and Growth Facility.* Washington, DC: International Monetary Fund. 5 February.

Interview. 2001. Former provincial secretary, Eastern Province, Freetown. 9 May.

Kalyvas, Stathis. 2001. "New" and "Old" Civil Wars: A Valid Distinction? *World Politics* 54 (1): 99–118.

Kaplan, Robert. 1994. The Coming Anarchy. *Atlantic Monthly,* February, 44–76.

Karimu, John. 1995. *Government Budget and Economic and Financial Policies for the Fiscal Year 1995/1996.* Freetown. 29 June.

King, David. 1975. Population Characteristics of Diamond Boom Towns in Kono. *Africana Research Bulletin* (Freetown), 60–75.

Lavalie, Alpha. 1983. SLPP: A Study of the Political History of the Sierra Leone Peoples Party with Particular Reference to the Period, 1968–1978. MA thesis, University of Sierra Leone.

————. 1985. Government and Opposition in Sierra Leone, 1968–1978. Paper presented at the Fourth Birmingham Sierra Leone Studies Forum, Birmingham, UK.

Muana, Patrick. 1997. The Kamajoi Militia: Civil War, Internal Displacement, and the Politics of Counter-Insurgency. *Africa Development* 22 (3–4): 77–100.

Mueller, John. 2000. The Banality of "Ethnic War." *International Security* 25 (1): 42–70.

Olson, Mancur. 1993. Dictatorship, Democracy, and Development. *American Political Science Review* 87 (3): 567–76.

Perry, E. 1959. Letter to Mr. Rowlands. 1 December [WAF 34/395/01, Strikes at the Sierra Leone Selection Trust's Diamond Mine at Yengema. PRO, CO 554/228].

Rosen, David. 1974. Diamonds, Diggers, and Chiefs: The Politics of Fragmentation in a West African Society. PhD diss., University of Illinois, Champaign-Urbana.

Sankoh, Foday. 2000. Speech delivered at Makeni, Sierra Leone. 1 February.

Sierra Leone. Department of Mines. 1957. *Report on the Mines Department, 1956.* Freetown: Government Printer.

Sierra Leone Intelligence Committee. 1959. Report [PRO, CO 554/1509]. Freetown. October.

Smillie, Ian, Lansana Gberie, and Ralph Hazleton. 2000. *The Heart of the Matter: Diamonds and Human Security.* Ottawa: Partnership Africa Canada.

Tilly, Charles. 1992. *Coercion, Capital, and European States, AD 990–1992.* Cambridge, MA: Blackwell.

United Nations. 1996. *A Peace Agreement between the Government of the Republic of Sierra Leone and the Revolutionary United Front of Sierra Leone.* New York.

————. 1998. *Second Progress Report of the Secretary General on the United Nations Observer Mission in Sierra Leone.* New York.

————. 2000. *Report of the Panel of Experts Appointed Pursuant to UN Security Council Resolution 1306 (2000), Paragraph 19 in Relation to Sierra Leone.* New York.

————. 2002. *Fifteenth Report of the Secretary-General on the United Nations Mission in Sierra Leone.* New York.

————. 2003. *Report of the Panel of Experts on Somalia Pursuant to Security-Council Resolution 1425 (2002).* New York. 24 February.

United Nations Drug Control Monitoring Programme (UNDCP). 2001. *Afghanistan Annual Opium Poppy Survey 2001.* Islamabad, Pakistan.

U.S. Department of State. 1998. *Sierra Leone Atrocities against Civilians.* Washington, DC: Bureau of Democracy, Human Rights, and Labor.

van der Laan, H. L. 1965. *The Sierra Leone Diamonds.* Oxford: Clarendon Press.

World Bank. 2002. *Transitional Support Strategy for the Republic of Sierra Leone.* Washington, DC.

Zack-Williams, A. B. 1995. *Tributors, Supporters, and Merchant Capital.* Aldershot, UK: Ashgate.

Rotten Fish

Polarization, Pluralism, and
Migrant-Host Relations in Guinea-Bissau

JOANNA DAVIDSON

O N 30 May 2000 the Diola population of Susana, a village in the extreme northwest of Guinea-Bissau, collectively demolished a mosque under construction by Susana's Fula population. After a Fula man attempted to intervene, the Diola group tore down three Fula houses. The Fula population gathered at Susana's army barracks, and upon the arrival of military reinforcements they were evacuated to the nearest town, where they remain today.

The physical violence in this episode was restricted to buildings. Although there were both threats and attempts to elevate the conflict to a more violent plane, these were fortunately circumvented. Some members of Susana's population were permanently removed from their homes, but no one died, and no one was even seriously injured. Only later did the Guinean police arrest and beat up several Diola men from Susana. The level and scale of the violence, compared with that in the rest of the continent, the region, or even recently in Guinea-Bissau itself, was relatively minor and forgettable. But if we put body counts aside, many of the same dynamics and problems that have led us to look at more gruesome events in other parts of the continent are also present, and equally problematic, in this case.[1]

In this essay, I examine some of the processes and events that led up to and followed the incident of 30 May. I explore the history of relations between

Fula and Diola in this area, the role of state authorities and national politics in shaping and interpreting events in Susana, and the different narratives
employed by people involved in the episode when they describe the conflict.
Detailing participants' and observers' narratives of this seemingly isolated
event exposes the extent to which it is enmeshed in a series of other violent
episodes, including Guinea-Bissau's anticolonial struggle, the postindependence violence of the one-party state, recent civil strife and military power,
long-term guerrilla warfare just across the Senegalese border, and the increasing autocratic brutality of postcolonial state power. References to all of these
events are woven seamlessly into residents' narratives about the Diola-Fula
conflict, and it becomes immediately apparent that in order to understand
Susana's day of destruction one must take into account these dimensions of
postcolonial experience in West Africa.

Although the conflict between Diola and Fula residents in Susana seems to
have clear-cut ethnic and religious dimensions, a microanalysis of the case reveals a more complicated and convoluted story. The incompetence and abuse
of power by a state-appointed local authority; the media focalization and
transvaluation (Tambiah 1996) of a complex story into an event framed along
ethnic and religious lines; the role of young men on both sides in exacerbating
tensions; and the fact that outside intervention and mediation efforts by state
authorities, military personnel, and other national political players divested
the situation of its local contours and molded it to fit often irrelevant—or
at least secondary—national concerns: all of these factors contributed to the
escalation and intensification of the conflict, which increasingly took on an
ethnicized tone, one not necessarily there to begin with. Such an understanding corroborates analyses of so-called ethnic conflicts from other parts of the
globe, as scholars have increasingly emphasized these dynamics in calling into
question primordial notions of ethnic-based animosity (Brass 1997; Daniel
1996; Malkki 1995; Mamdani 1996; Tambiah 1996; Wilmsen and McAllister
1996).

But although these factors help to situate and illuminate certain aspects
of the Susana conflict, they do not satisfactorily explain some of its more
troubling and enigmatic facets, particularly the continued insistence among
the Diola population on refusing to allow Fula families to return to Susana.
A deeper ethnographic analysis of the Diola-Fula conflict—through a consideration of microsocial interaction, migration stories, and some linguistic
twists and turns—reveals the extent to which structural and historical features
in Diola settlement patterns and precolonial processes for incorporation or
exclusion of strangers also help explain the seemingly rapid polarization between these two groups. By revisiting some earlier literature on ethnic polar-

ization and conflict (Simmel 1955; Kuper 1977; Southall 1971), I consider this case in light of the dynamics of distinction and exclusion based on perceived boundary confusion, rather than as primarily or exclusively the result of external manipulation of a fabricated and politicized sense of ethnicity.

The idea is not to regress into worn-out (and never particularly fruitful) debates over the primordial or constructed nature of ethnicity. Whether ethnic identity is constructed is beside the point; *of course* it is constructed. And of course ethnicity can be (and has been) manipulated for various political ends. But my goal is not to demonstrate, one more time, that ethnicity is the product of various efforts and inventions, that it is both traditional and modern, ephemeral and durable, affective and instrumental. Rather, a close analysis of this case, informed by broader ethnographic and historical patterns in the region, opens up the possibility of exploring dimensions of host-migrant (or landlord-stranger) relations through long-term ideas and practices of incorporation and exclusion. Ultimately, my explication of the Susana conflict both reinforces and challenges some current theories about ethnic conflict and in particular considers the possibility for pluralism in this region.

The Setting

Susana is the central village in Guinean Diola territory. Diola inhabit the coastal region of West Africa from the southern Gambia to the northwest corner of Guinea-Bissau, including the Casamance region of Senegal, where they have been spearheading a low-grade separatist war since 1982.[2] Diola live in an area of low-lying, lush forest and mangrove swamps, where they grow rice. Archaeological evidence suggests that Diola have been in this region of West Africa, and have been practicing their trademark wet-rice cultivation, for at least one thousand years (Linares 1981). Within Guinea-Bissau, Diola are referred to as Felupe.[3] Being geographically central, Susana links the outlying villages, which are roughly evenly divided between Diola that live in the forest and those that live on riverine islands, in what used to be a mutually interdependent trade of extracted goods: forest villagers would trade palm tree products (wine, oil, kernels) for fish.[4]

Susana's current population is approximately two thousand inhabitants, although there is seasonal variation based on the migration of family members attending school or seeking work in urban areas during the dry season and returning to Susana to help with the arduous labor involved in wet-rice cultivation during the rainy season. A 50-kilometer dirt road from São Domingos to Varela is the major artery that cuts through Guinean Diola land, and it is also the major source of its isolation from the rest of the country. In indescribably poor condition, the road is only served by a few flatbed truck drivers brave enough to venture onto it. This northern part of the country is further cut off from the capital, Bissau, by two rivers. Even though Susana is just 150 kilometers from Bissau, the trip often takes fourteen hours, with the result that Diola are isolated from the capital and their access to markets is hindered. This helps explain why most Guinean Diola orient themselves northward, across the Senegalese border to Ziguinchor, and even into the Gambia and other more accessible urban zones.[5]

Susana became the site of a Portuguese colonial outpost in the 1940s, although the Portuguese were at first rebuffed by Susana residents and set up in three other villages, before forcibly situating themselves in Susana. The same process was repeated in the following decade when Catholic missionaries first came to the area and wanted to make Susana their base of operations. Susana's elders again refused, and the mission was sent off to outlying villages before coming back and insisting (with Portuguese backing) on setting up in Susana. Now, Susana houses the administrative headquarters of the *secção*, the smallest unit of the postindependence Guinean administrative structure, as well as a large, fortresslike Catholic mission (sponsored by an Italian missionary diocese), the largest primary school in the area (and the only one going up to sixth grade), and the section's state health clinic, currently staffed by one nurse.

Susana is made up of two wards, Endongon and Utem, which are divided into three and two neighborhoods, respectively. There are three other recent additions to the Susana neighborhood structure: Santa Maria, the neighborhood of Diola Catholic converts, which skirts the mission walls; Centro, comprising an assortment of houses and administrative buildings along the main road; and Fulacunda, the now-abandoned row of houses adjacent to Santa Maria, where the Fula community lived until May 2000. These three neighborhoods occupy terrain that until the 1950s was dense forest separating Endongon and Utem. Portuguese colonial officials were the first to make serious inroads into this forest, followed by the Catholic mission, which cleared large tracts in order to build its own facilities and to offer a place of refuge where recent converts could build houses and hence escape both the temptations of traditional neighborhood ceremonial life and persecution from kin opposed to their conversion.

Susana has only recently been unified. Its two wards were federated in the mid-nineteenth century, during the height of internecine fighting among Diola villages. In Susana, neighborhoods remain the basis of most social and religious organization. All collective associations—age grades, work groups, women's groups, soccer teams, and so on—are neighborhood based. Each neighborhood has its own *hukulahu,* a clearing in which funerals, major ceremonies, and dances are conducted. Each neighborhood has its own cemetery, its own menstrual house (now largely abandoned), and its own maternity center (also largely unused, as explained below). Each neighborhood also has a secular representative on the village *comité de tabanka,* an administrative organ set up by the postindependence state to serve as a link between local and state power.[6]

Diola have residentially based patrifilial kin groups. Households are typically composed of a married couple and their unmarried children. Monogamy is by far the most common form of marriage, although polygyny is acceptable. Diola are virilocal; upon marriage, a bride is brought from her natal neighborhood (or village) to take up residence in her husband's family compound, where her new husband has recently built a house.[7] Most marriages are exogamous at the neighborhood level and endogamous at the village level.

Most authority is wielded within the *eluupai,* the house-based family. But beyond the largely autonomous household, the Diola political structure involves a combination of religious and administrative positions with varying degrees of authority. Each village typically has one "chief," or *ai* (pl. *ai-ì*). The Diola *ai-ì* are members of a priest class who hold ritual office over a spirit shrine that both safeguards and is the source of their right to reign.[8] Theoretically, *ai-ì* are bound by many restrictions: they are forbidden to enter the homes of laypersons (with the exception of *batolhabu,* members of the burial society lineage); to be seen eating, drinking, or performing any bodily activities (urinating, sleeping, etc.); to use anything that separates their bare feet from the ground (e.g., shoes, a bicycle, a car); to leave home anytime during the rainy season; to walk across salt water; and to travel by major paths or roads (they can only use secret bush paths). Because of the *ai*'s ritual power and the above-named restrictions, some observers have suggested that he is both "sacred and slave, all powerful and yet prisoner of his power" (Baum 1990, 375).[9] Many of these restrictions have been relaxed in the last fifteen years.

The head *ai* for all Diola lives in Karuay, a village several kilometers off the main road. He reigns over both Guinean and Senegalese Diola, although he rarely crosses over the Senegalese border now because of problems associated with the Casamance conflict. Beyond his religious duties, the Karuay *ai* is charged with spiritually uniting the Diola and serving as an arbiter in intervillage conflicts. Also, the Karuay *ai,* in collaboration with village elders, appoints other village *ai-ì* as needed.

In addition to an *ai,* Diola villages have a council of elders who hold ritual offices (*amangen*). This loose and informal group is primarily responsible for religious and ceremonial matters but can also be called on for advice and arbitration of matters relevant to the village. As previously mentioned, there is also a secular *comité de tabanka,* with one or two representatives from each neighborhood, which serves as a conduit for any official messages from within or outside the village. Sometimes the committee organizes collective labor on a neighborhood basis for villagewide projects, such as building a new school or constructing a community health facility.

Most conflicts are solved at the household level, among neighbors or kin who are called upon to witness or arbitrate. If a conflict cannot be solved by talking things through in this way, the parties involved may call upon the *comité* member or members in the affected neighborhood(s), or they may take the case to an *amangen* or a group of *amangen-í,* who will adjudicate the dispute through testimonials and ceremonies at a spirit shrine.

Only when all local channels have been exhausted do people consider taking a case to state authorities. Diola have what is, for the most part, a well-functioning system of conflict resolution and justice, and they are extremely reluctant to bring matters to the state's attention, so much so that they have a reputation for being backward, resistant to national integration, and "tribal-ist." Diola are concerned about these labels, but not enough to change their opinions and actions regarding state authority. So far, their geographic and administrative isolation has allowed them to resolve their conflicts through their local justice system.

The literature on Diola (from both Senegal and Guinea-Bissau) describes them as acephalous, lacking any centralized political structure (see, e.g., Brooks 1993; Forrest 1992; and Thomas 1959). This assessment does not accurately portray the many layers of political and religious authority and institutions extending from the neighborhood to intervillage networks. But power is loosely wielded by official authorities (such as the *ai* and *comité* members), and while elders (both men and women but especially men) are generally respected and listened to, younger men can certainly go their own way if they choose, so a strict gerontocracy does not exist.[10] Overall, Diola are ambiguous about the existence of leaders outside the household, and the restrictions on *ai-í,* as well as the no-rush approach to replacing them, can be seen as ways to confine or limit their authority.

Events Surrounding the May 2000 Conflict

Before the 1960s, a few Fula families lived in Susana. They had come from Guinea-Conakry as traveling merchants and settled in Susana as *jilas,* traders and small shop owners, in the 1950s. Some of them married Fula women living in the nearby settlement of Sangatutu, about five kilometers from Susana. When Guinea-Bissau's liberation war broke out in the 1960s, several Fula families in Sangatutu were killed by African Party for the Independence of Guinea-Bissau and Cape Verde (PAIGC) fighters.[11] By this time, most Diola villages had been mobilized by the PAIGC's war effort, but Susana and Elia remained exceptions, siding, or at least complying with, the Portuguese. There was a Portuguese army barracks in Susana, and Diola residents were often conscripted into participating in raids to ambush PAIGC "rebels" in the bush.

Accounts differ as to whether Fula in Sangatutu were rescued by Diola in Susana or escaped with the aid of Portuguese soldiers. According to several Susana Diola residents, when they heard about what was happening to Fula families in Sangatutu, they decided to rescue them by bringing them to Susana. Several of Susana's men went to the Fula settlement at night and brought the remaining Fula families back to Susana. AmpaDjaponor, a Diola man in Susana at the time, remembers, "We went to rescue them when the PAIGC were massacring them. . . . We went to rescue them, we brought them here, we put them here in our midst, we told them: 'Well, now this massacre that you suffered there [is over]; you are free.'"[12]

Mamadu Ba, at the time a recently married Fula man born in Sangatutu, recalls:

It was the war with the PAIGC. That's what took us out of Sangatutu. The PAIGC people, they came and attacked our village, they killed lots of people, so we ran to Susana. . . . I was there. At night they [the PAIGC] came. They burnt my older brother's house. . . . My older brother, he escaped and came and called to me, and said, "Ha, people want to kill me." We left and saw the fire coming out of the top of his house. I, I got up, I, Mamadu, I myself. I took a bicycle and went at night to Susana and arrived at the Posto [colonial administrative headquarters]. I went to enter the Posto, where the cottonwood tree is now. You see, Felupes would do night duty there. I called out: "Ooo-oooh. Ooo-oooh." Two times. The person from Susana responded. He said: "Who are you?" I said: "It's me, Mamadu." He said: "Come here. Don't be afraid." I told him: "People of the forest [PAIGC fighters] attacked us." We went from the Posto to the barracks. . . . We told the soldiers. . . . We got up and walked out until the bend in the road. When we got there, they told me to go back. I went back to Susana. They went in the night, they came to save our land. . . . The next day, I went there [Sangatutu] to see what to do. In the afternoon, they requested cars. [Portuguese] soldiers came to find us. . . . We, with families whose houses were burned, we came to Susana. . . . But many of them, they crossed over. They went to the Senegalese side. . . . Almost all of them [the population of Sangatutu] went to Senegal.

By that time, the mission and the Portuguese authorities had begun to clear the dense forest that separated Utem from Endongon in Susana. Diola provided the refugee Fula families with a plot of land in Susana's center and told them that if they wanted to stay, they could build houses there. The idea to place Fula families in the center of Susana was to ensure both their protection and their surveillance. Fula families were also given plots of forestland on which to plant small gardens of potatoes, corn, and beans. Over the next several years Fula built their houses and set up shops. The neighborhood became known as Fulacunda. As the families grew, several of the Fula sons born in Susana married Diola women. The resulting families were, by all accounts, more Fula than Diola—virilocality in both groups plays a big role here—and the children were brought up as Muslims, although Fula are quicker than Diola to mention their kinship links with Diola families.

The next few decades were apparently peaceful ones, although Diola accounts more often cite nascent problems between the two communities, generally revolving around their perceived exploitation by Fula merchants. Commerce is anathema to Diola sensibilities, and even though Diola became increasingly reliant on store-bought goods (oil, matches, and even rice), they were never comfortable with the idea of actually paying for such items, and much less so with the concept of profit. On the Fula side, the stores were their only means of livelihood; given Diola land tenure laws and the impossibility of obtaining sufficient land to sustain their families through agriculture, Fula depended on their commercial skills to eke out a living. Whether Fula actually exploited Diola through their commercial transactions is now a matter of conjecture. Diola narratives also express increasing resentment toward Fula, based on their perception that Fula considered themselves superior to Diola and treated Diola as "donkeys." One Diola informant insisted that Fula were out to colonize and subordinate Diola, saying that he had heard Fula residents proclaim: "We are their white people now. They will work for us." Although Diola narratives express a growing antipathy toward the Fula, it is difficult to ascertain whether these tensions existed at the time or are a product of postconflict revisionist history.

Also, at the end of the liberation war, a shift in orientation regarding land ownership swept across the country as PAIGC leaders declared that "matu ka ten dunu" (no one owns the forest). Like many people across newly independent Guinea-Bissau, Fula residents in Susana put this philosophy into practice by clearing tracts of forestland on the outskirts of Susana, near Kandembá, on which they eventually planted cashew groves. This land surrounded an important Diola spirit shrine of the same name, and Diola had left the forestland in this area intact, for both religious reasons associated with its sacredness and practical reasons associated with the war being waged around it. Although Susana's Diola residents were opposed to Fula occupation of this land, they had no means of protesting, given the national political climate at the time.

A brief diversion into changing national policies and practices regarding land use might be instructive here. Until recently Guinea-Bissau has had a particularly laid-back approach to land issues. During the colonial era, the Portuguese did not use Guinea-Bissau as a settler colony and never set up plantation systems as they did in their other African colonies; thus, land distribution was largely undisturbed throughout the colonial era.[13] As mentioned above, the immediate postindependence philosophy and practice regarding land was a kind of free-for-all approach; the PAIGC encouraged people to settle and utilize uncultivated land wherever they chose. Given the small population and large tracts of forestland, it was assumed that there would be enough land to go around.

Within the past several years, however, this willy-nilly approach to land use has come under severe pressure. A host of factors have made this approach untenable, including population growth and urbanization, but the single most important factor is the recent explosion of cashews as the nation's most successful export crop. In a country with limited natural resources and an ever-dwindling capacity to sustain itself through subsistence agriculture, cashew farming has become the only way to generate income at all levels of the society, and in many areas during cashew season raw cashew nuts have replaced cash as the most utilized form of currency. Now that everyone has an interest in planting acres of cashew trees, forestland has finally come to be seen as a finite resource, and one that needs regulating.

In March 1998, three months before the civil war broke out, Guinea-Bissau's parliament passed a land law that sought to protect peasant holdings and customary land tenure practices while introducing far-reaching privatization and taxation policies. The land law was shelved during the conflict and its aftermath. In 2001, given increasing land-based conflicts around the country, a new effort was mounted to put the 1998 land law into practice. With the financial backing of the UN Food and Agriculture Organization (FAO), researchers and policymakers began to revisit the new national land law. Although the 1998 land law stands as it was passed, the work of regulating and applying it, as well as building up local and national institutions capable of enforcing it and preventing land conflicts, remains to be done.

In the 1980s, Susana and other villages decided that they wanted to build an annex to Susana's health clinic. This has been alternately described as a maternity center or as a housing facility for resident health workers and patients visiting from other villages.[14] The latter project, a residence for both patients and health workers, emerged as an initiative based on two factors: Susana's population wants to have more health services but potential health workers have nowhere to live when they are posted to the village. Most Susana residents saw building a residence for posted health workers as a guaranteed way to attract them to Susana. The second purpose, to have a place where visiting patients from other villages could stay, probably emerged in the wake of two successive cholera outbreaks in Elia. Generally, visitors from other Diola villages always have a place to stay based on extended kinship networks and Diola hospitality conventions, but the cholera outbreaks strained such norms, and building a patient guesthouse was a way to finesse the issue. As one Diola man involved in the project put it:

We saw that . . . sickness, well people would say that there are contagious diseases, so if . . . someone for example had tuberculosis or other things like measles, these are contagious. So, what is one to do when there is no place to stay, just in the forest, so that the disease does not spread to others? That is why we saw that we should build that house. If that house exists, and someone comes from the forest with a contagious disease, then, when he arrives we will tell him, "You have to stay here in this place so that you do not spread this disease among your friends."

After repeated requests, in the mid-1990s Susana residents obtained permission from the state-appointed president of the *comité de estado* to use a plot of land in the center of the village, on the main road and directly across from the existing clinic. The land was considered to be state owned, as it was located in the administrative center of Susana and had been the site of successive Portuguese colonial and Guinean state projects.

Construction of the health facility began in 1997 with a state-mandated labor team of Diola men from Edjaten, a village eleven kilometers from Susana. In 1997 there was a rash of deaths of unmarried young men in Edjaten. As one Susana resident recalls, "Not a week would go by without [our] hearing about another boy who had died there, and we were constantly going up to Edjaten for funerals." At the corpse inquisitions conducted during the funerals, the determination of the cause was always the same: witchcraft. Diola witchcraft beliefs involve reciprocity of offerings among one's cohort of witches, and the deaths in Edjaten indicated that witchcraft contracts were being fulfilled by the concentrated killing of young men.

The state-appointed administrator in Susana at the time was a Diola man named AmpaDjitoto from the village of Djifunco. He decided that he was going to teach the men from Edjaten a lesson. AmpaDjitoto sent word to

Edjaten summoning all the men there to Susana. They presented themselves to AmpaDjitoto at the administrative post on the appointed day, whereupon he counted them and then, with military backing, locked them in the Susana barracks. In the afternoon, he told them, "Those who have brothers in Edjaten, go get them and bring them here. The only people who will sleep in Edjaten tonight are women." The men went to get their brothers. AmpaDjitoto kept them imprisoned, with no explanation, for four nights. During the day, they were let out and allowed to mingle in Susana and find something to eat, but each evening they were to report back to the barracks, where they were locked up. On the fourth day, AmpaDjitoto let the men go, but he said that they had not yet received their punishment; they were to return to Susana on a date that he named, bringing their machetes and axes.

When the Edjaten men returned to Susana, AmpaDjitoto set them to work on the construction of the health workers' house. First, they cleared and cleaned the area. Then they formed mud blocks and started building the walls. Each day, they worked from early in the morning until the afternoon and then walked back to Edjaten in the evening. This continued until the second level of the wall was complete, at which time AmpaDjitoto decided that they had paid their dues and he released them from further work. The punishment appeared to have had the desired effect, as the constant death of young men in Edjaten stopped.

Other villages organized work teams to contribute to the effort, and by the end of the year the walls were almost complete. According to Diola in Susana, Fula residents did not participate in the building project, although they were aware of the proceedings. That Fula did not contribute labor to community projects from which they ultimately benefited is a consistent Diola complaint. In 1995, for example, Susana's population built a community primary school. Diola insist that Fula residents did not participate, even though their children later attended the school. As one Diola resident claims:

Well, that school, we did not hide it. We told everyone who was here. But when we went to build the school, but not a single day did they [Fula] come. Not even a little bit did they work, not even a wheelbarrow did they use to wet mud. At least they could take a mound of mud so they could say, "Here, this is to make the wall." We were not interested, we threw ourselves into the work, we made the school here where you can see it. . . . But we never said "Ha, Mamadu, you are Muslim, or you did not participate in the construction so your child cannot attend school." We never said that. . . . We did not tell them, "Hey, we worked, and you refused." No, their children attended the school . . . in that very same building that we made.

The same complaint was lodged against Fula when Diola residents began to build the health facility. But all work stopped in 1998, first because Susana's Diola population was fully consumed with its male initiation,[15] and then because of the 7 de Junho War, an eleven-month popular uprising against the nineteen-year-long regime of President João Bernardo "Nino" Vieira. Many of Susana's men joined the military junta led by Brigadier General Ansumane Mané, which eventually removed President Vieira from power. Other Susana residents were consumed by the extra obligations of providing for their swollen households, as Guineans from Bissau sought refuge in the interior. During the intervening rainy season the health facility's mud walls crumbled.

When the building project started, one of the Fula men, Braima, who had been born in Susana and whose father had come there at the time of the Sangatutu massacre, claimed that the land on which the health center was being constructed belonged to him. He said that his father had been given the land by the postindependence state and that he had inherited it. Although Braima had no proof to back up his claim, and although most Diola and non-Diola residents in Susana insisted that he had invented it, AmpaDjitoto was concerned to treat him equably in order not to raise suspicion of ethnic favoritism in his administrative practices. AmpaDjitoto suggested that since the health facility took up only a portion of the plot, the young Fula man could build his house on the other side. Braima built his house contemporaneously with the health facility collective building project and arranged highly coveted zinc sheets (bought, some Susana Diola claim, from Casamance rebels on the Senegalese border) to cover it provisionally during the rainy season. Thus, although the health workers' house fell, Braima's house remained intact.

In 1999 the Fula community decided to build a new mosque. Fula residents had a small mosque in Fulacunda, but their numbers were growing and they wanted to have a mosque in a more central and visible location. They chose to build the mosque on the land where the health care facility had fallen down, assuming that the project had been aborted or would be moved elsewhere. This assumption was based in part on the fact that the land in question had been a Diola burial ground and that Diola had found that they could not build successfully on such terrain. As one Fula man explained, when the men from Edjaten were forced into the building project,

they started to dig a hole there, and they found people's bones and skulls. That's taboo for Felupes. That's why they left it; stopped working. . . . They could not go on. They left the house and it fell down. That's when we requested to put our mosque there. We, ourselves, those bones, we would return the bones that had been dug up there. We would return the bones and cover them with dirt. There was a small tree that stood there—I, myself, went and put those bones by that tree. We buried all of those bones, those human skulls there. All of them.

Diola agree that the land was a former cemetery, but they contend that this does not present a problem for building on the land as long as any encountered bones are removed appropriately. Diola residents in Susana also insist that Fula residents did not inform them of their intentions to build the mosque. As one man recounted,

When they started to build that mosque there, they did not tell any of us. There is no one in Susana who can say, "They told me." We did not know what was going on. . . . But we saw that Fulas were beginning to use the mud from the fallen health workers' house. We thought, since there was plenty of it, perhaps they were using it to build their "prayer house" . . . . So we watched them until . . . we saw them starting to measure that plot of land. So people said, "Mbeh! But we had reserved this land already for the health workers' residence. But they, our friends . . . our brothers . . . what's going on?"

Another Diola man corroborates, "If they had seen that they wanted to build a mosque there, they should have consulted us: 'So, brother, we want to build this thing here, so you tell us if you have intentions of building the health workers' residence that you told us about.' But they went ahead and just raised the house and built their mosque there."

When Diola realized what was happening, they went to the state-appointed administrator in Susana, a Mandinga man named Lamine (Ampa-Djitoto had died in 1998). A Diola delegation explained that they had already been allocated the land for a building project that they had every intention of resuming. The state authority concurred and told the Diola delegation not to worry, that he would discuss the matter with the Fula and they would stop building there. Time passed, Fula did not stop building, and Diola became more anxious as the building started to take shape. They returned to the state authority and were once again assured that he would put a stop to the Fula building activities. This happened two more times with no results. Fula continued building the mosque's walls, and Diola continued sending delegations to the state authority. Fula, for their part, contend that no one ever told them about the Diola complaints or suggested that they stop building.

After several meetings with no results, a Diola delegation held a meeting with Fula elders. These Fula elders explained that Fula residents wanted to build the mosque on that site because it was on the main street and anyone passing by, day or night, would know that there was a place to pray. Diola argued that they had already designated that site for the community health workers' residence. Fula elders backed down, agreeing to leave the site alone and build the mosque elsewhere. They told their sons that they had agreed to do this, but their sons refused to change their plans and continued building there.

When the walls were complete and the long wooden poles to be used for roofing arrived at the site, Diola decided to take matters into their own hands. AmpaDjaponor explains, "We had meetings at the shrine [Acuio, the male initiation shrine for the Nhakun neighborhood]. We said, 'We sent people [to the state administrator], we returned and returned, but nothing. How many times did we go there? Now, we are fed up. Now we will go to our own court. Now justice is in our hands.'"

Diola planted a forked stick at the building site. In Diola custom, if a dispute arises over a plot of land, be it rice paddy, forestland, or residential land, one step in mediating the conflict is for one of the parties concerned to plant a stick at the disputed site. This stick signals to all those who are using the land that there is a concern over rights to do so, and that any work being done at the site must stop immediately and all parties involved must meet and discuss the matter. The dispute may be settled among only the parties involved, or other witnesses and mediators, such as *comité* members, elders (*amangen*), or the *ai,* may be asked to intervene. In Fula versions of the dispute, the stick Diola placed at the site is called a *mandjidura,* which is a generic Crioulo word for a stick invested with spiritual power from a particular shrine. Some older Fula men called it a *xina,* which is an abbreviated Diola word for a spirit or intermediary god (from the Diola *bakinabu*). In Diola there are several different words for various sticks and the signals or objectives they represent. The general Diola word for a stick with any kind of meaning attached to it is *hubalenahu.* A stick used in land disputes is called a *hutukâhu,* and there are separate words for sticks used by women and by men for different secular and supernatural purposes. When referring to the stick that was planted at the Fula mosque site, Diola sometimes use the word *ehakai,* meaning a stick used both in land disputes and for ceremonial purposes in male initiation forests, and sometimes they use *hubalenahu.* When speaking in Crioulo, they often call the stick used at the mosque site a *mandjidura.* But Diola are consistent in their explanation that the stick was placed there to call for a meeting between the two groups.

A young Fula man, upon seeing the stick, tore it from the ground and threw it away in the part of the initiation forest from which he knew it had come. As discussed above, since the time the majority of Fula families had moved to Susana, a generation of Fula men and women had grown up there, many of them born of Fula fathers and Diola mothers. They were aware of Diola customs and in all likelihood knew the meaning and intent of the stick placed at the mosque construction site. Diola point to the fact that the Fula man who removed the stick returned it to its place of origin as evidence that he knew exactly what the signal was for and blatantly provoked Diola wrath by discarding it. This act ended any attempts at mediation between the two groups.

Diola men met in the initiation forest and decided on their action plan. The elders concurred that once the roof structure was in place, they would collectively knock down the mosque. The night before the appointed day, the Diola elders spread the word around the village for people to meet at Acuio early the following morning and to bring sticks.

On 30 May 2000, at approximately 8 AM, the *bombolom* sounded in each of Susana's neighborhoods.[16] Fula recall hearing the *bombolom* and thinking that they had never before heard *bomboloms* sound in all of the neighborhoods simultaneously. An older Fula man, Tcherno Ba, asked his young neighbor Angelo, a Bagnun man born and raised in Susana, what was happening. Angelo told him that Diola were going to tear down the mosque. When Angelo told another Fula neighbor the same thing, the neighbor gasped and said, "So, they are going to finish us off today." Angelo reassured him that they would just tear down the mosque and then leave.

All of Susana's adult Diola men, including members of the Catholic community, gathered at Acuio, on the outskirts of Nhakun. They were armed with sticks and machetes. The elders instructed them to collectively tear down the mosque but insisted that no one was to hit anyone or kill anyone or engage in any other kind of violence. The Diola men marched into the center of the village and proceeded to beat on the mosque's walls, hacking at them until they started to come apart. According to Fula and other non-Diola accounts, Diola men, women, and children participated in the tearing down of the mosque, but according to Diola accounts, only adult men participated, although women stood nearby and encouraged them by singing songs.

While Diola were tearing down the mosque, Tcherno's grandson, a man in his early twenties born in Susana, who had joined and then deserted the military junta that had recently overthrown Nino Vieira, retrieved a grenade from his house and moved toward the crowd. Tcherno called out to Angelo, who was sitting on his veranda, and told him to stop his grandson, "or they'll really finish us off." When the young man attempted to climb over the fence, Angelo grabbed him and pinned him to the ground, then tied him up in the yard, thus preventing what surely would have turned into a bloodbath.

After the mosque was demolished, a Fula man rode his moped into the crowd and started insulting Diola men. No one touched him. Another man came running toward them, shouting, "Before they kill me, I'll kill ten of them." A few older Fula women grabbed him and detained him.

The Diola men returned to Acuio to discuss what had happened. A chorus of young men said, "If the State comes to kill us, it's the young people they will kill, and they will leave the old people alone. But these people causing trouble, we don't want to see them ever again, so we're going to break down their houses." The elders tried to talk them out of it, but the young men insisted. Within an hour of mobilizing the Diola population, the elders were supplanted by the younger generation in spearheading the activities. The young men led the crowd back to Fulacunda and tore down three houses belonging to Fula men who were considered the instigators of the conflict. After demolishing the houses they returned once again to the initiation forest, where the elders told them: "Well, our plan was just to knock down the mosque. But now the mosque includes all those houses. War has been declared. Everyone should realize that this is war."

Fula uniformly express incredulity at the tearing down of these houses. They understand why Diola tore down the mosque, but they do not understand (or at least do not admit to understanding) why they then demolished the houses. Asked why Diola men had destroyed the houses, a Diola participant explained: "We throw away a rotten fish so that it will not damage the rest of the catch. . . . We don't have a jail where we imprison people, but we expel people so that they will never return to this place." Tearing down an offender's house is the ultimate Diola punishment, tantamount to excommunication. Diola employ such disciplinary measures among themselves when community members break Diola law, especially in cases of theft.

During the events described above, most Fula residents remained in their neighborhood, and when the Diola men scattered to their forest groves, Fula congregated at the army barracks. One young Fula man whose house had been torn down rode his moped to Varela, a village seventeen kilometers from Susana and the site of another Guinean army barracks. Susana's soldiers had been conspicuously absent throughout the morning's events; they were in the nearby village of Cassu conducting a routine border check for signs of Casamance rebel activity. Some informants contend that the soldiers absented themselves on purpose, having been informed of Diola plans ahead of time, in order to avoid responsibility and culpability for the proceedings. The soldiers in Varela radioed military reinforcements from São Domingos and Ingore, and Susana was soon swarming with Guinean soldiers.

An army commander who had previously been based in Susana urged all Fula families to evacuate immediately to São Domingos because he was planning to bomb Susana to punish Diola for their actions. Fula families, especially the older ones, said that they did not want to leave, but they were pressured to do so by the army commander and by the younger Fula. Later that same day, 171 Fula men, women, and children left for São Domingos, and they have not returned since.

The next day, Tcherno Ba's house burned down, as did the Fula youth club in Fulacunda. But instead of finding Diola culprits, the soldiers allegedly caught a member of Susana's Muslim community—a Serekule man—in the act of arson. According to one non-Diola resident in Susana, when the soldiers brought the Serekule man to the barracks, the commanding officer told them to release him and to keep his capture to themselves. The commander supposedly was still bent on bombing Susana, but his second-in-command refused, stating that it was now clear that Muslims themselves were provoking the problem. The facts of this exchange remain unclear, and a minority of Diola in Susana do not believe that the Serekule man burned down the buildings. Nonetheless, the soldiers left after four days in Susana. As one non-Diola Susana resident commented, "The fact that the soldiers caught [the Serekule man], this was Susana's salvation. If they had not caught him, people would have assumed that it was 'Susana's children' who were burning the houses. They would have shown no mercy. . . . Susana would have been bombed. No one could have stopped it."

In the days following 30 May, younger members of the Fula community reported to the Bissau and foreign media that they had been attacked by Diola because they were Muslim. They said that Diola had felled palm trees across the road and destroyed the plank bridge a few kilometers from the village so that the Guinean army and other state authorities would be unable to enter Susana. All of this was reported in the Guinean newspapers, which framed the conflict as one of "Felupe versus Muslims" (*Diário de Bissau,* 28 June, 6 July 2000). In subsequent weeks journalists from Bissau, including BBC and Radio Televisão Portuguesa (RTP) stringers, went to São Domingos and Susana to interview Fula and Diola. Both Fula and Diola claim that journalists spoke only to the other side, and each group complained that its perspective was not taken into account.

The weeks and months that followed 30 May were filled with meetings and various mediation efforts in Susana. All agricultural work was suspended as Susana's residents held meetings to discuss the matter. During the week, men and women met separately at their respective shrine sites, and on market day they joined in community-wide meetings at the central *hukulahu* in the Katama neighborhood. These meetings largely comprised discussions about what had happened and reports on any meetings that had been held with outsiders. Regional and national officials, including several ministers, came to discuss the case. Even Ansumane Mané, the brigadier general who had led the 1998 uprising against Nino Vieira and who was at the time the head of the military junta in control of the country, traveled to Susana to evaluate the situation. After meeting with both Diola in Susana and Fula in São Domingos, he proclaimed that Diola were in the right but said that they should forgive the Fula population and allow them to return to their homes in Susana. At this, an often outspoken Diola elder told Mané that Diola would welcome Fula back to Susana as soon as Mané welcomed Nino Vieira back to Bissau.

Fula insist that Mané sided with the Diola population because of his debt to Casamance Diola rebels, whom he had recruited to fight in the military junta campaign against Nino Vieira and with whom he had long been closely associated in his gunrunning activities. One Fula man whom I interviewed in São Domingos insisted that Ansumane Mané had orchestrated the conflict because he wanted to use Susana as a rear base to aid the rebels in the Casamance conflict. Ansumane Mané was killed shortly after his visit to Susana, in an alleged shootout between the troops of the newly elected President Kumba Yalla and Mané's own loyalists. The facts surrounding his death are still murky, and President Yalla has refused to allow any outside investigations into the episode.[17] Among many other consequences, Mané's death marked the end of any state mediation efforts in Susana.

Whereas the general perception at the national level is that Diola expelled Fula from Susana, Diola insist that they never intended for Fula to leave. They simply wanted to stop the building of a mosque on the site of a planned community project, and they wanted to discipline members of the Fula population who had egregiously violated community norms. The Diola actions, in the form of demolishing houses, were targeted at particular individuals, not at the Fula community as a whole. One Fula family refused to go to São Domingos, and Diola point out that that family has remained unharmed. However, although Diola did not intend for Fula to leave, and although Fula say that they would like to return to Susana, Diola unequivocally reject such a return, generally putting the matter in the following terms: "They chose to leave. They made their decision. So now they cannot come back."

All outside negotiation efforts were aimed at peaceably reintegrating Fula families back into Susana. But in the wake of the 30 May events Diola positions hardened, and attempts by state authorities to mediate the case ended without a consensus. Even though elders from both sides demonstrated an eagerness to resolve differences early in the mediation process, they were soon silenced by younger men, and the younger men on the Diola side worked actively to prevent the Fulas' return. One Diola man involved in the negotiations explained that when state authorities had tried to persuade Diola to receive the Fula back in Susana, he had said to them, "If you bring them here, we will not refuse. But whatever happens tomorrow, you are responsible for it. . . . If tomorrow an even more serious thing happens than what already exploded here, you are to blame. . . . If you return them [Fulas], fine, we will not refuse you, the State, who are second to God."

The Diola-Fula conflict remains unresolved, although such a state of abeyance really only affects the Fula, who are living in São Domingos as refugees. Many of them are unable to pay the rent for their temporary houses, and most of them, especially the older members, long to return to Susana, which they consider their rightful home. Their abandoned houses in Fulacunda are slowly being occupied by itinerant Fula merchants from Guinea-Conakry. Susana's Fula do not blame Diola for their prolonged refugee status and insist that they feel no vengeance toward them. Fula hold "the State" entirely responsible for their current predicament. Since they moved to São Domingos under state orders, they feel that they cannot return to Susana until the state resolves the situation.

In October 2002 a series of community-wide meetings were held in Susana to move ahead with plans to build a maternity clinic and health workers' residence. Collective work started in December 2002. A group of women cleared the brambles and brush behind the existing clinic in order to make space for the maternity center, while a group of men cleared the controversial plot of land across from the clinic, which will be the site, once again, of the health workers' dormitory. Diola men in Susana, led by the secular neighborhood representatives who make up the *comité de tabanka,* drew up plans for the facility and obtained clearance from the state-appointed administrator, a Manjaco man. The official who had represented the section during the conflict had left of his own accord shortly before 30 May. Both Diola and Fula accounts concur that, sensing rising tensions and fearing that he would be held accountable, he had feigned an illness and left Susana to get treatment. He has not returned since. Some Susana residents suggest that his exit was linked to the shift in national politics in the aftermath of the 2000 presidential runoff, specifically the ascendancy of the Social Renovation Party (PRS) to presidential power, implying that the PAIGC's defeat also entailed his own loss of backing and authority.

Both Diola men and women worked collectively for several weeks to construct their respective buildings, and the walls of the spacious health workers' and patients' dormitory were completed in early February 2003, shortly after the women completed the maternity clinic. Both structures were roofed in June 2003, just before the onset of the rainy season. Diola are justifiably proud of their work, which was no doubt spurred on by the collective sense of urgency to utilize the controversial plot of land before any further claims were laid upon it. In some ways, building these facilities represents a kind of closure for Diola on what they call "our problem with Fulas"; in addition, the buildings serve as tangible proof of the Diola claim that the land was intended for a project that would benefit the entire community. Fula are quietly resentful of these recent activities. For the most part, however, they no longer concern themselves with that specific plot of land. They are more concerned with returning to their houses and orchards and the peaceful lives they enjoyed in Susana.

Narratives of Violence and Structural Bases of Division

Both Diola and Fula narratives about their conflict reveal the extent to which the events of 30 May are steeped in other violent experiences. No matter who is telling it, the story of the 30 May tearing down of the mosque and the subsequent removal of Susana's Fula population begins thirty years earlier, with the Sangatutu massacre, and is peppered throughout with references to almost every kind of well-known and well-documented form of violence in Africa. The Sangatutu massacre and liberation war remind us of the recent colonial and anticolonial violence experienced across Guinea-Bissau. Matter-of-fact references to PAIGC repression reveal the extent to which postcolonial Guinean lives, even in the isolated provinces, have been conditioned by the postindependence violence of the one-party state. Even more recently, the 7 de Junho war in 1998 speaks to civil unrest, the fragility of the state, and military junta power, while allusions to the Casamance conflict evoke the separatist, low-grade, long-term guerrilla warfare on Susana's doorstep. The postconflict arrests and beatings of Diola men in Susana, as well as Ansumane Mané's death, highlight problems with police brutality and the increasing autocratic displays of postcolonial state power in Guinea-Bissau (see Mbembe 1992). But violence is not related just to state and national politics. The problem in Edjaten exposes how witchcraft beliefs and their attendant violent behaviors affect lives in the region, and the recent cholera epidemics and lack of sufficient health services speak to the excess burden of disease familiar throughout the continent.

Such saturation suggests that we cannot treat violence as episodic but must regard it as part of a matrix of events extending over place and time. Even this seemingly isolated conflict is enmeshed in a recent history of violent occurrences, and participants' experience of it, as well as actions within it, and cannot be disentangled from these surrounding incidents. With this in mind, let us now consider how this relatively benign riot speaks to larger issues of collective violence, polarization, and pluralism.

Not an Ethnic Conflict?

Many of the dynamics in this case call to mind similar instances of conflict in other regions of the world and thus allow for an interpretation of this episode that reinforces much contemporary thinking about collective violence, especially in an interethnic context.

For example, both preconflict provocation and postconflict intransigence were fueled by specific members of each community, namely, younger men. This corroborates Paul Brass's (1997) analysis that in moments of collective violence a small faction of agents provocateurs, typically young men who mobilize enmity between groups, play a significant role in stimulating or exacerbating tensions. Identifying these particular actors and their motives is critical for both preventing and resolving such conflicts, especially as it locates accountability in individual actions and steers away from "leveling" tendencies to collectivize agency and blame, which often produce the empirically inaccurate perception of ethnic-based conflict when the facts point to specific individuals—in Brass's terminology, "riot specialists."

Brass demonstrates that the "ethnic nature" of many instances of collective violence, rather than instigating the problem itself, is often born out of postconflict processes:

When examined at the actual originating sites of ethnic and communal violence, it is often the case that the precipitating incidents arise out of situations that are either not inherently ethnic/communal in nature or are ambiguous in character, that their transformation into caste or communal incidents depends upon the attitudes toward them taken by local politicians and authorities. The "official" interpretation that finally becomes universally accepted is often, if not usually, very far removed, often unrecognizable, from the original precipitating events. (Brass 1997, 6)

Diola, too, are often at pains to demonstrate that the conflict was not ethnic based, as one informant insists: "They said that we were against the Fula . . . [but] we do not understand why it is said that this was Felupe against Fula. . . . People say that we chased out the Fulas. But we did not chase out anybody. Just those three people who were authors of the problem."

In a similar vein, Stanley Tambiah offers a useful analysis from his study of ethnonationalist conflicts in South Asia, and introduces the conceptually rich terms *focalization* and *transvaluation*:

These are linked processes by which a series of local incidences and small-scale disputes, occasioned by religious, commercial, interfamilial, or other issues, and involving people in direct contact with one another, cumulatively build up into larger and larger clashes between growing numbers of antagonists only indirectly involved in the original disputes. . . . Focalization progressively denudes local incidents and disputes of their contextual particulars, and transvaluation distorts, abstracts, and aggregates those incidents into larger collective issues of national or ethnic interest. (Tambiah 1996, 81)

Such processes are evident throughout the Susana case. Accounts of the conflict based on simplistic journalistic renderings reduced the case's complexity and aggravated the situation by distorting and exaggerating Diola attitudes and actions. Furthermore, outside intervention and mediation efforts by state authorities, military personnel, and other national political players stripped the situation of its complex and multifaceted local texture and twisted it to align with extraneous personal and/or national concerns.

Perhaps even more pertinent is the way in which national political concerns appear in participants' narratives of the events. Most individuals with whom I spoke readily attributed others' actions to political interest but did not link their own attitudes or behavior to such motivations. Angelo, the Bagnun man born and raised in Susana, placed both Fula and Diola actions squarely within the national political playing field. According to his interpretation, Fula residents stubbornly refused to alter their plans regarding the mosque site because they believed they had political patronage in the form of Malam Ba, a Fula police officer posted to Susana who was in tight with the Nino Vieira regime. Malam Ba "had full power in Susana . . . and he knew Nino personally and had his full backing. He did whatever he wanted to do in Susana; abused his power . . . beat people up." According to non-Fula accounts, Fula residents in Susana thought they could act with impunity regarding the mosque construction because they assumed that Ba would favor members of his own ethnic group. Likewise, Fula and non-Diola commentators on the case insist that Susana's Diola never would have torn down the mosque if the PAIGC had still been in power. But the vacuum created in the aftermath of the 1998 uprising against Nino Vieira allowed Diola to take matters into their own hands without fear of PAIGC reprisals. These narratives demonstrate that the members of each group viewed the other group as motivated by national political interests, whereas they considered their own actions untainted by these forces.

At first, I found such assertions puzzling and misplaced. Not only is Susana extremely isolated and undisturbed by anything resembling a state administrative structure, but Guinea-Bissau is most readily characterized as a weak state, one whose authority barely exists within the capital and certainly does not extend into the interior (see Forrest 2003). I was tempted to characterize people's claims that others' actions had something to do with state power as paranoid, or at least misguided. But I eventually came to understand that such perceptions had much more to do with Guinea-Bissau's being a weak *bureaucratic* state but a powerful *patronage* state, if only in the public imagination. That is, the "state" to which people referred when evaluating others' actions was embodied by the particular military and police personnel posted to Susana, whose behavior was based not on the "rule of law" or any other official state mandate but on personal power and patronage. Susana's residents perceived people's interests and behavior as linked to state actors, regardless of whether those state actors actually wielded de facto bureaucratic power in Susana or elsewhere in the country.

One tempting conclusion based on these observations is that the immediate postconflict events within the medium of a perceived patronage state transformed the conflict, for both outsiders and participants, from one focused on a particular plot of land into one with ethnic, religious, and political dimensions. A postconflict hardening of attitudes, most evident in the Diola's unequivocal stance on the impossibility of the Fula's return, has exacerbated and prolonged the problem.

This interpretation would square nicely with received wisdom on ethnicity and conflict in many areas of the world (e.g., Brass 1997; Cohen 1969; Lentz 1995; Wilmsen and McAllister 1996). But although these analyses no doubt serve to illuminate certain aspects of the Susana conflict, they do not satisfactorily explain many of the dynamics that lie beyond a superficial rendering of this case. There is no doubt that the state administrator posted to Susana failed to perform his duty, that journalists simplified their accounts, that young people on both sides spearheaded the collective action of both groups, and that actions on both sides were influenced by changes in the national political field. All of these factors contributed to the escalation and intensification of tensions. But this easy analysis obscures tougher questions about tensions already present, ready for igniting. Through the explication of many similar cases we have learned that ethnicity is political and invented, that people use identity and history to serve present needs and ends, and that state or national political agendas often exploit and "transvalue" local cases. These are all important lessons, but they fall short of what Leo Kuper (1977) calls the "structural principles" already at play and ripe for politicizing.

One of Kuper's main concerns is the relationship between social structure and polarization, "the extent to which the structure of the society provided the context conducive to the accentuation of division" (Kuper 1977, 248). He tries to find an intermediate approach between structural determinists (like the writers on the Algerian revolution who insist that decolonization can only be possible through violence) and those who minimize the role of broad structural factors and place responsibility for polarization on the struggle for power by elites. This latter perspective does not account for the fact that something already needs to be present to resonate with politicized ethnicity. Explanations that require elites to shoulder the entire burden of responsibility for polarization also require "a view of ordinary people as devoid of judgment and totally manipulable" (Kuper 1977, 249). In a vital corrective to the over-emphasis of the role of both outsiders and insiders in politically fabricating ethnic solidarity, Kuper states:

I take it to be highly probable that with representative government in ethnically or racially plural societies, there will be politicians ready to exploit to the maximum the politics of ethnicity for personal power, whatever the political formula under which they act. But I take it to be equally axiomatic, that the ethnic appeal will have little resonance, unless there is a significant structural basis of division and discrimination. Ethnic politics cannot be fabricated out of a harmonious integration by pure ideology; nor is the mere presence of members of different ethnic groups within a society a sufficient basis for ethnic appeals. . . . I have no difficulty in accepting an emphasis on the significant role of the élites in inflaming and manipulating ethnic hatreds. . . . But I would add that they were harnessing real social forces, embedded in the structure of the society, and in the perception of many of its members. (Kuper 1977, 104–6)

Many recent books on collective violence focus on cases in which significant polarization has already taken place (e.g., Daniel 1996; Das et al. 2000; Malkki 1995; Tambiah 1996). They help illuminate some of the dynamics of increasing polarization and violence, especially in terms of elites' roles, the cycles of reprisals and reciprocal violence, the involvement of wider political forces, and the institutionalization and normalization of violence. But Kuper's book written nearly thirty years ago asks us to take several steps back and examine what—at the levels of social interaction, structure, and systems of symbols and values—might form the bases of these later-stage processes. In order to examine these attitudes, I now turn to some of the dynamics internal to Susana Diola society that helped shape the conflict as much as the external forces discussed above.

Narrative Contrasts

What remains most perplexing about this case is the consistency and conviction of a seemingly contradictory Diola statement: "We did not kick the Fula out. And in *no way* can they return." Much of what happened in May 2000 and in its aftermath can be explained, as above, by conventional and contemporary social science analysis or even common sense. But this apparent incongruity in Diola narratives continued to nag at me. The longer I stayed in Susana, however, and the more Diola comments I heard (and overheard) that at first blush seemed to have nothing to do with the Fula case, the better I understood how complicated it is to be a long-term stranger among Diola landlords.

Since I was living among Diola in Susana, I was first exposed to their unsolicited narratives about the events, and I naively thought I had a clear picture of the proceedings. But I remember my reactions when I first interviewed Fula men and women living as self-described "dislocated members of Susana" in São Domingos. Upon returning to Susana, I scribbled in my field notes:

When [a Fula elder] was recounting his continued disbelief, even after three years, that such a thing happened, and his continued hardship in São Domingos—poor health, lack of food, unstable and expensive housing, all classic refugee problems—the conflict finally took on a real, human quality. . . . I could not help feeling a little mad, a little disappointed, in the Diola, whose recounting of it never stirred me beyond a fact-finding and analytical bent. They were unemotional about it . . . never, in my discussions with them about the conflict, did they reflect once on the plight of the Fula in São Domingos. Never was there a shred of empathy or concern or even connection, whereas the Fula were profoundly emotional about their loss—of Susana as their rightful residence, of their livelihood in the cashew groves, and of their neighbors, friends and family. The Fula refugees recounted, unsolicited, their kinship links to various Diola families whom I know. None of these families has ever mentioned their kinship links to the Fula.

Fula narratives on the events surrounding the mosque destruction cast a different light on many of the details I had learned from Diola and non-Diola alike in Susana. For instance, on the topic of intermarriage between Diola and Fula the narratives of both groups use almost the same words, but their differing tones give them opposite meanings. Fula narratives often stress that the majority of the younger generation of Fula men, those born in Susana, married Diola women. "We *even* married their daughters," Fula often proclaim, in their expression emphasizing their integration in Susana. There is no doubt that Fula considered intermarriage a positive phenomenon for all parties involved. When Fula identify their kinship links with Diola, they are making a case to themselves and their interlocutors that they belong in

Susana. Diola residents' silence regarding their kinship ties with Fula speaks volumes about their attitude toward Fula incorporation (or lack thereof) into Susana society. And when I asked Diola residents in Susana about intermarriage between Fula and Diola families, they uniformly stressed that while Fula men married Diola women ("They married *our* daughters"), Diola men were prevented from marrying Fula women. They did not see intermarriage as strengthening ties between the two groups and paving the way to enhanced community relations, as it is often cast in analyses of West African interethnic interaction. Rather, Diola viewed the marriage of "their" women by Fula men as a form of theft, especially since in such marriages the bride was required to convert to Islam, and they resented the implicit fact that if a Diola man were to marry a Fula woman (which never happened), he too would be required to convert.[18]

These Diola perspectives reflect a deeper attitude regarding incorporation into Susana Diola society. The reigning trope on West African coastal groups is that they are hospitable to strangers and eager and willing to incorporate them (see esp. Brooks 1993; and Mark 1999). As George Brooks contends,

Two sociocultural paradigms of immeasurable significance are found throughout western Africa. The first involves "landlord-stranger reciprocities," which promote safety of movement and hospitality for travelers wherever they go. . . . The origins of landlord-stranger reciprocities are lost in antiquity, but their tenets are embedded in the fundaments of the societies of western Africa. . . . Hospitality and appropriate behavior toward strangers are ensured by the responsibilities of kinship affiliations (real and fictive), by customary law believed to be supported by divine sanctions and reinforced by long usage, by the socialization of children, and by oft-repeated sayings, proverbs, and heuristic stories. . . . One of the most important features of landlord-stranger reciprocities is the privilege of marrying local women, accorded valued strangers. . . . In short, western Africans opportunistically redefine their identities in response to changing circumstances. Remote, even fictive, kinship ties, special bonds between groups such as "joking relationships," indeed social or cultural advantages one can claim or contrive have for centuries facilitated human relationships and expedited trade, travel, migration, and settlement in western Africa. (Brooks 1993, 37–39, 28)

Such versions of West African history reflect the predominant view of African ethnicity as inherently fluid, opportunistic, and situational, and boundaries between groups as porous (e.g., d'Azevedo 1971; Mark 1999). Although this view may accurately represent some areas and aspects of West Africa, it does not ring true for Diola in Susana. There is an assumption in much Africanist literature (as in Brooks) that intermarriage indicates inexorable progress toward the universal goal of integration. "Marriage," states T. O. Beidelman, "converts strangers to kin" (Beidelman 1986, 20). But perhaps Diola, rather than encouraging such integration, were concerned about this trajectory and its implications for collective identity, and were reacting, consciously or not, to a perceived state of boundary confusion. An alternate view to one emphasizing the political aspects of ethnicity is one that considers boundaries between groups, no matter what they are based on, as essential for the production and reproduction of identity. Frederik Barth (1969) generally receives most of the credit for this insight. This perspective, however, can be recognized in a number of earlier works, including Georg Simmel's discussion of conflict. As Simmel rightly (and presciently) notes, the most intransigent forms of conflict often occur between groups that are not strangers to each other. "Where enough similarities continue to make confusions and blurred outlines possible, points of difference need an emphasis not justified by the issue but only by that danger of confusion. . . . The degeneration of difference in convictions into hatred and fighting only occurs when there were essential similarities between the parties" (Simmel 1955, 42). This observation is echoed in Michael Watts's discussion of the "narcissism of minor differences" (Watts 1999), as well as in Aidan Southall's (1971) study of twinship in East Africa. The point here is that the construction and emphasis of difference among groups takes on particular importance and strength in contexts that risk such boundary confusion; difference is instituted and emphasized when similarity threatens to obscure it. Tambiah asks whether we can push this point even further in an attempt to explain ethnic conflict:

The greater the blurrings of and ambiguities between the socially constructed categories of difference, the greater the venom of the imposed boundaries, when conflict erupts, between the self and the other, "us" and "them." . . . Can we push this process of creating and repudiating the intolerable "other" in current ethnonationalist conflict any further? Can we say that it is because that component of "sameness" that the ethnic enemy shares with you, and because your enemy is already a part of you, that you must forcibly expel him or her from yourself, objectify him or her as the total other? Accordingly, that component of "difference" from you, whether it be allegedly "religious," "linguistic," or "racial," is so exaggerated and magnified that this stereotyped "other" must be degraded, dehumanized, and compulsively obliterated? (Tambiah 1996, 276)

Although such a drive certainly did not *cause* this conflict, perhaps Tambiah's wary hedging provides some insight into why Diola so adamantly oppose the return of Fula residents. To be sure, there are other, more easily identifiable factors involved in such a stance, the reclamation of land surrounding Kandembā being foremost among them. But it might be worthwhile to consider the postconflict hardening of Diola attitudes as, in part, a reaction to increasing boundary confusion between the two groups.

I have argued that elements in this case challenge the predominant view of West African ethnicity as inherently fluid and politically fabricated. Even Mahmood Mamdani, who finds fault with the overemphasis in recent scholarship on the colonial creation of ethnicity, asserts that colonial rule in Africa, through the establishment and differentiation of customary law, changed the tenor of the relationship between host and migrant. According to Mamdani, precolonial Africa was characterized by more incorporative, multiethnic relations, especially with regard to access to land. While my study of the Diola-Fula conflict in Susana generally supports Mamdani's approach to ethnicity and ethnic conflict, my consideration of the complexity of host-migrant relations in this case suggests a modification of Mamdani's analysis that such polarized relations between host and migrant are the legacy of late colonialism's "regime of differentiation" (Mamdani 1996, 7). Rather, I suggest that Diola exclusionary practices predate colonial rule in this region.

The history of Susana's consolidation as a unified village provides a clue to these dynamics. Susana became an integrated entity relatively recently. Susana is a federation of villages that were joined together during the long period of internecine fighting among Diola villages, throughout the seventeenth, eighteenth, and nineteenth centuries, by a somewhat mythic culture hero named Ambona. During Ambona's time, about the early 1800s, Diola in this area were scattered in small forest hamlets, often made up of a single lineage. Hamlets would often raid one another, and incessant fighting among Diola villages is recorded both in Diola oral history and in colonial accounts (Dinis 1946; Lopes de Lima 1836; Girard 1969; Taborda 1950).

Ambona hailed originally from Cassu, a Baiote village about eight kilometers from Susana, but he was brought to one of Susana's as yet unfederated villages as a young boy to herd cows for a distant uncle. Ambona grew up to be a great warrior and conducted many successful raids on outlying hamlets and villages, either scattering their residents or bringing them to settle in one of Susana's villages. After several successful campaigns, Ambona decided that he would make Susana invincible, but in order to do so he would need to unite Susana's still distinct and autonomous wards, as well as its mixed "firstcomer" and "newcomer" population. By this time, most of Susana's neighborhoods were permanently hosting families from conquered villages. In a strategic attempt to strengthen Susana's fragile sense of unity, Ambona and other elders officially prohibited the open expression of "immigrant" origins, hoping to erase such distinctions and create a common identity among Susana's residents.

To this day, ancestral origins from one of the outlying and conquered villages, such as Caipa or Sebutul, are not discussed openly. Susana residents downplay "original" and "newcomer" distinctions in the service of greater unity, although these distinctions are still known and can be recognized through names, lineage histories, landholdings, and whispered (and quickly suppressed) conversations. I was often told, especially by members of "original" Susana lineages, that it was deemed highly inappropriate to openly discuss the fact that one was a "real" Susana resident, whereas others were "not from here." In some cases, a person making such a remark could be disciplined through a hearing at a spirit shrine and a fine. Susana residents even pride themselves on having done away with a status distinction that is preserved in neighboring villages, the distinction between original inhabitants and slaves, or *amikelau* (pl. *emikelai*). *Amikelau* can be glossed as both "slave" and "stranger," so it holds the simultaneous meaning of "someone bought or sold" and "someone from another village."[19] In Susana, no such distinctions are made, and no one can call anyone else an *amikelau*.

Susana's suppressed immigrant past provides a telling example of how history is manipulated to serve present ends, in this case the consolidation and unification of a village population for defensive purposes in the context of omnipresent war. But the unexpected result is that the suppression of such distinctions helps pickle them in a particularly potent brine; what is meant to be forgotten simmers just below the surface and subtly intrudes into social interactions in myriad ways. This phenomenon recalls Igor Kopytoff's discussion of frontier societies, in which an outward appearance of status equality among all members was upheld and strangers in host societies thus became "internal secrets." This was especially important given the need to maintain adherents in frontier societies through "good treatment" of new members, regardless of their formal status. As Kopytoff notes, "An important aspect of good treatment was to make knowledge of their precise status a strictly internal matter. A secret guarded by autonomous kin groups, particularly in the uncentralized African societies, has always been the secret of 'who is' and 'who isn't' a real relative, as opposed to a 'stranger' or 'slave.' Vis-à-vis the outside world, the strangers could hold their heads high by being publicly defined as relatives" (Kopytoff 1987, 48).

Although Susana residents regard their having abolished *emikelai* distinctions as placing them on the moral high ground relative to neighboring villages, Susana's Diola make distinctions among various kinds of strangers, encoded in both behavioral and linguistic practices. In addition to *amikelau*,

Diola have several other terms to describe different types of strangers. *Amasorau* refers to either a guest or a stranger and implies a reciprocal, almost proprietary relation between guest and host. An *amasorau* is a person who stays in one's home, and vice versa, when one visits the other's village. *Amasorau* also has a temporary feel to it; it describes someone who visits for a short time but does not settle in the host village. An *abilabilau* is similar to an *amasorau* but can stay for a longer time and can come from farther away, even Europe. *Alulumau* refers to urban, or in one Diola glossing, "civilized," people. This is the term most often employed when referring to whites or to other Africans (Diola or non-Diola) trying to emulate whites. Finally, *apasianau* refers particularly to African strangers, including those from other ethnic groups, who become longtime or permanent residents in Susana. Descendents of such families are likewise considered *epasianai,* even if they intermarry with Diola. Fula families in Susana were often called *epasianai.*

The most relevant aspect of these linguistic and attitudinal observations is that they expose the difficulty of incorporation into Susana society for Diola and non-Diola alike. Incorporation and integration, even for other Diola, is not the simple and straightforward affair that it is made out to be in much of the literature on West African coastal societies. It is an extremely prolonged and sometimes impossible process, and although Susana's Diola readily portray themselves as receptive and tolerant hosts, their deeply ingrained collective reluctance to erase or even diminish the boundary between landlord and stranger—which is invisible to the casual observer—cannot help but be felt as exclusion and rejection by longtime residents, especially those who, by virtue of their birthright, consider themselves to be full and equal Susanans.

With regard to the Fula population, this tension is perhaps best expressed in the different narratives regarding Fula arrival and settlement in Susana. When discussing the 30 May conflict, Diola readily point out that Fula, especially those of the younger generation, have "forgotten their own history." From a Diola perspective, the comportment of certain segments of the Fula population smacks of amnesia or, worse, ingratitude. As one Susana Diola resident reasoned: "If you invite someone into your home, does he then have the right to claim the house for himself and push you out onto the veranda?" In Diola reckoning, Fula were permanent guests on Diola land. But Susana's Fula population, especially those born in Susana, clearly did not perceive themselves as guests in Susana. Rather, Fula accounts of the conflict are saturated with a sense of belonging, not as guests or strangers but as "children of Susana."

At the heart of the problem lies a question about the possibility for pluralism. At what point do "outsiders" or "newcomers" become outright members of a community, even if they are in the minority, and does their continued marginal status eventually if not inevitably create fertile ground for polariza- tion? Although the facts of this particular case suggest that it might have been resolved or prevented through effective administration or a host of other well- timed interventions, this question lurked closely behind attitudes and actions on both sides. Most Diola in Susana readily admit that had the Fula resi- dents not built a mosque on the controversial site, a conflict of the same scale would have erupted over almost anything else. Although such after-the-fact assessments are impossible to verify, they suggest that there had been friction between the groups for a long time. Even those who claim that Diola actions were tied to changes in the national political climate are quick to point out the long-standing tensions between the groups. As one non-Diola Susana resident observed, "If Nino had stayed in power, no Diola would have dared to do anything like this. . . . Fula would have built their mosque and nothing would have happened to it. They would have left it alone. They were afraid of the PAIGC regime. But after the PAIGC regime left, that's when this started. But the real problem started long before this mosque business. Long before. The change of regime opened up the opportunity to do something that was a long time in coming."

In the Susana case, the roles of a range of social actors—young men, state administrators and politicians, journalists, and military personnel—shed light on certain aspects of postcolonial experience in Africa, especially in shaping and interpreting so-called ethnic conflict. But perhaps more intriguing—and more troubling—is that the structural and historical features in Susana, es- pecially those that have a bearing on the conditions of possibility for incor- poration and pluralism, help explain why such seemingly rapid polarization between the groups might have actually been brewing for quite some time. The analytic value of this case lies less in the moment of collective violence on 30 May, which briefly captured and focused national attention on this out- of-the-way place, and more in the ongoing processes of incorporation and exclusion that continue to challenge postcolonial Guinea-Bissau in its effort to become a peaceful pluralistic society.

Notes

This essay benefited from insightful comments by participants in the Sawyer Foundation's September 2003 international workshop, "Africa and Violence: Identities, Histories, Rep- resentations." The Social Science Research Council's Program on Global Security and Cooperation, the Wenner-Gren Foundation for Anthropological Research, the National Science Foundation, and Emory University's Internationalization Fund provided financial support for my research in Guinea-Bissau. Finally, I thank my friends and colleagues in Guinea-Bissau for generously sharing their experiences and insights with me.

1. Information about this case is based on ethnographic and historical research conducted in this area. I spent twenty-two months (October 2001–July 2003) in Guinea-Bissau, the bulk of this time as a resident in Susana. The first time I visited Susana, however, was in July 2000, shortly after the events described above, and although my stay was brief and I did not conduct any systematic inquiries, my impressions from this time helped shape my subsequent research plan. I should also make clear that my own knowledge is uneven regarding the groups involved in this case. I lived and worked and studied among an almost exclusively Diola population in Susana, since by the time I arrived the Fula population had already moved to São Domingos, a town thirty-six kilometers down a sometimes impassable road. Although I did befriend and interview Fula men and women who had previously lived in Susana, I did not study Fula society (in São Domingos or in its previous incarnation in Susana) in the same way that I studied Diola society in Susana, and so my analysis is weighted toward the Diola. This does not mean, however, that my judgment is inevitably biased in favor of the Diola; however, because I know them much better, I am more deeply attuned to both their admirable and their problematical attributes that are manifest in this case, and the resulting orientation is a combination of ethnographic appreciation and, as Richard Handler puts it, "destructive analysis" (Handler 1985).

2. Precise population statistics are difficult to obtain. Regarding Diola in Senegal, estimates range from 200,000 to 250,000 (Mark 1985, 6), to 400,000 (Baum 1987, 1). Linares (1992, 5) suggests a middle ground of 260,000–340,000. Although Diola are the majority ethnic group in the Casamance, they are a minority in Senegal overall, where they make up 6–8 percent of the total population (Linares 1992). Diola are a minority group in Guinea-Bissau, numbering approximately 13,971 (*Recenseamento geral da população e habitação* 1991), although Scantamburlo (1999) estimates a total Guinean Diola population of 15,000. Based on initial survey data, I believe both of these numbers to be too low, and suggest a total Guinean Diola population of approximately 20,000 (not including the resident refugee populations of Casamance Diola currently spread throughout Guinean Diola villages).

3. I have opted to use the label "Diola" instead of "Felupe" because this is the term currently preferred among Diola themselves, who consider "Felupe" to be a Portuguese misnomer. The word "Diola" most likely came from Wolof or Mandinga travelers to the area and only became accepted internally in the nineteenth century. The reader will note that Fula typically use "Felupe" to refer to Diola in their narratives. For the village, I use "Susana," a Portuguese mislabeling of the Diola name Esana. Diola residents in this area use "Esana," "Sesana," and "Susana" interchangeably, depending on the context and interlocutor. I have chosen to use the Portuguese name because it is more commonly recognized both within and outside Guinea-Bissau.

4. In the past several years, as people have become more integrated into the cash economy, residents from fishing villages have shunned the traditional barter market, preferring the more lucrative cash markets in Elia (a nearby Baiote village), São Domingos, Ziguinchor, and even Bissau. Susana, as a result, is often without fish. Some members of

other villages (notably Varela, in which there is a resident population of Mandinga and Wolof fishermen from Senegal) claim that Susana is without fish because the fishing villages are punishing Susana residents for their actions against the Fula.

5. Another reason that Diola orient themselves (and their products) northward is that laborers are better paid and rural products bring more in Senegal and the Gambia than in Guinea-Bissau.

6. See Forrest 1992 for an excellent discussion of Guinea-Bissau's village committees.

7. The Diola word *eluupai* (pl. *siluupasu*) means both "family" and "house." So closely tied are an adult man and his house that upon his death his house is torn down. This usually takes place a year or more after his death, to give his wife (or wives) time to remarry or build a small widow's house (*hungumahu*). Virilocality extends even after the death of the husband, as a widow's house is built in her husband's compound (*hankahu*) rather than in her natal neighborhood, and a woman's funeral and burial take place in her in-married neighborhood.

8. Similar shrine societies exist throughout the Senegambian region; see, e.g., Brooks 1993 and Forrest 2003.

9. In the nearby Baiote village of Elia the *ai* is not subject to many of these restrictions, but he can never leave the bounds of his own village.

10. See Eric Gable's study (2000) of the intergenerational dynamics of Manjaco, a nearby and related ethnic group in Guinea-Bissau, which offers a compelling demonstration that youth challenging elders' power has a long history in Manjaco cultural production—rather than being a "modern" innovation—thus providing a corrective to nostalgic versions of West African gerontocracies.

11. The PAIGC is the nationalist revolutionary party founded by Amílcar Cabral. After winning the eleven-year war for liberation against the Portuguese, the PAIGC went on to rule Guinea-Bissau as a one-party state. Nineteen ninety-two marked the first year that other political parties were allowed to enter into the Guinean political field. The PAIGC lost its first election since independence in 2000, in the aftermath of the 7 de Junho war in 1998. The PAIGC regained control of the parliament in the 2004 legislative elections.

12. All personal names, except those of widely known figures in the national political arena, have been changed. All quotations from Diola, Fula, and other residents in Guinea-Bissau have been either transcribed and translated by me from tape-recorded interviews or were reconstructed in my field notes immediately after conversations.

13. This does not hold true for the liberation-war period. Many of the current land conflicts stem from the period of instability during the 1960s and 1970s, when major dislocations—by Guineans who fought during the war and those who sought refuge in neighboring countries—led to confusion over proprietary rights to land.

14. The decision to build a centrally located maternity center represents a significant shift in Diola practices regarding childbirth. Women's reproduction is a highly secret subject, and Diola men and uninitiated women (e.g., those who have not yet given birth) are supposed to be completely ignorant of such matters (see van Tilburg 1998 for an illuminating discussion of secrecy and silence surrounding Diola pregnancy and childbirth). Each neighborhood has a separate maternity house, fenced in by tall palm fronds

and completely off-limits to men, where in-married women give birth, assisted by elder women and traditional midwives. However, with access to modern health practices within the past twenty years (through both the state health post and the Catholic Mission's clinic), birthing practices have shifted as Diola have become aware of decreased mortality in childbirth at such facilities, and most of Susana's women currently give birth in one or the other of these clinics. Nonetheless, Diola remain uncomfortable giving birth in such public settings, both of which are used by men and women for all health concerns. The construction of a separate maternity center reconciles the issue by providing a compromise between the sacredness and secrecy of women's reproduction and the need for improved and professional health services.

15. Diola male initiation takes place only once every thirty years in each village. (For detailed descriptions of Diola and Baiote male initiation practices in the Casamance, see Mark 1992; Schloss 1992; and Thomas 1970.) Preparations involve complicated coordination among residents to accumulate and distribute the massive resources involved in sustaining the increase in population—because of returnees and guests. Initiates and most of the adult male population typically remain in the initiation forest for three months. In Susana's 1998 initiation, men opted to add another month onto their stay.

16. The *bombolom* (in Diola, *kagataku*) is a large slit gong used in several Guinean coastal societies as a form of long-range communication. Among the Diola the *bombolom* is most often used for funerals and major ceremonies, although in the past it was used to announce an outside attack or to organize a war effort.

17. After his election in February 2000 Yalla's presidency has been marked by increased instability in all government institutions. Yalla was deposed in a popularly supported bloodless coup on 14 September 2003 and replaced by an interim government. Parliamentary elections, which were slated and canceled four times after Yalla dissolved the parliament in November 2002, took place in March 2004.

18. Most Diola women who had married Fula men left Susana with the other Fula families in May 2000, but some have since returned. The experiences of these "interethnic" families, although beyond the scope of this essay, deserves further study.

19. Historically, being an *amikelau* did not necessarily imply that one's work was any different from one's owner's. Currently, these status distinctions rarely manifest themselves in daily life, and most younger residents in villages that preserve these labels are unaware of who belongs to each group. The distinction surfaces only during betrothal rites (*emikelai* can only marry other *emikelai*) and burial practices, in which an *amikelau's* grave is marked by a string that comes out from the ground and is tied to a stick near the gravesite. In one village near Susana in which *amikelau* status is preserved in such marital and funerary practices, residents claim that *emikelai* arrived in the village in the form of fish excrement (or, in some versions, fish vomit).

References

Barth, Frederik, ed. 1969. *Ethnic Groups and Boundaries.* Prospect Heights, IL: Waveland.

Baum, Robert M. 1987. A Religious and Social History of the Diola-Esalalu in Pre-Colonial Senegambia. PhD diss., Department of History, Yale University.

———. 1990. The Emergence of a Diola Christianity. *Africa* 60 (3): 370–98.

Beidelman, T. O. 1986. *Moral Imagination in Kaguru Modes of Thought.* Bloomington: Indiana University Press.

Brass, Paul R. 1997. *Theft of an Idol: Text and Context in the Representation of Collective Violence.* Princeton, NJ: Princeton University Press.

Brooks, George. 1993. *Landlords and Strangers: Ecology, Society, and Trade in Western Africa, 1000–1630.* Boulder, CO: Westview.

Cohen, Abner. 1969. *Custom and Politics in Urban Africa: A Study of Hausa Migrants in Yoruba Towns.* Berkeley and Los Angeles: University of California Press.

Daniel, E. Valentine. 1996. *Charred Lullabies: Chapters in an Anthropology of Violence.* Princeton, NJ: Princeton University Press.

Das, Veena, Arthur Kleinman, Mamphela Ramphele, and Pamela Reynolds, eds. 2000. *Violence and Subjectivity.* Berkeley and Los Angeles: University of California Press.

d'Azevedo, Warren L. 1971. Tribe and Chiefdom on the Windward Coast. *Rural Africana* 15:10–29.

Diário de Bissau. 2000. 28 June, 6 July.

Dinis, A. Dias. 1946. As Tribos da Guiné Portuguesa na História. *Portugal em Africa* 2:206–15.

Forrest, Joshua B. 1992. *Guinea-Bissau: Power, Conflict, and Renewal in a West African Nation.* Boulder, CO: Westview.

———. 2003. *Lineages of State Fragility: Rural Civil Society in Guinea-Bissau.* Athens: Ohio University Press.

Gable, Eric. 2000. The Culture Development Club: Youth, Neo-Tradition, and the Construction of Society in Guinea-Bissau. *Anthropological Quarterly* 73 (4): 195–203.

Girard, Jean. 1969. *Genèse du pouvoir charismatique en Basse Casamance (Sénégal).* Dakar: Institut Fondamentale d'Afrique Noire.

Handler, Richard. 1985. On Dialogue and Destructive Analysis: Problems in Narrating Nationalism and Ethnicity. *Journal of Anthropological Research* 41:171–82.

Kopytoff, Igor, ed. 1987. *The African Frontier: The Reproduction of Traditional African Societies.* Bloomington: Indiana University Press.

Kuper, Leo. 1977. *The Pity of It All: Polarisation of Racial and Ethnic Relations.* Minneapolis: University of Minnesota Press.

Lentz, Carola. 1995. Tribalism and Ethnicity in Africa: A Review of Four Decades of Anglophone Research. *Cahiers des sciences humaines* 31:303–28.

Linares, Olga. 1981. From Tidal Swamp to Inland Valley: On the Social Organization of Wet Rice Cultivation among the Diola of Senegal. *Africa* 51 (2): 557–95.

———. 1992. *Power, Prayer, and Production: The Jola of Casamance, Senegal.* Cambridge: Cambridge University Press.

Lopes de Lima, J. J. 1836. Memoria dos Felupes. *Jornal de Sociedade dos Amigos das Letras* 3:68–69.

Malkki, Liisa H. 1995. *Purity and Exile: Violence, Memory, and National Cosmology among Hutu Refugees in Tanzania.* Chicago: University of Chicago Press.

Mamdani, Mahmood. 1996. *Citizen and Subject: Contemporary Africa and the Legacy of Late Colonialism.* Princeton, NJ: Princeton University Press.

Mark, Peter. 1985. *A Cultural, Economic, and Religious History of the Basse Casamance since 1500.* Stuttgart: F. Steiner.

———. 1992. *The Wild Bull and the Sacred Forest: Form, Meaning, and Change in Senegambian Initiation Masks.* Cambridge: Cambridge University Press.

———. 1999. The Evolution of "Portuguese" Identity: Luso-Africans on the Upper Guinea Coast from the Sixteenth to the Early Nineteenth Century. *Journal of African History* 40:173–91.

Mbembe, Achille. 1992. Provisional Notes on the Postcolony. *Africa* 62 (1): 1–37.

Recenseamento geral da população e habitação. 1991. Bissau: Instituto Nacional de Estudos e Pesquisa.

Scantamburlo, Luigi. 1999. *Dicionário do Guineense, Volume I.* Lisbon: FASPEBI.

Schloss, Marc R. 1992. *The Hatchet's Blood: Separation, Power, and Gender in Ehing Social Life.* Tucson: University of Arizona Press.

Simmel, Georg. 1955. *Conflict.* Translated by K. H. Wolff. Glencoe, IL: Free Press.

Southall, Aidan. 1971. Twinship and Symbolic Structure. In *The Interpretation of Ritual: Essays in Honour of A. I. Richards,* edited by J. S. La Fontaine. London: Tavistock.

Taborda, António da Cunha. 1950. Apontamentos etnográficos sobre as Felupes de Suzana. *Boletim cultural de Guiné Portuguesa* 5:187–223.

Tambiah, Stanley. 1996. *Leveling Crowds: Ethnonationalist Conflicts and Collective Violence in South Asia.* Berkeley and Los Angeles: University of California Press.

Thomas, Louis Vincent. 1959. *Les Diola: Essai d'analyse fonctionelle sur une population de Basse Casamance. Mémoires 58–59.* Dakar: Institut Fondamentale d'Afrique Noire.

———. 1970. Mort symbolique et naissance initiatique (Bukut chez les Diola-Niomoun). *Cahiers des religions africaines* 7:41–71.

van Tilburg, Mariette. 1998. Interviews of the Unspoken: Incompatible Initiations in Senegal Fieldwork. *Anthropology and Humanism* 23 (2): 177–89.

Watts, Michael. 1999. Geographies of Violence and the Narcissism of Minor Difference. In *Struggles over Geography: Violence, Freedom, and Development at the Millennium,* edited by Michael Watts. Hettner Lectures. Heidelberg: Department of Geography, University of Heidelberg.

Wilmsen, Edwin N., and P. McAllister. 1996. *The Politics of Difference: Ethnic Premises in a World of Power.* Chicago: University of Chicago Press.

Youth, Gender, and Generation

"Survival Is Political"
History, Violence, and the Contemporary Power Struggle in Sierra Leone

MARTHA CAREY

Every generation must out of relative obscurity,
discover its mission, fulfill it or betray it.

—Frantz Fanon, *The Wretched of the Earth*

I N many respects, the violence that has plagued Sierra Leone since 1991 must be read as part of a larger, truly regional conflict (Hirsch 2001; Opala 1998; Reno 1995; Richards 1996). Local mercenaries, natural resources, and weapons move fluidly through international borders and lines of affiliation, while civilians continuously cross and recross into neighboring countries. Yet this violence also refracts into different patterns as it unfolds within the specific history and context of each nation, simultaneously creating very local accents. The trait that came to characterize international discourse on the Sierra Leonean chapter of the war is amputation.

In January 2002 President Tejan Kabbah declared that Sierra Leone's war was officially over (Human Rights Watch 2003, 3). Such a statement contains many implicit meanings, most notably that there are winners and losers in this confrontation and that power is no longer under contestation. David Keen warns us not to be so quickly deluded. Contemporary "civil wars are not simply declared, and they cannot simply be declared over," he argues (1996, 22), suggesting that the *cessation* of open violence may not in fact be equated with an *end* to conflict. This begs the questions, first, whether the war is really over, and then, if that is in fact the case, who perceive themselves, and are perceived by others, as controlling power in Sierra Leone today. In this essay, I attempt to discover who the "winners" of Sierra Leone's civil war are. To do so, I focus less on what started the war and look more closely at what kept it going.

There are no doubt myriad complex reasons why Sierra Leoneans took up arms when they did, but the history of this nation also suggests that there are concerns and sociopolitical tensions that have persisted in Sierra Leonean culture over time. Others have explored some prominent underlying themes, including the markedly unequal distribution of wealth gained primarily through the exploitation of rural regions by urban elites, the inadequate infrastructure throughout most of the country, and a glaringly ineffective and corrupt government (see William Reno's essay in this volume). Paul Richards was one of the first to tackle the question of disenfranchised youths as an important part of the armed insurrections. He explains that ex-combatants describe the war "in terms of an intergenerational struggle for a fairer society," and goes further to identify education and class as among the most important motivating factors prompting them to fight (Richards 1996; Richards and Peters 1998, 187). While scholars have since problematized the idea of class as one of the fundamental causes of this war, the notion of common motivations seeping through all armed groups persists (Abdullah et al. 1997). I argue here, in an attempt to contribute to unraveling the complexities of this war, that it is within the space of generational tensions that some of the underlying reasons for the *persistence* of the contemporary war can be found.

The longevity and level of Sierra Leonean's social concern over generational friction are affirmed by the existence of well-established mechanisms to regulate such discordance and stories about the dangers of uncontrolled juniors. It is important to clarify that in Sierra Leone there is no fixed definition of "youth." Initiation, generally a marker for the passage from childhood, generally begins between the ages of 13 and 20 for boys (Ijagbemi 1976; McGovern 2003). Assuming an initiation period of seven years, young adults thus returned to their villages at between 20 and 27 years of age. In some instances, people "up to the age of 35 were considered youth" (McIntyre, Aning, and Addo 2002, 8). This is striking, in light of a current average life expectancy of 40.8 years (UNDP 2005). Therefore, "youth" needs to be seen as a social category with a sliding definition.

In reaching back into Sierra Leone's history, we can pluck at threads woven into the fabric of the contemporary war to unearth those ideas and frustrations that have resonated through time and space and that were important factors in the renewed outbreak of violence in the 1990s. Richards has eloquently portrayed this war both dramaturgically and textually (1996). Using his idea of looking at "war as a type of text" or "a violent attempt to . . . 'cut in on the conversation' of others from whose company the belligerents feel excluded" (Richards 1996, xxiv), I will analyze this conflict as the continuation of an ongoing dialogue between people with a shared past who hold common ideas about power. Bringing together the trickster-hero myth of Musa Wo,[1] secret societies, and the act of forced amputation as points of commonality in the Sierra Leonean theater, I will examine different layers of possible objectives of this war to discuss whether the war is really over and to determine who controls power in postwar Sierra Leone.

The myth of Musa Wo is part of the oral traditions of all ethnic groups in Sierra Leone and reflects a past heavily influenced by Mande cultures. In Sierra Leone this particular mythological character seems to have developed traits that are unique to this country (Cosentino 1989). Musa Wo, the trickster-hero, illuminates the possibility that the objective of fighting may not, in fact, be to win in the Western sense. Open conflict and its subsequent chaos may be considered ends in themselves. The gender-specific secret societies found throughout most of this region of West Africa are central in this analysis in that they provide an autochthonous system that embraces the need to control intergenerational tensions and combines the provision of education with ideas of power and its containment. Poro, the male-based association, provides "the intelligence, co-ordination, and hierarchy for the organization of war" (Leach 2000, 588).

Atrocities have been recorded in all the countries affected by widespread violence in the Mano River region, yet the acts of systematic amputation are distinctively Sierra Leonean. That such acts of violence often were committed against people belonging to the same ethnic group as the perpetrators (Dufka 1998; Médecins Sans Frontières 1998a, 1998b)[2] suggests a very intimate discourse, a dialogue concerning local ideas of community and concepts of power.

The significance of committing amputations is a slippery subject indeed, and it is not my objective here to understand exactly why mass amputations were perpetrated. Rather, we must look below the surface of the products of hostility, for terror and violence, as Mamdani reminds us, are not perpetrated for their own sake but must be seen as a language or a tool of communication (Mamdani 2001). By reading these acts through the context outlined above and juxtaposing them to the dialogue between the fighters and their victims, I shall attempt a partial vernacular translation of these "artifacts of political violence" (Mamdani 2001, 3). Using the human body as a means of communication is not uncommon, as the "body is man's first and most natural instrument" (Mauss 1979, 104). Even in terms of warfare, the human body "both of victims and perpetrators—is the privileged terrain for staging violence" (Ferme 1998, 555), and is a "strategic target . . . of war" (Nordstrom

1998, 105). Therefore, the amputee can be seen as a vehicle through which fighters in this conflict communicated and displayed their own objectives in the war and their relationships to power. As reported in Elaine Salo's analysis, in this volume, of youthful violence in a South African township, violence has become "an alternative means" for asserting personhood and creating a new identity for oneself in a rapidly changing and unfair world. Continuing Richards's line of thought about the youthful combatants of Sierra Leone's war, I will step into this 1996 conversation, both where Richards's *Fighting for the Rainforest* leaves off (a postscript was added in 1997) and where the amputations began.

Richards states that "this war is a terror war fought with local cultural resources. Those selfsame resources . . . [are] essential to the task of rendering the terror understandable" (1996, xxix). Here, these resources become useful for understanding local ideas about the power behind the terror—its manifestations, manipulations, and communications—within a historical context, showing how old patterns of tension have ceased to be contained and why a youth-filled rebellion emerged from this brew. I will show how this most recent period of fighting can be considered one battle in a war that originated in the deep past and how it is the members of this young generation, irrespective of their political and military affiliations, who are today's victors. It is the youth who have the potential to disrupt all order at will, to destroy established mechanisms of maintaining balance, and to start the war again. This potential makes them unexpectedly powerful in postwar Sierra Leone.

Trickster, Heroes, and Local Representations of Power

In this essay I investigate the category of Sierra Leonean power that has been manifested in the recent conflict and is represented in part in the specific example of the amputee. Because of the seemingly limitless interpretations of the concept of power, it is necessary to clarify the *who,* the *what,* and the *how* of power in Sierra Leone. As in other African societies, in Sierra Leone power is not seen as originating from any single source and therefore does not continually reside in one unique location or with one type of agent. Rather it is seen as all-pervasive, its source being located "in the interaction between natural, social and supernatural realms" (Arens and Karp 1989, xvii). It is to this space between visible and invisible permeable realms, where boundaries are blurred, that we must turn our gaze.

Why choose to look at oral narratives? Scholars such as Luise White have shown that different layers of oral narratives exist and that by reading them from a local perspective we can gain insights into past experiences that may not be apparent to those on the outside. These stories tell us where "power and uncertainty" reside and also "explain what was fearsome and why" (White 2000, 5). It is partly here, in these stories, that we find the manifestation of concepts of power and the violent legacy of Sierra Leone. The narratives are anchors that speak of those troubles considered to be inherent in Sierra Leonean life.

Various forms and perceptions of power are described in Sierra Leonean myths and legends. One example common to the region is the shape-shifting, transformative ability to move between human and animal form, a power belonging to the elephant-man of the Mende foundation myth of Serabu, Bumpe Chiefdom. Here we find the chiefdom's founder "out prospecting in new country one day, when he met a Banta hunter. The latter gave him charge of the new country, after they had made friends, and it turned out that this Banta man was an elephant, 'because in those days, elephants had the power of changing themselves into human beings'" (Little 1951, n. 26).

Other folktales speak of important life lessons. The Sundiata epic, known throughout western Africa, which tells of the founding of the empire of Mali, is told in multiple versions across Sierra Leone. However, in all its Sierra Leone variations Sundiata takes on the specific configuration of a trickster-hero known among the Mende as Musa Wo (Cosentino 1989, 29). The unwanted son and heir to the chief, Musa Wo is born, after an abnormally long gestation period, with supernatural strength and the ability to converse with animals, but he seems unable to grow up, either physically or socially. His first order of business is to avenge his and his mother's wrongful exile and humiliation and to regain his rightful place in the political sphere of his father's chieftaincy, thereby restoring social continuity. This revolt against his father, Musa Wo's first heroic act, exemplifies the "primal struggle between the overbearing father and rebellious son" that is at the heart of all his labors (Cosentino 1989, 34).

Yet Musa Wo is not a typical mythological hero. Rather, he is an *enfant terrible* who "descends to the level of a relentless, obscene, and amoral monster" and seems to "represent the dark side of . . . social values" (Cosentino 1989, 22). While he is trying to put the world right, something happens and Musa Wo becomes an "unrestrained psychopath." He is accused alternately (or simultaneously) of horrible acts, such as "fratricide, patricide, genocide" (Cosentino 1989, 27), making him both hero and trickster.

The story of Musa Wo is a story of youth's potential "longing for free expression in a tightly constructed society" (Cosentino 1989, 36). His anarchic qualities ironically give him the potential for both creation and chaos, and also offer "the antidote to endless social rigor," an "entropic stasis" seen in the father-son relationship, or the "promised relief . . . of the *tabula rasa*" (Cosentino 1989, 32). Musa Wo's tale tells us that in Sierra Leone "to be contained is to be controlled" (Hardin 1993, 98). When this youthful potential is no longer bound by society and its institutions, it becomes uncontrolled, creating disorder and inverting relationships.

Conflict between generations is not, of course, unique to West Africa. For example, the ancient Greek story of Oedipus and the biblical tale of the prodigal son both concern this tension. Yet the political weight that this unresolved intergenerational struggle carries is unique in the contemporary African context, where demographics illustrate the importance of this issue. An estimated 44.7 percent of the population of Sierra Leone is under age fourteen (CIA 2005), a statistic not unlike those in most sub-Saharan societies. Musa Wo personifies the bifurcation of power as a man-child who moves between worlds, much like the Banta elephant-man, and has an oscillating relationship with order, yet is an integral and necessary part of the whole unit of social life. It is not difficult to find similarities between this mythological character and the young fighters in present-day Sierra Leone, who are themselves trying to negotiate between the world of modernity, with its associated expectations, and that of a local space, with its limited capabilities.

Musa Wo's unique destructive character represents a particular manifestation of societal tension that is specific to the Sierra Leonean context. In comparing the Sierra Leonean versions with other regional versions of this Mande epic, Dan Costentino notes, "Sundiata creates and sustains a great empire; Mwindo learns the nature of perfect chieftaincy; but Musa Wo destroys the very institutions of office and state" (1989, 30). We are left, however, with the question what it is in contemporary Sierra Leone that supports a continued focus on the violent contestation of power between generations.

Poro and Youth

The known history of Sierra Leone is one of movement, violence, and uncertainty. From at least the time of the collapse of the Songhai state, various pressures, most caused by violence, have prompted population migrations throughout this region of West Africa. Historical accounts of early European explorers speak of "invasions" of Mande-speaking people sometime in the late 1500s (d'Almada 1594). With the advent of the transatlantic slave trade and the arrival and eventual settlement of European traders, lucrative economic and political opportunities developed for local business people. Both the international and indigenous slave trades were vital in this new global economy, and they were in large part responsible for maintaining the atmosphere of uncertainty, hostility, mistrust, and displacement (Shaw 2002b).

As European demands for cash crops and forest products—palm oil, kola, rice, and wood—grew, so too did the need for larger labor forces. Big Men needed work groups not only to cultivate or collect these resources but also to transport them to market. Labor was acquired through slave raids that also led to alliances with other authority figures. The result was the formation of shifting confederacies whose periodic collapses made conflict, dislocation, and uncertainty aspects of everyday life. This pattern continued at least until 1928, when the British government outlawed indigenous slavery and the brokerage systems of these Big Men began to crumble. Within this shifting and heterogeneous environment, we find the secret societies.

Divided along gender lines, secret societies function within all facets of Sierra Leonean life and offer communities ways to socialize youth, integrate strangers, and maintain social order. Poro, the ubiquitous male society, is universal, initiating basically all boys in local communities. It is also hierarchical, offering only a select few entry to the highest and politically most influential levels. Poro's female counterpart, known as both Sande and Bundu in Sierra Leone, similarly trains girls, and offers certain senior women opportunities to become wealthy through the negotiation of marriage ties. I focus on Poro here, for it is charged with the transformation of boys into trustworthy men who can be loyal fighters, as well as with the coordination of war (Leach 2000).

Citing a relatively early anthropological study of Poro, Kenneth Wylie remarked that in "a highly mobile and diversified adaptive situation," Poro forges and solidifies hierarchical relationships between elders and youths through initiation and the passing on of esoteric knowledge. Its success in providing stability in a confused and shifting world can be seen in the fact that in contemporary Sierra Leone Poro has continued to control political and religious hierarchies within local communities (Wylie 1977, 23).

Yet not all members of a group perceive social regulations as positive. This is especially true when it comes to systems of controlling power. Poro elders directly influence the social, economic, and political potential of young members of local communities. Such a role can be seen either as benevolent or invasive, depending on the perspective of the agent. This tension around controlling the production of youthful agency and the desire to wrest it from the gerontocratic power systems is at the heart of the recent civil conflict. How, then, does this control affect the daily reality of an up-and-coming generation?

It is the Zoes,[3] or elders of Poro, who mediate between the visible and invisible worlds, who communicate between the spirits and the community in both secular and nonsecular matters, and who control the passage into adulthood from adolescence. For the vast majority of youths in Sierra Leone, the first, most crucial step on the road to becoming an adult is initiation into

Poro or Sande (Bundu). It is during this period of seclusion that initiates learn the secrets of the society and are taught the lessons that will enable them to function as members of the community.[4] It is only after leaving the sacred Poro bush that individuals are considered adults, that is, capable of handling social responsibility without being selfish and destructive (Hoffer 1975; Mac-Cormack 1980). One of the tasks of the Poro, then, is to lead the young generation away from the path of Musa Wo.

Poro's position of power, and the Zo elders' indispensability to the vibrancy and well-being of the community, are maintained in several ways, one of the most important being secrecy. Many scholars report that when all is said and done, the elders actually withhold more knowledge than they impart to their initiates. The realization that knowledge, and therefore access to many forms of power, remains restricted must be for some both disappointing and frustrating. The Zoes use secrecy as "a boundary mechanism separating members of different social categories or groups" (Murphy 1980, 193). But in a society where Musa Wo can be expected to emerge at any time, the elders have many reasons not to reveal everything to the young generation. "The man who lays his secrets before the world shows his rivals how to become his enemies" (proverb quoted in d'Azevedo 1962, 34).

During their long seclusion in the forest, the minors' lives are filled with hard work for the chiefs and Zoes, farming and weaving mats, baskets, and hammocks that these elders then sell in the market for personal profit (Murphy 1980). C. P. Meillassoux explains this "economic privilege" very clearly: "The authority of the elders rests on withholding knowledge, and it is this which supports and justifies the control of youth's labor products" (1960, 49). Such a patron-client relationship, based on the exploitation of labor, echoes strongly the Big Men system and indigenous slavery. Between the lack of household labor that the youths' absence represents (labor that is absolutely essential for adequate rice production) and the huge sums families must pay to Poro, acquiring knowledge and becoming an adult is an expensive process in Sierra Leone.

There *is* some possibility for moving up the ranks of Poro hierarchy and becoming a member of the inner circle of Zoes, but acceptance is based on a combination of heredity and costly ritual initiations (Fulton 1972; Little 1966). The fees for initiation into these higher-ranking Zo positions are usually so prohibitive that "only a very wealthy man of advanced years could hope to pass initiation into these higher degrees" (Little 1965, 359), which allows the Zoes to control the ranks of their own leadership.

Not only is mystical power associated with the Zoes, but they also wield considerable control over secular power. Poro gives legitimacy to the chiefs by approving all of their political activities, including those concerning the choice to partake in wars (Fulton 1972; Little 1965). In 1896 the British colonial government decided to create the inherited position of paramount chief as a local representative to the government and to handpick those who would assume this new role and maintain them for life. In this way, local positions of authority became official extensions of the centralized government (Hardin 1993). This environment also created different relationships between secular and nonsecular power and drew traditional leaders much closer to the parasitic central government, either in opposition to it or in support of it. Many Zoes of Poro became entwined with this state system by putting their sacred powers up for sale to advance the careers of politicians, both local and central (Dorjahn 1960; Shaw 2002b). Between the lineage restrictions to the inherited secular position of chief and the combination of genealogical requirements and cost restrictions associated with attaining high-ranking positions in Poro, access to political and nonsecular power is virtually unattainable for the majority of young Sierra Leoneans.

Poro also regulates the more pedestrian avenues to adulthood, authority and success. Once initiation has finished, the people departing the bush are called "those who may procreate," making them eligible for marriage (Mac-Cormack 1980). It is primarily through marriage, and obtaining a wife's land, that men who do not own land (and therefore are nonsettlers and do not belong to a chiefly lineage) are able to stop being clients to the ruling houses. A wife and children also mean more labor potential, removing one of the biggest obstacles in cash-crop farming and increasing the household earning capacity. However, marriage remains dependent upon the ability to pay brideprice. Those men who are members of non-landowning families (the majority today) are often unable to garner financial support from their impoverished families, and so resort to internal migration within Sierra Leone, usually to the capital, Freetown, or to the mines, in order to earn money (Jackson 1977; MacCormack 1982). The consequences of economic decline and the resultant increasing disenfranchisement of the youth were clearly visible just prior to the recent war. "In situations of relatively scarce resources, when most sons know their chances of inheriting either resources or position are slight . . . the pressure . . . is intense. Anxiety, tensions, and anger are words that crop up in a young unmarried man's discussion of his relationship with [his parents]" (Hardin 1993, 72).

Still, having the bride-price, which today is paid primarily in cash rather than in local commodities, is not always enough to allow a man to marry the woman of his choosing; marriage is also regulated in part by the secret societies. Sande has a monopoly on "certifying women as eligible wives," and marriages are often negotiated and sanctioned through the two associations (MacCormack 1980). By maintaining control of marriage ties, the elders also maintain control of the power of land rights, lineage, individual economic advancement, and, therefore, authority.

We see that Poro elders have "a finger in every pie" in Sierra Leonean society (Little 1965) and can represent the at times insurmountable barriers facing the young generations today. Yet, to be clear, it is not being debated that many of Sierra Leone's young generation respect and appreciate these cultural mechanisms. Surely not every boy who goes through Poro perceives these social structures in negative terms. However, in any community, not all will submit "passively to the law of elders" (Bayart 1993, 113). In the modern context, feelings of frustration and resentment toward traditional institutions and community elders have been exacerbated, engendering the "conflict within the individual and between him and the older members of the family or kin group" (Conteh 1973, 59).

Oral tradition reminds us that every village and every family potentially has in its midst a Musa Wo, an individual capable of destroying order and bringing about total chaos. One of the major objectives of the regulatory mechanism of Poro is to contain such individuals and prevent them from getting out of control. Thus, it is through Poro that generational tensions become tied to indigenous ideas of access to power and controlling agency: *wealth,* obtained by controlling people or their labor; *production,* in terms of access to land and marriage; the *supernatural,* by managing access to knowledge through secrecy; and *politics,* via association with the paramount chiefs and the central government. In the modern context outlined above, Poro seems to have failed to fulfill both its restorative responsibilities toward the community and its supportive and transformative responsibilities toward the youth.

Sierra Leonean Youth and War

There is no question that youth were at the center of the rebel movements. This has been clear from the first months of the conflict. The questions people have struggled with are the *who* of the rebel movement, the *why,* and the *how.* In an attempt to answer these questions, Richards describes this lumpen proletariat as members of marginal, forest-dwelling, diamond-mining communities, forgotten by a distant central government and locked into a life of basic survival. He stresses that the impetus for these youth to partake in war was their resentment at being marginalized economically, geographically, and socially. This is only partly true. Richards himself suggests that there is more, when he explains that "it hardly matters to which faction a combatant belongs" (Richards 1996, 174). In the evolution of the war and the composition of the ranks of the various armed movements, the stimuli of class, ethnicity, and economic category take a back seat to the older, deeper divisions between senior and junior generations. For this reason, when discussing the armed combatants I purposely use terms such as "fighter" or "rebel" to avoid suggesting that reasons for conflict must be compartmentalized and based on some partisanship.

Who were the rebels? Like most armed groups, Sierra Leone's rebels included a relatively small number of leaders in command of a larger fighting force. These leaders seemed to be in endless supply throughout the war, and a few charismatic individuals carved out names for themselves. Their rise to power followed closely the patterns for those seeking positions of authority in precolonial times, when a man "had to get power by war and by proving himself as the first among the warboys. He could then get farms and wealth, because all feared him and respected him, and his warriors protected him" (Wylie 1969, 297). Like other violent periods of Sierra Leone's history, the modern conflict provided avenues through which power and wealth could be acquired, if only for the short term.

In contemporary Sierra Leone the expanding cash economy has resulted in an ever-rising demand for market goods (corrugated iron sheets, metal cooking pots, etc.), and in all expenses, including those of a traditional nature, being paid in cash. When the national economy crumbled in the 1980s, people were caught between what was expected of them by their society and trying to be their own person in a modern world (Finnegan 1965; Hardin 1993; Jackson 1977). By the late 1980s, it was difficult for men to find work, which led to an economic situation that nurtured this disparity, forcing individuals to try to "control or come to terms with the tensions and conflicts engendered by the clash of objectively imposed and subjectively developed ideas of who they are" (Hardin 1993, 77). The result was an environment in which, just below the surface of cooperative social life in Sierra Leone, "lies the potential for chaos and uncertainty" (Hardin 1993, 100).

From this context sprang a young and angry generation, whom Jean-François Bayart refers to as the "juvenile underworld" (1993, 240). While most members of this group were perhaps not the masterminds behind the atrocities and violence of the recent war, many of them "did not need a second asking to be enthusiastic participants in the bloodletting" (Abdullah et al. 1997, 211). This said, it is also impossible and dangerous to categorize all of these armed juveniles as willing participants. Many of the fighting forces swelled their ranks primarily by kidnapping and abducting youths from the areas they plundered. These youths, who were held against their will and forced to carry out brutal acts, often against familiars, under threat of death, seem to have accounted for a large part of the fighting ranks, a trend that most likely increased over the course of the war. Melissa Leach explains that this recruitment strategy is part of a "regional military history" in which people, having been forced to "break the strongest laws governing social . . . order, . . . invite devastating effects on their future . . . and they become locked into subordinate relationships to those who can claim the power to . . . protect them" (2000, 590). These children became trapped in the world of the fighters and participated in the carnage in order to survive.

Why Now?

The institution of Poro does not in itself produce the differences and tensions between the generations; it is simply the main mechanism for controlling them. Yet, in so doing, Poro helps perpetuate this struggle. All interpersonal relationships are qualified by Poro, which is also charged with maintaining "conformity with traditional concepts of ideal social order involving absolute obedience to authority as represented by the hierarchies of age, lineage status, and official position" (d'Azevedo 1973, 133).

Bayart points out that "what is being fought for is the exclusive right to the riches claimed by the holders of 'absolute seniority.' The young challenge this claim" (1993, 241). We have seen that within the social framework solidified by the secret societies, where knowledge is controlled by the Zoes of Poro, "wealth and power are derived from knowledge, and those who possess the one are believed to have the other within their grasp" (d'Azevedo 1962, 29). If we define riches more broadly, to encompass that power which is represented and controlled by Poro, then we see that the relationship this creates between elder and youth is one of "domination-subordination," a relationship that now extends beyond its original context (Price 1974, 177).

Sierra Leoneans' construct of power mirrors Bayart's system of "closed" or "absolute" seniority, in which "the younger generation is permanently denied superiority except through individual achievement, secession or manipulation of genealogy" (1993, 113). Then why is Sierra Leone not constantly embroiled in conflict? Although the precipitants to this war are not the primary focus here, a brief history of recent political and economic trends illustrates how the field was prepared for tapping into this youthful potential, removing it from autochthonous mechanisms of control, thus bringing Musa Wo to life.

The period 1968–85 was the time of Siaka Stevens's rule, also known as the "17-Year Plague of Locusts" (Hirsch 2001). This period of blatant governmental corruption resulted in what Reno refers to as a "Shadow State" (Reno

1995) operating largely on profits obtained through selling natural resources via parallel, unofficial markets, which funneled the majority of income into the pockets of politicians. Following Stevens was his handpicked successor, Joseph Momoh, also known as the "Fool." Although younger than the octogenarian Stevens, Momoh was a clear case of "Same taxi, different driver" (Opala 1998). The total breakdown of any semblance of capable governance is exemplified by the commencement of civil war in May 1991 and a military coup that overthrew the Momoh regime in April 1992.

The Revolutionary United Front (RUF) officially began the civil war in May 1991, when Foday Sankoh and a small group of armed men crossed into Kailahun District from Liberia. The early days of the incursion found Liberian mercenaries among their ranks. This was openly admitted by Sankoh himself (RUF/SL 1995). Several prominent scholars have blamed the violent methods of this war on the presence of these outsiders in the RUF. Joseph Opala disputes this idea, explaining that there were "many angry, disaffected youths crossing into Liberia," fleeing political violence in the urban areas of Sierra Leone, during the early 1980s (Opala 1998, 7). Many were from Southern Province and would later help to found the RUF. In some areas, the RUF initially received "some popular support for exacting retribution against people who had exploited the local community in the past" (Reno 1995, 173).

In response to the incursion, Momoh started a massive recruitment of soldiers in the streets of Freetown. These new soldiers included "hundreds of disaffected urban youth, and many young Mende [from Southern Province] whose people were suffering the brunt of the [RUF] attacks" (Opala 1998). It was young officers from within this new army who staged a coup d'état in 1992, making twenty-seven-year-old Valentine Strasser president of Sierra Leone and twenty-three-year-old "SAJ" Musa his aide-de-camp (Reno 1995). This hodgepodge of youth also made up Strasser's national army. In the early years, the civilian population called Strasser "The Redeemer" because he was seen as "delivering them from a corrupt and callous government that had treated them just as Strasser had described his treatment as a soldier" (Reno 1995, 174). Calling themselves the National Provisional Ruling Council (NPRC), this army embodied the power of youth, including the potentially positive "tabula rasa" condition typified in the myths of Musa Wo. Although some older people found it difficult to be ruled by people the same age as their own children, "most acknowledged that since their own generation had failed to set a standard of honesty in public life, the youths deserved their chance" (Opala 1998). Soon after the NPRC took power, it became clear that it was yet *another* case of "Same taxi, different driver." They, too, took their turn at plundering, continuing the legacies of Stevens and Momoh.

The NPRC was still faced with the challenge of the RUF incursion and so deployed its ragtag army to the southern and eastern frontline areas of the war. By 1994 people in the rural areas of Southern Province, the areas under the heaviest military action at that time, were beginning to speak of "sobels"—soldier by day, rebel by night. Initially, the expatriate community defined these "sobels" as undisciplined soldiers who were simply taking advantage of a hostile environment, while the local choice to designate this group as a combination of soldiers and rebels suggested an actual mixing of the ranks of the two forces. The local definition was confirmed with the coup of 1997. The potential of the young army leaders and the hopes of a nation disintegrated, and the power of the youth began its steady destructive spiral.

The youthful militarization of the country was indicative of the "strain and stress generated by social change in a political environment of scarcity between value expectations among all socio-economic groups and value capabilities" (Conteh-Morgan and Dixon-Fyle 1999, 5), as well as the failure of autochthonous cultural systems vis-à-vis its youth. Angela McIntyre, Emmanuel Kwesi Aning, and Prosper Nil Nortey Addo are surely correct that this war "thrived" and that certain youth were drawn to it, not because this was a generation with an inexplicable propensity to violence, but because "constructive social incentives offered to youth were insufficient" (2002, 12). Their modern-day aspirations were "structurally and psychologically connected to global capitalism's tendency to create desires or needs it cannot satisfy" (Conteh-Morgan and Dixon-Fyle 1999, 4). They lacked the financial support necessary to attend school and had no assistance in finding work. One young boy shot his parents, yelling, "You made me suffer. You never sent me to school" (Voeten 2000, 260). Chiefs, elders, and elite were "doing wrong" by the youth, and "nobody was willing to help the young men, especially the politicians" (Archibald and Richards 2002, 349). Even the Zoes used their sacred powers to further the careers of the very politicians who were literally consuming the futures of the young generation. Social systems were simply unwilling and unable to cope with the needs of the youth, resulting in "exclusion and instability" (Archibald and Richards 2002, 359). For those whose future was a life of urban poverty or subsistence farming, the ever-expanding modern world must have seemed unfair.

Reading Amputations

Studies have shown very clearly how the combination of a failing state, its predatory practices, and the resultant socioeconomic decline created an untenable situation (see Reno 1995, Zack-Williams 1989, Opala 1998, Hirsch

2001, and Abdullah et al. 1997). Youths, already marginalized geographically, psychologically, and economically, saw their future as bleak when juxtaposed to the possibilities advertised by the global market economy. While the above-mentioned studies are vital to an understanding of the recent precipitants to the war, we still do not have answers to the questions why the war continued for ten years and why youth committed these atrocities and deliberate mutilations.

The intimacy of the systematic amputations, a form of violence found only in the Sierra Leonean chapter of this war, implores us to look deeper, to other layers of conversation taking place in this conflict. The importance of these amputations is not the act itself, although it is obviously devastating for the survivors. Rather, the amputee is the nexus of a conversation that engages those involved at all levels of the war.

Amputations were rumored to have been carried out from the beginning of the war, in 1991, but cases were not documented until its first widespread appearance in 1995–96. We can identify three peak periods of amputations, each coinciding with open military and political contestation: prior to the presidential elections of 1996; between April and August 1998, following the fall of the RUF–Armed Forces Ruling Council (AFRC) coalition government; and in January 1999, when the RUF–AFRC forces attacked Freetown in an attempted, and almost successful, coup d'état. It is important to stress that these were *peak* periods, identified by medical workers as periods when there were marked increases in amputations; people were amputated at other times throughout the war as well.

The conflict in Sierra Leone had a violent impact on every one of its ethnic groups, and atrocities were carried out by and against people of all ages, classes, and genders, with victims generally chosen at random. The total number of people who suffered amputations or attempted amputations is not known. These acts often took place in remote areas where there was no access to health care, and, undoubtedly, many people died without receiving treatment. There was also a large movement of refugees into neighboring countries, and many amputees were among these groups. Estimates of the number of amputees vary wildly, with the highest quoted figures being 4,000 hospitalized and an additional 16,000 dying before reaching a medical facility (Robinson 1999).

September 1995–October 1996

The first round of mutilations took place in Southern Province just in advance of the 1996 presidential elections in Sierra Leone, in which Tejan Kabbah, an elder statesman, was elected for the first time. These elections were meant to provide the RUF the opportunity to enter into the political arena as an official party, and thus to put an end to the war. That never happened (Opala 1998; Richards 1996). Amputations in this period were associated with deliberate messages aimed at the government and/or the international community. The following is the testimony of survivors of the pre-election violence:

We were on the road to Mokollaywo when we fell into an ambush. . . . They stripped me naked and tortured me. . . . They tried to cut off my arm but did not succeed. I was then told to go to Moyamba town and say to the people that the rebels would attack the town. (Médecins Sans Frontières 1996a, 12)[5]

They told me that they did not kill me so that I could go to Bo and tell the people that they [the RUF] were in the region. (Médecins Sans Frontières 1996b)[6]

These quotations make clear the obvious intent of the rebels to communicate their presence and their horrific capacity to destroy by sending human reports to the district governmental headquarters at Bo, the capital of Southern Province, and to Moyamba. In the months leading up to the presidential elections, the RUF had announced repeatedly that it opposed the elections. The clear association between the amputations of hands and voting in the upcoming elections was even more poignant, as Kabbah's campaign symbol was two hands clasped in a sign of national unity (Dufka 1998). Médecins Sans Frontières sources, for example, report, "A large group of more than 200 dressed in military fatigues and armed with AK47s, RPGs [rocket-propelled grenades] and shotguns entered the village. . . . At 6 AM the attackers attempted to amputate the hands of five men saying it was 'to prevent voting'" (Médecins Sans Frontières 1996a, 13).

Are these the only messages being communicated? Similar sentiments are present in many violent contexts on the continent and throughout the world where amputations do not occur. Other, more indigenized hypotheses have been put forward. This first period of amputations coincided with the harvest season for rice in Southern Province, linking this act directly to ideas of food production and livelihood. Rice, indigenous to this area of West Africa, is extremely important in local society, making up as much as 90 percent of the diet (Spencer 1981, 179). In order to comply with the pre-election ceasefire, the RUF had stopped raiding villages and so was in short supply of food. Richards reports that hungry soldiers began defecting from the RUF in order to return home to take part in the harvest and therefore receive a portion of the yield. He speculates that, to prevent a large defection, the amputations were carried out to scare the community and the fighters so badly that the harvest would be suspended (Richards 1996, xx). Others have highlighted the weakness of this theory, as the rebels were also reliant upon the rice harvest for their own sustenance, so that if the harvest were suspended, they too would be faced with a serious food shortage. In any event, this was the only time that mass amputations coincided specifically with the rice harvest.

If we consider the centrality of rice in Sierra Leonean life, we can see that this was a conversation, not about one specific rice harvest, but about the reproduction of crops, community, and agency. The importance of rice was noted by Europeans in the years prior to manumission, when during busy periods of the rice-farming calendar local rulers suspended all trading so that their laborers could concentrate solely on the rice crops (Richards 1996, 65). The heavy reliance on rice is also evident in the ways in which the plant has been anthropomorphized, using terms "such as gestation and birth for different stages of ripeness, to labels such as 'legs' and their joints given to the plant's stalk" (Ferme 2001, 44). In chopping off the hands of rural farmers the RUF effectively showed that farming and food production would be allowed to take place where and when the RUF decided, a position exemplified in the photograph of a young fighter with "War is my food" painted in red nail polish on the butt of his AK-47.[7]

Still, some of these fighters were challenging more than just the perpetuation of the village through rice harvests, or even the reproduction of the state via elections, as the following quotations illustrate:

I begged them to leave my [daughters]. But they didn't want to. One of them came towards me, he pulled me violently by the arm, pulled out a machete and cut off my hand. Another killed my two girls in front of my eyes. (Médecins Sans Frontières 1996b)

I pleaded but Commander Don't Blame God said that he was going to kill me. . . . "Don't kill me, please don't kill me" . . . I pleaded with him and he then said, "I've changed my mind, I'm going to give you a letter." Once we got there I saw many more rebels, about twenty . . . they asked me to sit down and wait. Commander Don't Blame God said: "I have a letter for you but wait for the cutlass [machete] man to come." Then the one with the machete came and told me to put out my left arm. It took them three chops with the cutlass to cut off my arm. After this I begged them not to cut my other arm but they struggled with me and a rebel held it down and cut it off. The cutlass man said, "We belong to Foday Sankoh's group [the RUF]." Then one of them took my left arm and put it under my vagina and kicked me twice in the vagina . . . very, very hard. (Human Rights Watch 2003, 36)[8]

Such actions were grotesque, and "a feature of the grotesque is that it plays out the dramaturgy of power at the lowest bodily levels, the sites of sexuality and reproduction" (Ferme 2001, 178). The testimony quoted above speaks to a much more local and personal reproduction. It is clear that without access to land or able-bodied people to work the farms a family cannot survive. "How can I hope to feed my family?" asked one victim. "I have no hands" (Dufka 1998). A person's adult status, (re)productive capacity, and therefore lineage also depend upon the ability to marry, procreate, and raise children. After surviving amputation, one fifteen-year-old girl lamented, "Now I don't think I'll ever find someone to marry me" (Dufka 1998). The killing of a woman's two daughters and the placing of another woman's amputated hand under her vagina spoke of reproduction, traditionally controlled in part by the elders of Poro, now linked to and brutally dominated by the fighters.

Who exactly were the rebels at this point in the conflict? It is known that the RUF swelled its ranks primarily by kidnapping children and teens from areas it attacked and captured (Dufka 1998; Dufka, Ezetah, and Wardwell 1999; Hirsch 2001; Richards 1996; Richards and Peters 1998), and that a significant number of the "sobels" were from Southern Province, where these atrocities occurred. "The majority of amputees who are now living around Bo and Gondama will tell you that their hands, arms, fingers . . . were . . . cut . . . by people who were formerly resident in their own villages" (Abdullah at al. 1997, 212). Even some among the rebels were referred to as "our brothers who engage in atrocities, those who do bad things to our people" (Abdullah et al. 1997, 191).[9] This narrows the gap between the perpetrators and the victims in these stories, making the action that much more intimate and horrific. In two swift kicks the young fighter identified the RUF as the destroyer of both familiar social categories and familiar structures of power.

Not all those fighting were from Southern Province. By 1992 the RUF had successfully captured Kono, home to the richest diamond mines in Sierra Leone. The mining areas were full of *san-san* boys, or illicit miners searching the gravel of other mining operations, mostly youths from around the country who were no longer in school and could not find gainful employment elsewhere. In this eclectic mixture three types of youths have been identified as having taken part in the fighting, "the urban marginals . . . 'san-san boys' . . . and socially disconnected village youth" (Abdullah et al. 1997, 172). This fits with Richards's description of Sierra Leonean youth as a poor, marginalized generation, tired of being forgotten and cheated by corrupt traders and politicians from the patrimonial, centralized government in Freetown (Richards 1996; Richards and Peters 1998). Yet this description does not give sufficient credence to the extreme heterogeneity of the fighters as a group.

Abdullah argues that their shared culture does not permit us to lump all the marginal youths of Sierra Leone into one category; that is to say, even if "the common culture of youth in Sierra Leone cannot be contested," this does not mean that it is "non-negotiable" (Abdullah et al. 1997). Not every san-san boy joined the RUF, and not every child in Freetown joined a gang. Who, then, were the youth responsible for these atrocities? Abdullah asks, "Did those who join the RUF to participate in the orgy of violence have anything to lose? I think not—on the contrary they had everything to gain" (Abdullah et al. 1997, 183). These were the youths who, like Musa Wo, spread destruction and chaos when their youthful energy and potential spilled outside those structures, traditional and contemporary, designed to contain them.

March 1998–August 1998

In April 1997 junior officers from the remnant army staged another coup d'état and took over the government as the Armed Forces Ruling Council. At this time, they called the RUF to join them in creating a coalition government. This junta regime was deposed in February 1998 by the military forces of the Economic Community of West African States, or ECOMOG. It was after this defeat that the second, most widespread phase of amputations took place, beginning in March 1998 in the diamond-rich area of Kono, in Eastern Province. In April, this wave of violence began to spread out of Kono, first into the northeast and then into the northwest of the country. The RUF–AFRC forces were able to greatly increase their numbers by adding former members of government forces from these regions of the country to the rebel fighting ranks (Opala 1998).

This time the fighters were not battling voters, but retreating under heavy military pressure. In March 1998, the RUF–AFRC forces found themselves almost defeated in eastern Kono. In April, the first amputees from this area arrived in Freetown for medical treatment (Médecins Sans Frontières 1998b). Interviews indicate the continued practice of sending messages and the taunting with threats of imminent attack at some ambiguous future point. On the surface, this conversation was directly aimed at President Kabbah and his allies.

Many amputees were told to go to President Kabbah and ask him for new hands. "One patient was given a letter by the attackers, with the orders to give it to President Kabbah." Others reported "that the armed men would tell them to go now . . . to ECOMOG and tell ECOMOG, 'that we, the attackers, do not want them here, and that [we are coming] to ECOMOG soon'" (Médecins Sans Frontières 1998b).

Reno explains that "armed adolescents may find that warfare offers them liberation from a lack of opportunities, giving them a license to loot, and the chance to wreak revenge on their enemies and settle old scores in ways their parents could only dream of" (Reno 1995, 175). In this same vein, others have expressed how "handling a gun empowered them—it made them somebody" (Abdullah et al. 1997). Thus, war was used as an alternative way to construct identities and as an opportunity to hold immense power over anyone, even the president. "In the romances of the oppressed, to assert power, any power, is itself a triumph. . . . Killing and torture is the most primitive and personal assertion of ultimate power, and the weaker the rebel feels himself to be at bottom, the greater, we may suppose, the temptation to assert it" (Hobsbawm 1959, 56). That many of the rebels at this time were from the areas where the amputations took place again speaks of a very local and personal conversation.

In general, most patients told about attacks that started with groups of men arriving in their villages, calling out that they were ECOMOG, and that they were there to free the villagers. . . . Upon leaving their houses, the villagers then realized that these men did not belong to ECOMOG. . . . Villagers were rounded up, in groups or in lines. They were then, one by one . . . taken to the pounding block [a mortar for pounding food, especially for shelling rice] where . . . their hands were then amputated. Several patients reported that the attackers took the amputated arms with them. (Médecins Sans Frontières 1998b)

The groups of villagers gathered together by the rebels around their pounding block suggest Ferme's observation that "moments of violence always have their own distinctive, culturally and historically informed semantics" (1998, 558). Here, the local tool for preparing food for every meal, and the source of the most common sound in an African village, became a tool for devastating that same community and its means of production. By destroying the capacity of individuals, the rebels successfully reproduced the "hegemony of violence . . . in the minutia of everyday life" (Nordstrom 1998, 108). The survivors of amputations were no longer able to use a pounding block or to take part in many communal activities; instead they became burdens of society. Hands are "the interface between an individual and his or her social environment . . . the palms of the hands are the point of contact among people in greeting or, in prayer, among people, God, and the ancestors" (Ferme 2001, 182). Amputation destroyed a part of the humanness of the individual, while the person's life was purposefully preserved, perhaps echoing the rebels' own frustrations about being denied full, independent agency and a successful future in a new, modern world by the various parasitic local hierarchies of power.

The 1998 amputations differed from those in 1995, not only in the composition of the fighting forces or their military positions, but also in the much larger number of victims and the wider geographical range covered (Médecins Sans Frontières 1998a). The reaction among the national and international communities, including endless photographs, video images, and articles widely disseminated, had the unintended consequence of making amputations an effective tool for the rebels when they needed to assert their strength and power. It is not surprising that when the RUF–AFRC forces were almost defeated, they turned again to this tool.

What kind of power did these fighters embody? Amputations were not just a way to frighten the government and the international community, although they did this effectively. They were also an attack on local ideas of order and power communicated through common cultural markers. With this violent act, the rebels "offered a new system of social incentives to youth, of a negative, destructive variety, an answer to what the state and society failed to provide" (McIntyre, Aning, and Addo 2002, 8).

The militias formed their own systems of authority for the internal control of their particular power, and used arm amputations as one of the means of rising in their hierarchy. As one militia member explained,

In Kabala I was forced to do amputations. We had a cutlass, an ax and a big log. We called the villagers out and let them stand in line. You ask [the victims] whether they want a long hand or a short hand [the amputation closer to the wrist or closer to the elbow]. The long hand you put in a different bag from the short hand. If you have a large number of amputated hands in the bag, the promotion will be automatic. (Masland 2002)

They made mass destruction and control of individual agency, rather than lineage rank and expensive initiation, the requirements for advancement and access to more authority. This perversion of traditional mechanisms of containing power became the concrete proof of the fighter's potential—to create chaos, to destroy known order, and to reconfigure the rules of power to his liking.

January 1999

Throughout 1998 amputations and other violence continued sporadically in various rural areas, moving in a general westerly direction and culminating in the rebel attack on Freetown in January 1999. This last, most publicized phase of amputations occurred as the RUF–AFRC forces were being pushed from

the city following their almost successful coup d'état. Again, fighters punctu-
ated their atrocities with messages:

We are not able to do to you half of the things we do to people in the provinces. You
bastard civilians, you hypocrites; as soon as you see ECOMOG, you start to point
fingers at us. (Dufka 1998)

When they were cutting me, I heard one of them say, "Now you will know the rebels;
now you will know the bitterness of the war." (Dufka, Ezetah, and Wardwell 1999)

Then the one who seemed to be in charge called forward a fifteen-year-old boy they
called "Commander Cut Hands." (Dufka, Ezetah, and Wardwell 1999)

What is striking about the amputations of 1999 is that they took place
in Freetown, the location not just of industrial and corporate production
but also of the production of the socioeconomic and political systems of the
state. The fighters were able to disrupt the means of production of the nation and thereby take control of the "dynamic of increasing vulnerability,"
a dynamic that, as we have seen, was epidemic among the youth of Sierra
Leone (McIntyre, Aning, and Addo 2002). Having successfully toppled two
governments and paralyzed the country during almost ten years, the rebels
made an identity for themselves as a tenacious contradictory possibility to
the traditional and contemporary power structures. Their message carried in
it the weight of the knowledge that disorder would continue if they were not
included in the shaping of power and identity. One victim reported,

They surrounded my family and one of them said, "Since Pa Kabbah won't give us
peace, we have come to cut your hands." . . . They then marched me up the hill to
the grounds of St. Patrick's Catholic Church where I saw over one hundred rebels.
They ordered me to put my left arm on a tree trunk and then they swung the axe
from behind and hacked it off. They kept talking about President Kabbah and as they
ordered me to put my other hand. I screamed, "But I don't know anything about
politics" and one of them answered, "But you voted for Kabbah." Then he hacked off
my remaining hand. Blood was spurting out of my arms. . . . They started laughing
at me and I shouted, "Just kill me, kill me, look how you've left me." (Dufka, Ezetah,
and Wardwell 1999)[10]

Exactly what the rebels' threat held for the individual civilian was ambiguous
and blurred, but clearly horrific.

The majority of amputations throughout the war took place in open spaces in front of crowds (Dufka 1998; Dufka, Ezetah, and Wardwell 1999; Médecins Sans Frontières 1996a, 1998a, 1998b, 1999). The results were extremely visible and accessible to a national and international audience. What does this signify? If in local systems of thought legitimate power is considered that which is public and therefore contained and controlled, a new level of conversation had become visible. Locally, these fighters seemed to be saying that they had replaced the autochthonous organizations that had failed their generation. The longevity of the war and the atrocities of these new, young Big Men showed that they had replaced indigenous systems and leaders as the controllers of power, fulfilling the desires of Musa Wo "to play Child Triumphant in a world turned upside-down" (Cosentino 1989, 35).

This third cycle of atrocities was accompanied by new images. Young, angry teen fighters seemed surprised that, after years of bitter war, it was their own people who betrayed them and pointed fingers. This was an odd reaction from fighters responsible for years of terror and slaughter. But what if Opala is right and "All humans crave order" (1998)? From this view, war and the act of amputation could be considered what Paul Bohannan calls "extra-processual events" taken to the extreme, or a social institution not approved of in and of itself. "Men who had acquired too much power or who were careless in the way they exercised their power were whittled down by means of [these extra-processual events]" (Bohannan 1970, 262). For some, perhaps, the rebels were an evil necessary to destroy all social and political systems. Fighters often stressed that "before the war there was corruption, misuse of power," and that the task of the rebels was in part to combat "bribery and corruption" (Archibald and Richards 2002, 349). Steven Archibald and Paul Richards argue that the rebels were "making claims . . . that whether or not young people make a successful transition to adulthood should not have to depend on the whims of patrons" (2002, 351). Perhaps total destruction, even of one's own kin, became a desperate attempt to restore balance and to bring about the positive effects of Musa Wo.

This violence and its horrific intimacy were not alien to people's ideation of power and its diverse manifestations. Survivors said that they tolerated the abuses, "as it was war" (Human Rights Watch 2003, 3). Musa Wo, Poro, and the young fighters all engaged in a conversation about local concepts of where power and its potential lay, and about the necessity and danger of keeping it contained. In the context of postconflict Sierra Leone, the reminders of the consequences of "neglect[ing] the energy and cunning of the young" (Richards 1996, 59) were everywhere. The scars of the wounded and amputees will be permanent markers of this chapter in a generation's history.

Sierra Leonean Youth Today

The marginal youth who were at the heart of this conflict and responsible for perpetuating many of these atrocities are still very much present in the region, yet today the war seems to be over. However, the persistence of the myth of Musa Wo tells us that this recent war was only one battle in an age-old conflict that can never be resolved and perhaps never should be. But who won this battle?

The way these young ex-fighters speak about the war and their place in present-day Sierra Leone shows that they have been successful in their quest to demonstrate their powerful potential, a potential that in their minds and the minds of many Sierra Leoneans they clearly still possess. When an eleven-year-old demobilized soldier was asked, "What would happen if Freetown were attacked?" he answered without hesitation, "I'd take up my arms again. I miss the sound of my gun" (Hammer 1995). Another interviewer spoke with aid workers trying to rehabilitate these minors. "When she gets angry, she says she will go back to the bush again," the interviewer was told. "It's a recurring mechanism with many of the children: they turn the bush into a kind of utopia. God knows what they really did down there" (Voeten 2000, 238). Even when faced with the reality of their atrocities, outside of the context of war, some of these youth remain indignant. "In Freetown, a rebel boy was grabbed by the scruff of the neck by a man whose left arm he had cut off. 'Be happy that I left you with an arm,' the boy yelled brazenly" (Voeten 2000, 211.)

Other Sierra Leoneans recognize that deep changes have taken place among these youth. "When we were kids, we had never seen a dead body," said one. "Now, if someone is lying dead out on the street here, the kids run out whooping with joy" (Voeten 2000, 235). In postconflict Sierra Leone, this raises the burning question whether there have been sufficient changes within the social systems to recontain this energy and to satisfy those who attained power through the war. The youth successfully wrested power out of the hands of both local and central authorities, even if in an unsustainable way. With the structure of the RUF at least greatly damaged, will the government be able to channel this youthful potential into constructive avenues, or will another uprising occur? Large groups of youth, especially in the urban sprawl of Freetown, "express frustrations (and sometimes despair) at their sense of having the potential for a middle-class, adult future, but few opportunities to achieve it" (Shaw 2002a, 8). Others have voiced disillusionment with traditional structures such as the secret societies, which "waste a lot of blood" and which during the war were not able to protect anyone from the violence, including the youth (Shaw 2002a, 10). Owing to the length of the war, and the fact that the vast majority of the fighters were quite young when they left their homes, many of Sierra Leone's youth were never initiated into Poro; instead, they were initiated into war, where they learned about chaos, violence, and the power of terror. This generation has been described as literally having no "betters" (Opala 1998).

Problems may arise if some of these rebels do not want to give up the power that the society of violence created for them and that they were able to maintain as fighters. "The children had a very strong identity. . . . They were soldiers; they carried a weapon, had power and authority. . . . In one way, their dreams had come true. . . . It's very hard for children to return to reality" (Voeten 2000, 240). The potential for a recurrence of a Musa Wo army is high in present-day Sierra Leone, as "life in the bush [for the youth] is a perfectly acceptable long-term option" (Richards 1997). In the bush they had a high degree of autonomy and were out from under the authoritarian rule of their families, their village, and Poro. The war also reinforced for them a "particular version of masculinity," that of the "macho gun-phallus-bearing killer" (Leach 2000, 592). The difficulty in preventing these youths from choosing the road of violence in the future is hauntingly described by a child psychologist working in Sierra Leone. "We can't teach them to be sissies. You can't just go up to an ex-murderer and say, 'You have to be a good boy, now. Learn a trade and become one of the millions of unemployed young people in Africa'" (Voeten 2000, 241). Many of these ex-fighters do not even have a sense of guilt for what they did during the war. "God must forgive boys like us. It was not our fault. It was the fault of the elders," said one (Masland 2002, 29).

Conclusion

The international community has repeatedly failed to respond in indigenously appropriate ways to the Sierra Leone conflict, its resolution, and the subsequent reconciliation. In the words of a U.S. official who wished to remain anonymous, "It seems we made some false assumptions . . . that the people who signed the peace accord actually wanted peace. That was a mistake" (Schuler and Vo 2002). Social positions are still being renegotiated as people return to their homes and to an environment where power is no longer located only within controllable constructs but could be usurped at any moment by the young generation. Although war is endemic to humankind, and so the potential for it to appear is ever-present, this inversion of power in Sierra Leone, with the young generation proving its potential to destroy all order, has placed it firmly outside the norms of institutional regulation. Having violated the known rules for the use of power, the youths' actions have become thoroughly unpredictable, so that active conflict could erupt anywhere and at any time. This has sparked within Sierra Leonean society feelings, such as the reintegration of ex-combatants being "a bone in the throat," or that the postwar nation is "desperately in a hurry" (Awoko 2003). This invokes an image of a country trying quickly to grasp the elusive peaceful future that seems possible, rather than one comfortable in its new-found stability. Can any country's gerontocratic conflicts be resolved? Should they be? Perhaps a certain level of such tension is necessary, as Musa Wo is a necessary part of the totality of community. Sierra Leone's war is not over. In fact, it never will be.

Notes

The title of this essay is a Sierra Leonean proverb.

1. For continuity, I utilize the Mende name for this character.

2. Survivors of rebel attacks often report that their attackers spoke their language, and many captured youth were forced to carry out exactions within their own communities.

3. There are several spellings of this term. For consistency's sake, I will follow d'Azevedo's "zo(e)s."

4. Traditionally, the period of seclusion is four years for boys and three years for girls, but now it is generally reduced (d'Azevedo 1973).

5. Often amputations were not complete and limbs were left attached by soft tissue, even though the bones were cut completely through.

6. Quotations from *L'horreur ignorée* have been translated by me.

7. This photo, taken by Molly Bingham in 1999, can be found at http://www.humanrightswatch.org.

8. This even occurred in Mattru village, Bo District, Southern Province, prior to the 1996 elections.

9. "Dem we broder way dae fet de badbfet, dem wan dem wae dae do bad to we pipul dem."

10. *Pa* is a term of respect in the lingua franca, Krio, and in this instance refers to the president of Sierra Leone, Tejan Kabbah.

References

Abdullah, I., Y. Bangura, L. Gberie, L. Johnson, K. Kallon, S. Kemokai, P. K. Muana, I. Rashid, and A. Zack-Williams. 1997. Lumpen Youth Culture and Political Violence: Sierra Leoneans Debate the RUF and the Civil War. *Africa Development* 22 (3–4): 171–215.

Archibald, Steven, and Paul Richards. 2002. Converts to Human Rights? Popular Debate about War and Justice in Rural Central Sierra Leone. *Africa* 72 (3): 339–367.

Arens, W., and Ivan Karp. 1989. Introd. to *Creativity of Power,* edited by W. Arens and Ivan Karp. Washington, DC: Smithsonian Institution Press.

Awoko. 2003. Save a Generation. http://www.awoko.com/news/features/Save%20a%20 generation.htm.

Bayart, Jean-François. 1993. *The State in Africa: The Politics of the Belly.* London: Verso.

Bohannan, Paul. 1970. Extra-processual Events in Tiv Political Institutions. In *Man Makes Sense: A Reader in Modern Cultural Anthropology,* edited by E. Hammel. Boston: Brown.

Conteh, J. Sorie. 1973. A dissertation prospectus. Diamond Mining and Secret-Sacred Ritual Institutions: The Kono Experience; A Study in Social Change. *Africana Research Bulletin* 3 (4): 51–67.

Conteh-Morgan, Earl, and Mac Dixon-Fyle. 1999. *Sierra Leone at the End of the Twentieth Century: History, Politics, and Society.* New York: Peter Lang.

Cosentino, Donald. 1989. Midnight Characters: Musa Wo and the Mende Myths of Chaos. In *Creativity of Power,* edited by W. Arens and Ivan Karp. Washington, DC: Smithsonian Institution Press.

d'Almada, André Álvarez. 1594. Brief Treatise on the Rivers of Guinea. In *University of Wisconsin Madison Libraries—Africana Digitization Project.* Reprint, Madison: University of Wisconsin Madison Libraries, 1984.

d'Azevedo, Warren. 1962. Uses of the Past in Gola Discourse. *Journal of African History* 3 (1): 11–34.

———. 1973. Mask Makers and Myth in Western Liberia. In *Primitive Art and Society,* edited by A. Forge. London: Oxford University Press.

Dorjahn, V. R. 1960. The Changing Political System of the Temne. *Africa* 30 (1): 110–40.

Dufka, Corrine. 1998. Sowing Terror: Atrocities against Civilians in Sierra Leone. *Human Rights Watch Report* 10 (3).

Dufka, Corrine, Chinedu Ezeath, and Davis Polk Wardwell. 1999. Sierra Leone: Getting Away with Murder, Mutilation, Rape. *Human Rights Watch Report* 11 (3).

Ferme, Mariane. 1998. The Violence of Numbers: Consensus, Competition, and the Negotiation of Disputes in Sierra Leone. *Cahiers d'études africaines* 150–52 (2–4): 555–80.

———. 2001. *The Underneath of Things.* Berkeley and Los Angeles: University of California Press.

Finnegan, Ruth. 1965. *Survey of the Limba People of Northern Sierra Leone.* Vol. 8. London: Great Britain, Department of Technical Cooperation, Overseas Research Publication, HMSO.

Fulton, Richards. 1972. Political Structure and Function of Poro in Kpelle Society. *American Anthropologist* 74 (5): 1218–33.

Hammer, Joshua. 1995. Teenage Wasteland. *New Republic* 212 (15): 10–11.

Hardin, Kris. 1993. *The Aesthetics of Action: Continuity and Change in a West African Town.* Edited by W. Merrill. Smithsonian Series in Ethnographic Inquiry. Washington, DC: Smithsonian Institution Press.

Hirsch, John. 2001. *Sierra Leone: Diamonds and the Struggle for Democracy.* International Peace Academy Occasional Paper Series. Boulder, CO: Lynne Rienner.

Hobsbawm, Eric. 1959. *Social Bandits.* Glencoe, IL: Free Press.

Hoffer, Carol. 1975. Bundu: Political Implications of Female Solidarity in a Secret Society. In *Being Female: Reproduction, Power, and Change,* edited by D. Raphael. The Hague: Mouton.

Human Rights Watch. 2003. "We'll kill you if you cry": Sexual Violence in the Sierra Leone Conflict. *Human Rights Watch Report* 15 (1): 1–75.

Ijagbemi, Adeleye. 1976. *Naimbana of Sierra Leone.* Edited by O. Ikime. African Historical Biographies. London: Heinemann.

Jackson, Michael. 1977. *The Kuranko: Dimensions of Social Reality in a West African Society.* London: Hurst.

Keen, David. 1996. Sympathy with the Devil (War and Warfare). *Anthropology in Action* 3 (3): 22–24.

Leach, Melissa. 2000. New Shapes to Shift: War, Parks, and the Hunting Person in Modern West Africa. *Journal of the Royal Anthropological Institute* 6 (4): 577–95.

Little, Kenneth. 1951. *The Mende of Sierra Leone: A West African People in Transition.* London: Routledge.

———. 1965. The Political Function of the Poro, Part I. *Africa* 35 (4): 349–65.

———. 1966. The Political Function of the Poro, Part II. *Africa* 36 (1): 62–71.

MacCormack, Carol. 1980. Proto-social to Adult: A Sherbro Transformation. In *Nature, Culture, and Gender,* edited by Carol MacCormack and M. Strathern. Cambridge: Cambridge University Press.

———. 1982. Control of Land, Labor, and Capital in Rural Southern Sierra Leone. In *Women and Work in Africa,* edited by E. Bay. Boulder, CO: Westview.

Mamdani, Mahmood. 2001. *When Victims Become Killers: Colonialism, Nativism, and the Genocide in Rwanda.* Princeton, NJ: Princeton University Press.

Masland, Tom. 2002. "We beat and killed people . . ." *Newsweek,* 31 May 2002, 24–29.

Mauss, Marcel. 1979. Body Techniques. In *A Category of the Human Mind: The Notion of Person, the Notion of "Self."* London: Routledge.

McGovern, Mike. 2003. Personal communication. 8 April. Atlanta.

McIntyre, Angela, Emmanuel Kwesi Aning, and Prosper Nii Nortey Addo. 2002. Politics, War, and Youth Culture in Sierra Leone: An Alternative Interpretation. *African Security Review* 11 (3): 7–15.

Médecins Sans Frontières. 1996a. *Diamonds and Terror in Sierra Leone.* Brussels.

———. 1996b. *L'horreur ignorée.* Brussels.

———. 1998a. Archives. Paris.

———. 1998b. *Atrocities against Civilians in Sierra Leone.* Freetown.

———. 1999. *Sierra Leone mutilations: Un mois d'activites à l'hopital Connaught de Freetown.* Paris.

Meillassoux, C. P. 1960. Essai d'interprétation de phénomène économique dans les sociétés traditionelles d'auto-subsistance. *Cahiers d'études africaines,* no. 4:38–67.

Murphy, William. 1980. Secret Knowledge as Property and Power in Kpelle Society: Elder versus Youth. *Africa* 50:193–207.

Nordstrom, Carolyn. 1998. Terror Warfare and the Medicine of Peace. *Medical Anthropology Quarterly* 12 (1): 103–12.

Opala, Joseph. 1998. Sierra Leone: The Politics of State Collapse. Paper presented at the "Irregular Warfare in Liberia and Sierra Leone" conference, Denver, Colorado, 30 July–1 August.

Price, Robert. 1974. Politics and Culture in Contemporary Ghana. *Journal of African Studies* 1 (2): 173–204.

Reno, William. 1995. *Corruption and State Politics in Sierra Leone.* Cambridge: Cambridge University Press.

Revolutionary United Front, Sierra Leone (RUF/SL). 1995. Footpaths to Democracy: Toward a New Sierra Leone. N.p.

Richards, Paul. 1996. *Fighting for the Rainforest: War, Youth, and Resources in Sierra Leone.* Edited by A. D. Waal and S. Ellis. African Issues. Reprint, Portsmouth: Heinemann, 2000.

———. 1997. Letter to Her Majesty's government. 10 October. London.

Richards, Paul, and Krijn Peters. 1998. "Why we fight": Voices of Youth Combatants in Sierra Leone. *Africa* 68 (2): 183–210.

Robinson, Mary. 1999. Meeting the Challenge of Human Rights. Sounding the Century lecture. London. 23 September.

Schuler, Corinna, and Minh T. Vo. 2002. UN's Largest Force Loses Control. *Christian Science Monitor,* 10 May, 1.

Shaw, Rosalind. 2002a. Fighting the Underworld: The Militarizing of Imaginative Practice among Pentecostal Youth in Sierra Leone. Paper presented at "Youth Policy and the Policies of Youth in Africa," conference at Northwestern University, Evanston, May.

———. 2002b. *Memories of the Slave Trade: Ritual and the Historical Imagination in Sierra Leone.* Chicago: University of Chicago Press.

Simmel, Georg. 1997. *Simmel on Culture.* Edited by D. Frisby and M. Featherstone. Theory, Culture, and Society. London: Sage.

Spencer, Dunstan S. C. 1981. Rice Policy in Sierra Leone. In *Rice in West Africa: Policy and Economics,* edited by S. R. Pearson, and C. P. Humphreys. Stanford: Stanford University Press.

Stevens, K-Roy, and Bernadette Cole. 1996. Sierra Leone's Date with Destiny. *West Africa,* 4–10 March 1996, 337–38.

United Nations Development Program (UNDP). 2005. *Human Development Report.* http://hdr.undp.org/statistics/data/countries.cfm?c=SLE.

U.S. Central Intelligence Agency (CIA). 2005. *The World Factbook.* Washington, DC. http://www.cia.gov/publications/factbook/geos/sl.html.

Voeten, Teun. 2000. *How de Body? One Man's Terrifying Journey through an African War.* Translated by R. Vatter-Buck. Amsterdam: J. M. Meulenhoff BV.

White, Luise. 2000. *Speaking with Vampires: Rumor and History in Colonial Africa.* Berkeley and Los Angeles: University of California Press.

Wylie, Kenneth C. 1969. Innovation and Change in Mende Chieftancy, 1880–1896. *Journal of African History* 10 (2): 295–308.

————. 1977. *The Political Kingdoms of the Temne: Temne Government in Sierra Leone, 1825–1910.* New York: Africana.

Zack-Williams, A. B. 1989. Sierra Leone, 1968–1985: The Decline of Politics and the Politics of Decline. *International Journal of Sierra Leone Studies* 1:122–30.

Violent Vigilantism and the State in Nigeria
The Case of the Bakassi Boys

DANIEL JORDAN SMITH

I N much of contemporary Africa, violence scars the promise of youth. Young people are not only the victims of violence but also its perpetrators. Young people participate in violence as soldiers for the state (Rabwoni 2002); as rebels against the state (Carey, this volume; Richards 1996); as members of gangs and campus cults (Bastian 2001; Gore and Pratten 2003; Salo, this volume); and as urban thugs and ordinary criminals (Marenin 1987; Momoh 2000). In Nigeria, vigilantism, led by young men primarily in urban areas and marked by thousands of extrajudicial executions, has emerged as one of the most troubling forms of violence since the transition to democratic rule in 1999. The O'odua People's Congress in the southwest (Human Rights Watch 2003), the Egbesu Boys in the Niger Delta, and the Bakassi Boys in the southeast (Harnischfeger 2003; Human Rights Watch 2002; Smith 2004) are among the most notorious of many vigilante groups to appear in recent years. These vigilante groups ascended and became popular in response to public perceptions that crime was out of control.

But much more than a popular response to crime, vigilantism lies at the center of complex tensions and interconnections between the state, politics, power, and popular understandings of the roots of inequality and injustice in Nigeria. Public support for vigilantism builds on notions of local sovereignty, on people's ambitions and frustrations with regard to participation in Nigeria's nascent democracy, and on a sense that inequitable access to resources controlled by the state undermines traditional mechanisms of reciprocity associated with long-standing systems of patron-clientism. Indeed, vigilante groups in Nigeria were for several years extremely popular among ordinary people because they represented a brand of "people's justice" in the face of the corruption and inequalities associated with politics and state institutions. But the story of vigilantism in democratic Nigeria is equally one of co-optation by politicians and the eventual disillusionment of the masses with vigilante groups because the vigilantes themselves were perceived as becoming political and therefore corrupt.

In this essay, I examine the case of the Bakassi Boys in southeastern Nigeria, arguably the most notorious of all of the vigilante groups in the country. I explore the complex intersections between violence, vigilantism, and the state. In analyzing these interconnections, I build on a literature that interrogates the relationship between postcolonial state practices, inequality, and ordinary people's perceptions of and responses to perceived injustice (Bayart 1993; Chabal and Daloz 1999; Ekeh 1975; Geschiere 1997; Mbembe 1997). On the one hand, both vigilantism and the widespread popular support for it can be read as a response to the practices of the Nigerian state and the failures of democracy to deliver expected political and economic dividends. As I show below, vigilantism is extolled in local discourse as an indigenous alternative to the corruption of the state. On the other hand, vigilantism must also be read as an expression of discontent with regard to more traditional structures of patron-clientism as they play out in an era of centralized state power and heightened inequality in a population that is younger, more educated and urbanized, and full of frustrated ambitions. Popular support for vigilantism draws both on dissatisfaction with the supposed democratic state and on critiques of traditional patronage structures that are voiced, partly, in the language of democratic ideals.

The rise of violent vigilantism, particularly youthful urban-based vigilante groups like the Bakassi Boys, is not unique to Nigeria. Similar phenomena have occurred in Cameroon (Argenti 1998), Kenya (Anderson 2002), South Africa (Baker 2002a; Haysom 1990), and elsewhere, suggesting a wider relevance of some of the connections in Nigeria between youth, vigilantism, and popular understandings of inequality and power in an era when the promise of democracy is belied by the ineptitude of the state and the willful injustices perpetrated by its leaders. Indeed, Ray Abrahams (1996, 1998) has demonstrated many historical and cross-cultural parallels in the relationship between vigilantism and the state, suggesting that vigilantism is a common response to ambiguities and ambivalence regarding the authority of the state. The role

and authority of the state seem to be particularly problematic and provoca-
tive for African youth, who are both inspired by the promises of democracy
and frustrated over the way state institutions continue to be manipulated
by powerful politicians. As elites utilize state institutions to turn traditional
patron-client structures into mechanisms for massive individual enrichment,
the anger of youth is double edged. They have been disappointed both by
patron-clientism and by the mechanisms of the neoliberal state.

The irony of the Bakassi Boys is that although they ascended to popularity
based on perceptions that they were incorruptible crime fighters, they were
eventually discredited precisely because they came to be seen as co-opted by
politicians. Although violent vigilantism expressed the anger of youth about
inequality and injustice in Nigeria, ultimately, vigilantism served to deflect or
obscure the role of politicians and the state in perpetuating the conditions that
produce crime, insecurity, and inequality. Rather than targeting elite politicians
who might be said to be most responsible for inequality and injustice, or
working to reorganize Nigeria's complex political economy in ways that better
benefited the young and the poor, vigilantism channeled frustrations against
ordinary criminals, who were themselves as much victims as perpetrators.

Public Support for Vigilantism in Nigeria

Popular local explanations for the emergence of vigilante groups like the
Bakassi Boys focused on the extremely high rates of violent crime that plagued
Nigeria's cities in the late 1990s. While high rates and great fears of violent
crime provide an obvious context for understanding the rise of vigilantism
in Nigeria, they are not a sufficient explanation. A number of other political
and symbolic processes are central to explaining the widespread popularity
of vigilante groups like the Bakassi Boys. Particularly important are competing idioms of accountability at work in local support for and eventual ambivalence about the Bakassi Boys (Comaroff and Comaroff 1999; Gore and
Pratten 2003). The youthful vigilantism of the Bakassi Boys and the massive
popularity they initially enjoyed reflect the complex and contradictory ways
in which ordinary Nigerians experience and understand inequality. To put
it too simply, Nigerians juggle two seemingly irreconcilable idioms of accountability (Ekeh 1975), one grounded in a moral economy of reciprocal
patron-clientism rooted in ties to kin and community of origin (and reinforced by notions that the ultimate sanctions for immoral human conduct
are supernatural), the other adopted with the emergence of the modern nation-state and tied to Weberian and neoliberal ideals about bureaucracy and
democracy.

Of course, in reality these systems are intertwined. Ordinary Nigerians fashion their understandings of inequality in a social world where politicians must prove (or pretend) they are both good democrats and good patrons. Common folk simultaneously condemn the corruption of politicians and cultivate corruption in their own patrons as the only means by which their interests are served (Joseph 1987; Smith 2001). All these contradictions are connected to youthful (and broader societal) anger over poverty, inequality, and corruption. Further, the sense of insecurity created by poverty and inequality is exacerbated, but also powerfully symbolized, in fears about crime. Anxieties about crime crystallize people's collective sense of insecurity. They also mobilize violence against these perceived threats in ways that both lash out against inequality and, sadly, reflect and reproduce some of the ways violence has been inflicted on the wider population by the state. To understand vigilante violence as rooted in but also a rejection of state violence, it is necessary to examine Nigerians' experiences and collective representations of the deployment of state-controlled means of violence, primarily by the police and the military.

Vigilantism and the Legacy of State Violence

Popular experiences with and perceptions of the Nigerian military and the Nigerian police both normalized everyday violence and created a climate in which people believed that institutions of the state were not only incapable of combating crime but often complicit in its commission. Since Nigeria's independence in 1960, the military has ruled for more than twenty-five years, and during that time Nigerians have experienced numerous forms of everyday violence. Arrests, imprisonment, and extrajudicial executions of political opponents have been widely reported in the national and the international press. Over the years, many ethnic and political demonstrations and riots have been put down through violent military responses in which many hundreds of civilian citizens have been killed. During the regime of General Sani Abacha, from 1993 to 1998, the extrajudicial executions of the activist Ken-Saro Wiwa and eight colleagues generated extensive media coverage and wide popular discussion (Bastian 2000; McLuckie and McPhail 2000). While such high-profile actions symbolized the capacity of the military to impose its will through control of the means of violence, it is the more everyday forms of state-sponsored brutality that have both normalized violence and created an expectation that violence is an acceptable means for dealing with threats to the social order.

Perhaps the most notorious and most popularly recognized example of the everyday violence of the state against its citizenry is the checkpoint. During military rule, heavily armed soldiers set up roadblocks at which vehicles would be stopped, drivers harassed, and passengers searched. Many Nigerians were subjected to police and military checkpoints daily, and anyone who utilized Nigeria's roads, whether in private cars or public transportation, encountered them frequently. Most people interpret these checkpoints, which continue under civilian rule, as means for police and soldiers to extract money from the public, symbolizing larger processes of control and exploitation through which elites enrich themselves and their cronies at the expense of the larger population. During the six years I lived in Nigeria, during a period spanning 1989–97, hardly a month passed without media reports or oral testimony from my friends and informants about people who had been harassed, beaten, or shot in confrontations at checkpoints with the police or the military.

Stories about checkpoints, regardless of whether they were all true, became an important form of folklore that represented wider interpretations of military rule and the everyday violence it produced. One popular story, of which several versions circulated during General Abacha's rule, represented public consciousness about the capriciousness with which the military resorted to violence, but also the notion that violence could be an acceptable way to solve problems. The story alleged that when Abacha was a young colonel a policeman stopped and delayed him at a roadside checkpoint. When the young policeman failed immediately to yield to Abacha's identification of himself as a military officer, the then Colonel Abacha simply shot the man dead and continued on his way. Whether the story is true or apocryphal, local interpretations illustrated an ambivalence that juxtaposed concern about violence as an instrument of power with a widely shared sense that the country requires an iron hand to assure discipline and order. Despite the irony that the military itself was responsible for many checkpoints, the idea that the head of state was brazen and powerful enough to kill a policeman blocking his way held a certain appeal to many Nigerians, in large measure because police checkpoints are powerful symbols of corruption and indiscipline. Though Nigerians often lament the violence of the state, many people also participate in discourses that construct certain kinds of violence as ethical and necessary for the maintenance of an otherwise unruly society. Certainly such discourses dominated initial positive reactions to the Bakassi Boys, as illustrated below.

Before turning more directly to the Bakassi Boys, their popularity, and their eventual demise, we must recognize the importance of local perceptions of the Nigerian police as a context for understanding the positive reception of the Bakassi Boys. In contrast to the military, about which Nigerians seem to have extremely ambivalent feelings, the police are overwhelmingly perceived negatively. In addition to their widely shared experiences of roadside extortion at ubiquitous checkpoints, Nigerians perceive the police as being unconcerned about investigating crime, quick to unleash violence on uncooperative citizens (even when they have committed no crime except resisting police extortion), and even complicit in the very epidemic of violent armed robbery that gave rise to the Bakassi Boys. A few journeys on Nigerian public transportation are enough to familiarize one with the negative images Nigerians have of the police. Bus and taxi loads of passengers collectively condemn the police at virtually every checkpoint, at which drivers and passengers are greeted with all too familiar extended hands backed up by menacing scowls and freely wielded weapons. A number of widely publicized media stories about police collaboration with criminal gangs have fueled such perceptions, and while the role of police in crime may well be exaggerated in popular discourse, the fact that the police are perceived as corrupt and ineffective definitely contributed to the dramatic rise and positive reception of vigilante groups like the Bakassi Boys.

Who Were the Bakassi Boys?

In late 1998, in the commercial southeastern Nigerian city of Aba, shoemakers and traders angry over the extent of extortion and violent robberies perpetrated by an increasingly powerful group of criminals organized a vigilante force known as the Bakassi Boys.[1] Initially made up of young traders and other young men paid with contributions provided by the traders' association, the Bakassi Boys embarked on a mission to rid Aba's main market of violent criminals, publicly executing dozens of alleged criminals in Aba. These executions, dubbed "instant justice" in popular discourse, typically took place in prominent public spaces, such as major intersections or market centers, attracting large crowds of observers. The Bakassi Boys killed these alleged criminals with machete blows, dismembering their bodies and then burning them at the site of the execution (Smith 2004).

The original Bakassi Boys vigilante group in Aba probably numbered no more than fifty to one hundred men, but over the next several years, as the Bakassi Boys expanded their coverage to include other cities in the southeast, their numbers increased to perhaps several hundred. Demographically, the Bakassi Boys were typically between the ages of eighteen and forty, and while some of the leaders were married men with families, most of the rank-and-file vigilantes were single young men. They appeared to be from relatively poor backgrounds, and few had extensive education. Almost all were recruited from urban areas, and after the Bakassi Boys eventually lost popularity many local people observed that there seemed to be little difference in overall profile between the Bakassi Boys and the criminals they fought. My own impression was certainly that the Bakassi Boys and the criminals had a great deal in common in terms of background, with the violence of each fueled by anger and frustration over the unfulfilled promises of Nigerian society. Indeed, many people speculated that after the Bakassi Boys were disbanded the erstwhile vigilantes resorted or returned to lives of crime.

It is hard to say how individual Bakassi Boys were recruited and even how the vigilantes were organized, as secrecy was part of the aura of supernatural power that they manipulated to increase popular fear and awe. But as they spread their coverage to several cities in the southeast, power struggles emerged between the original leaders in Aba and new leaders who competed for power in other towns. While the Bakassi Boys tended to portray these struggles in terms of claims over supernatural legitimacy, in practice these struggles led to more than one instance of intragroup violence and murder. In the end, most disturbing to ordinary Nigerians was the revelation that the Bakassi Boys were ultimately pawns of the very corrupt politicians whom people had hoped they were independent of. But for several years the Bakassi Boys enjoyed wide popular support, and they depended on their appearance as supernaturally powered crime fighters to sustain their popularity.

Vigilantism and Supernatural Power

Against a history in which the police and the state are viewed as ineffective, corrupt, and even complicit in violent crime, but in a society where supernatural judgment is perceived as the ultimate mechanism of accountability and where violence by the state has been normalized and even celebrated as an ethical and effective response to disorder, the Bakassi Boys were not only well received, but constructed as heroes. Their hero status seemed to blind the local public to very clear early signs of the risks that vigilantism posed to achieving justice, including the possible loss of innocent individual life and the misuse of extrajudicial "prosecutions" and executions to settle personal and political scores. In the rush to celebrate the apparent curtailment of violent crime, most people were initially impervious to evidence that the Bakassi Boys were being co-opted by politicians and manipulated in political, ethnic, and sectionalist disputes. In addition, for almost three years the local public largely overlooked indications that the Bakassi Boys themselves seemed increasingly to resemble a criminal gang as much as a supernaturally inspired vigilante force. Before examining the relationship of the Bakassi Boys to politicians and the state, it is important to analyze the processes through which the Bakassi Boys achieved hero status, particularly the belief that they had supernatural power.

While vigilantism may have had real effects in reducing crime (Baker 2002b; Smith 2004), the Bakassi Boys' popularity is only partly explained by their empirical impact on crime. Once the Bakassi Boys were formed, they represented themselves and were represented in the media and in popular discourse in ways that fueled their symbolic status as heroes enforcing an idiom of accountability tied to an ultimate authority, the supernatural. The Bakassi Boys' physical appearance—their black attire, their dark glasses, their amulets, their weapons, and the tone of their facial expressions (which ranged between menacing and without affect at all)—contributed to their image of invulnerability. They looked dangerous and intimidating, and this image clearly impressed the public. Further, the aura of invincibility surrounding the Bakassi Boys and the popular imagery of them ridding society of armed criminals was promoted by various forms of media attention, in newspapers and magazines but especially through popular media like videos and posters. In 2001 I purchased a three-part series of home videos produced in Nigeria called *Issakaba*. *Issakaba* is almost *Bakassi* spelled backwards. These films, in the genre of docudrama, present fictional stories that draw on the real-life exploits of the Bakassi Boys, and they were very popular. In them the Bakassi Boys are represented as vigilantes protected by charms that enabled them to avoid injury from criminals' bullets and to detect innocence or guilt through the magical use of their machetes. The process of determining magically a suspect's innocence or guilt was ironically dubbed in popular discourse a "lab test" (Harnischfeger 2003).

The belief that the Bakassi Boys had supernatural powers was vital to public confidence in their abilities to catch criminals and distinguish the innocent from the guilty. Key to their initial popularity was the belief that they were incorruptible in a hopelessly corrupt society and that their incorruptibility was supernaturally assured. In a detailed analysis of the case of the Bakassi Boys' extrajudicial execution of Eddy Okeke, a Christian "prophet" widely suspected of using ritual murder to attract followers and propitiate his own wealth, Johannes Harnischfeger (2003) argues persuasively that the Bakassi Boys asserted their legitimacy by demonstrating their capacity to fight not just ordinary criminals but the evils of the occult. Indeed, Abrahams (1996) argues that the capacity to fight "witches" is part of what gives many vigilante groups the legitimacy that the police and other state law-enforcement agents lack. Put another way, the Bakassi Boys tried to prove their worthiness in an idiom of accountability that in the minds of many ordinary Nigerians trumps that of the state. In this idiom of accountability, incorruptibility is supernaturally assured, but supernatural power is only proven by incorruptibility. Each is easily undermined when doubts emerge about the other. As experience with the Bakassi Boys grew, doubts about both their incorruptibility and their supernatural powers emerged.

The importance of the association of incorruptibility and supernatural powers surfaced in many ways. The two or three occasions when members of the Bakassi Boys were reportedly killed in battles with criminals (and later with police) challenged their supernatural status. These stories evoked great debate, as some people dismissed the reports as untrue, others opined that those killed were likely not to have been "real" Bakassi, while a very few suggested that the Bakassi Boys were not, in fact, protected by charms. In June 2001 I found myself unexpectedly caught in the middle of a demonstration by several thousand people in the city of Owerri over the launching of a vigilante service by the Imo State government. When I asked people in the crowd what the demonstration was about, I was surprised when they told me that they were demonstrating against the launching of the Bakassi Boys. It took several more conversations to discover that the anger was not over the Bakassi Boys or vigilantism per se, but instead over a widely shared suspicion that the vigilante group being introduced was not the "real" Bakassi Boys but rather a group sponsored by the state's increasingly unpopular governor. "These ones are fake," one young man in the crowd told me, "let us see if their bodies can resist bullets. If not, they are not real Bakassi." The idea that the Bakassi Boys were supernaturally endowed with extrahuman capabilities helps explain not only the confidence people placed in their capacity to combat crime but also the initial lack of public concern about the possible loss of innocent lives.

Vigilantism and the State

Popular support for the Bakassi Boys hinged on their perceived role as supernaturally powered heroes fighting violent criminals and evil forces of the occult that the police were unable or unwilling to apprehend. From the first months after the Bakassi Boys' founding, politicians seized on their popularity and attempted to co-opt vigilantism for political gain. When news of the "success" of the Bakassi Boys in combating crime in Aba spread to other Igbo-speaking cities in the southeast, traders' associations and other citizens' groups in places like Onitsha, Nnewi, Awka, and Umuahia clamored for similar anticrime vigilantism. The governors of Abia and Anambra states responded by inviting the Bakassi Boys to fight crime in major cities under their jurisdiction. Newspaper, radio, and television news services reported that the state governments provided the respective vigilante services with funds and vehicles, and in Anambra the government passed a law officially creating the Anambra Vigilante Services (AVS) (Baker 2002b). So close were the ties between the governor and the Bakassi Boys in Anambra that the AVS had an office inside Government House, the official compound of the state governor.

Politicians clearly used the Bakassi Boys to boost their own popularity. The governors and other local politicians cast vigilantism as an example of local state prerogative in Nigeria's federal system, and state politicians countered federal government pronouncements about the dangers of "ethnic militias" with statements about threats to the autonomy of states in Nigeria's federal system (Baker 2002b). Though southeastern governors resisted applying the label "ethnic militia" to the Bakassi Boys, popular discourse about the group did evoke issues of ethnicity and religion, painting the Bakassi Boys as the Igbo alternative to Sharia in the Islamic north. From 1999 until well into 2002 politicians succeeded in capturing the popularity of the Bakassi Boys for their own benefit. But eventually accusations that the Bakassi Boys were used to settle political scores, hired as thugs and assassins for the political patrons, became increasingly widespread and led to enough popular discontent with the abuses of vigilantism that the federal government's decision in August and September 2002 to disband the Bakassi Boys and arrest its members was politically feasible.

Vigilantism and the Democratic Dispensation

On 29 May 2001 the Bakassi Boys in Onitsha slaughtered more than thirty alleged criminals in a public mass execution. The twenty-ninth of May is a public holiday in Nigeria, designated "Democracy Day" to mark the transition to civilian rule in 1999. The mass extrajudicial execution on Democracy Day, perhaps calculated by the Bakassi Boys to emphasize their power in Anambra state politics and society, symbolized important issues central to the relationship between vigilantism and the state, highlighting divisions within the Nigerian polity. The dramatic expression of violent vigilantism on Democracy Day in Onitsha literally drew in blood a picture of the fault lines in Nigerian society exposed by the transition to democracy and the rise of vigilantism.

The Bakassi Boys were first invited to Anambra by local leaders in the commercial city of Nnewi in April 2000. Indeed, by late June of that year, barely two months after the Bakassi Boys "cleansed" Nnewi, Governor Mbadinuju invited them to extend their vigilante services to the entire state. The widespread sense of insecurity caused and symbolized by high rates of violent crime created a climate in which populist political rhetoric that called upon people to take back the streets appealed to the public.

In the wake of the first wave of killings by the Bakassi Boys in Anambra in 2000, in which scores, and perhaps hundreds, of alleged criminals were ex-trajudicially executed, some federal authorities expressed concern over these events. In late July a spokesman for the Federal Executive Council announced that it had instructed the Nigerian police to halt the activities of the Bakassi Boys in Onitsha:

The Federal Executive Council (FEC) yesterday in Abuja directed the Nigerian Police Force (NPF) to stop the activities of the Bakassi Boys, who were invited to contain armed robbery in Onitsha. Announcing the directive after yesterday's FEC meeting, Minister of Economic Matters, Mr. Vincent Ogbulafor said the "council has directed NPF, through the Minister of Police Affairs, to flush out all Bakassi Boys from Onit-sha immediately." He said the FEC's decision followed reports that the Bakassi Boys, who were invited by the Governor of Anambra State to put a check on the mayhem perpetrated by armed robbers in the commercial city, had taken "laws into their hands and were killing innocent people." According to him, the Bakassi group had been infiltrated by "bad eggs" who were being used to perpetrate havoc on innocent people who fell victim in the process of settling scores. (*Vanguard* 2000)

Several things must be said in relation to the initial announcement autho-rizing police to intervene. First, the fact that the federal government chose Vincent Ogbulafor, an Igbo-speaking minister from the southeast, to pro-nounce its position signified its recognition of the potentially divisive effect of banning the Bakassi Boys. Having an Igbo minister announce the plan to disband the Bakassi Boys was clearly aimed at mitigating interpretations that this was an anti-Igbo decision. Second, the intent of Ogbulafor's assertion that "bad eggs" had infiltrated the Bakassi Boys seems to have been to avoid the appearance of questioning the public's faith in the efficacy of the "real" Bakassi Boys. Third, and most significant, the crackdown never occurred. Local public reaction to the federal government's announcement was swift and strong, with public opinion in the southeast clearly favoring the preser-vation of the Bakassi Boys. The following excerpt from a Nigerian newspaper story about interviews with residents in Onitsha contains quotations similar to comments I heard from people in Owerri and Umuahia, where I was when these events unfolded:

A cross-section of the people who spoke on the development express dismay over the decision of the federal government to flush out the Bakassi Boys whom, they now regard as their "messiah." Ogbuefi Okonkwo a trader in Ontisha told *Vanguard* that "The federal government appeared to be unfair to the people of this area, otherwise how can one ever think of exposing the citizenry to armed robbers who have laid siege on the state recently." Okonkwo wondered why the government kept quiet all these while that men of the underworld were terrorizing innocent citizens in the state, saying it was completely wrong for government to order the police to flush out the Bakassi Boys when adequate security arrangement has not been made for the state. He stated that since the Bakassi people came to Onitsha, the town has been crime-free and asked the federal government to try to feel the pulse of the people. (Edike 2000)

It is not clear why the federal government failed to follow through on its plans to clamp down on the Bakassi Boys. Harnischfeger (2003) reports stories circulating in Onitsha, almost surely apocryphal, that the Bakassi Boys repelled federal forces at the outskirts of the city. Governor Mbadinuju presented the federal government's inaction as the outcome of his personal lobbying of President Obasanjo, "I have sufficiently explained to President Obasanjo about the activities of the Bakassi Boys and he has lifted the ban and this presidential approval of Bakassi Boys was received with joy by people of Anambra State" (Onwubiko 2000). Although the governor's version of what transpired was obviously politically inspired, it is nonetheless true that in Anambra, as well as in Abia and Imo states, the federal government did not initiate steps to check the activities of the Bakassi Boys until the crackdown in August and September 2002.

The federal government's long tolerance of the Bakassi Boys reflected its wariness over the many fault lines that divide the country, including ethnicity, regionalism, and religion, as well as its reluctance to challenge powerful local idioms of accountability when its own legitimacy seemed so precarious. The Bakassi Boys' popularity and the success with which politicians in the southeast cast vigilantism in populist terms meant that disbanding them had potentially destabilizing political repercussions. To the federal government, leaders in the southeast presented the Bakassi Boys as an anticrime force without political or ethnic agendas. From the federal government's perspective, the populism expressed in vigilantism was most dangerous precisely because of its potential to exacerbate already powerful cleavages in the Nigerian polity. Federal authorities faced a dilemma. Allowing the Bakassi Boys to exist posed risks that they could be mobilized for political purposes; banning them might stoke the very ethnic and regional polarization they hoped to avoid. Ultimately, the Bakassi Boys diluted their own popularity by actions that undermined their heroic status. The proliferation of stories that they acted as thugs for their political patrons, that they could be hired to intervene in local disputes, and that they abused their status to extort money from the public weakened their popular support. The increasing association of the Bakassi Boys with the state (in the person of the governors) tainted their image. The more they looked like a political and hence corrupt organization (or perhaps equally accurate, the more they looked like a corrupt and hence political organization), the less supernatural their powers seemed and the more unpopular they became. By the time the federal government clamped down on them in late 2002, popular reaction was at least as much relief as outrage.

Vigilantism, Ethnic Militias, and Religion

A final aspect of the Bakassi Boys' popularity must be explored before we can assess the longer-term effects of vigilantism in Nigeria. While politicians in the southeast did everything possible to represent the Bakassi Boys to the federal government in nonethnic terms, in local discourse the image of the Bakassi Boys as an Igbo organization was powerful. Igbos took pride in the national reputation of the Bakassi Boys as a "dreaded" force—dreaded by criminals but also inspiring great fear in the larger society. In the aftermath of Nigeria's civil war, in 1967–70, in which Igbos lost their bid to secede from Nigeria and create the independent state of Biafra, Igbos have continuously decried their marginalization in Nigerian politics and governance. Letters and editorials in newspapers lamenting Igbo marginalization appear almost daily, and everyday political conversation in the southeast inevitably turns to the issue. Local discourse about the Bakassi Boys frequently cited the success of indigenous vigilantism as an example of how much better Igbos could do if they were left to govern themselves. The statement of one Ikechi, a fifty-six-year-old man who ran a small provisions store, exemplifies similar comments I heard from many people about the Bakassi Boys, "The police do nothing. Their only interest is lining their pockets with our money. They do not care about the welfare of our people. When the Igbo man works hard to earn a living they simply blackmail us into subsidizing their lives. Crime was ruining business. The Bakassi Boys have taken back the market. We are the ones who know how to deal with these problems. If the Igbo man were given a free hand in Nigeria there would not be so many problems" (pers. comm., 7 July 2001).

That the Nigerian police are a federal force is a significant part of the story. Police commanders in the southeast are most often non-Igbos, and police officers are usually deployed away from their places of origin. A federal police force reinforces the local sense that people are not in control of their own governance, and for Igbos this is exacerbated by the legacy of Biafra.

As part of their heroic image, the Bakassi Boys denied any political ambitions or affiliations. To stave off federal intervention, local politicians worked hard to avoid any perception that the Bakassi Boys were an "ethnic militia." Indeed, compared with the O'odua People's Congress in the Yoruba southwest or the Egbesu Boys in the Niger Delta, organizations that had explicit political and ethnic agendas, the Bakassi Boys seemed much less politically and ethnically oriented. Yet Igbo pride in the Bakassi Boys had clear ethnic dimensions, and the initial (aborted) federal decision to disband the vigilante group produced strong regional and ethnic sentiments that contributed to popular resistance to federal intervention. (In Onitsha, for example, thousands of traders marched to Government House to express solidarity with the Bakassi Boys.)

Igbo support for the Bakassi Boys is only partly attributable to regional and ethnic interests and pride. In many ways, popular support for vigilantism in Nigeria is undergirded by common experiences and idioms of accountability that transcend divisions based on the politics of identity. But while public support for vigilantism partly transcends social and cultural cleavages, it also builds upon them. Popular justification for the Bakassi Boys incorporated a religious dimension that reflected the increasing role of religious difference as a polarizing force in Nigeria, albeit in ways that intersect with ethnic and regional divisions. Since the transition to civilian rule in 1999, many mostly Islamic northern Nigerian states have instituted Sharia, justifying their right to do so under Nigeria's ostensibly decentralized federal system. The federal government's hands-off approach to Sharia in northern Nigeria is motivated by similar political calculations that underlie its three-year tolerance of the Bakassi Boys. Intervention would involve considerable political costs. The parallel between Sharia and the vigilante justice of the Bakassi Boys exists not only in calculations of government officials. I heard many Igbos discuss the Bakassi Boys as the Igbo alternative to Sharia. The words of Ferguson Nwoke, a fifty-two-year-old unemployed Catholic, are similar to several statements I collected about the parallels between the Bakassi Boys and Sharia: "Crime in Nigeria was out of control. The Hausas instituted Sharia law to restore order. That's their justice. They cut off people's hands when they steal and stone to death adulterers. Bakassi is our Sharia. The Bakassi Boys have restored sanity to the society. If government allows the north to have Sharia, why shouldn't we have Bakassi?" (pers. comm., 29 June 2001).

In fact, no one has actually been stoned to death under Sharia in northern Nigeria, and while Igbos, and Christian southerners generally, are apt to condemn Sharia as primitive and barbaric, the Bakassi Boys' actions were far more violent and deadly than anything that has resulted from Sharia. Nonetheless, the parallels that many Igbos drew between Sharia and the Bakassi Boys reflect the degree to which vigilantism was justified and federal intervention was resisted in the name of local rights and idioms of accountability that both called upon and transcended regional, ethnic, and religious identities.

The Legacy of the Bakassi Boys

Since Nigeria's Mobile Police Force, on orders from the federal government, attacked the Bakassi Boys in August and September 2002 in the main cities in the southeast where they operated, the vigilante group has disappeared from the Nigerian scene. The police killed an untold number of the Bakassi Boys and detained scores of others. The Bakassi Boys undermined their own popularity through their collaboration with politicians, their availability as thugs for hire, and their extortion of the very public they proclaimed to protect. Nevertheless, the idea of vigilante justice and the dream of a society in which criminals of all stripes, be they armed robbers or corrupt politicians, are subject to popular accountability remain extremely powerful among the masses. In the runup to Nigeria's elections in April 2003, many politicians in the southeast called for the reinstitution of vigilantism, albeit always arguing for "real" vigilantes. Since the elections, newly elected officials have promised to revitalize groups like the Bakassi Boys, and local traders in Onitsha apparently have recently formed a new vigilante force to protect the market. The embattled governor in Anambra State is reportedly protected by remnants of the Bakassi Boys. Almost surely, vigilante groups like the Bakassi Boys will rise again in Nigeria.

Disillusionment with the Bakassi Boys, along with continued distrust of the police and other institutions of state justice, has also led to new forms of extrajudicial accountability. For example, in Aba, the commercial city where the Bakassi Boys were originally formed, a new phenomenon of "street justice" has recently emerged. If a criminal is caught in the act of stealing, if a car accident occurs, or if two individuals' disagreement escalates to the point where onlookers take notice, "people's courts" are constituted immediately, the cases are "tried," and sentences are passed and carried out. Seemingly random onlookers and passers-by become lawyers, judges, and juries (and in the most disturbing cases, executioners). While the consequences of some of these cases of street justice seem innocuous enough (e.g., a car driver is made to pay the hospital costs of a motorcycle driver he collided with), the opportunities for injustice, including extrajudicial execution, abound. Indeed, the couple of incidents I witnessed myself (both of which resulted from traffic accidents) seem to suggest that the outcome was determined as much by the force of individual characters who were protagonists in these unfolding dramas as by any principles of justice.

But the popularity of these forms of people's justice in places like Aba is unmistakable, attributable largely to people's sense of disappointment in the institutions of the state. In June 2003 I asked numerous people in Aba how they felt about the demise of the Bakassi Boys. The response of a textile trader in Kent Market was the most common: "Now the whole of Aba is Bakassi." What he meant, and what many others expressed, was that the people have taken into their own hands the task of assuring public safety and punishing criminals. Just as the police and the state could not be trusted, neither could the Bakassi Boys. The irony is that it is people's expectations for, as well as their disappointments with, the promises of democracy that have created a situation in which opportunities for people to do injustice in the name of justice have become so profound.

Conclusion

The fact that the Bakassi Boys were young and male—as are so many of the world's soldiers, rebels, bandits, gang members, and other perpetrators of violence—probably requires explanations of an order of magnitude that transcends what can be offered in this case study. But the violent vigilantism of the Bakassi Boys clearly grew out of and gave vivid expression to frustrations over a widespread sense of insecurity in Nigeria. The pervasive sense of insecurity in the country must be explained as a result of the twin pressures of poverty and inequality and the suffering they engender. This suffering is doubtless experienced disproportionately by the young, both because they are less well positioned to navigate Nigeria's clientelistic political economy than their seniors and because they are growing up with a sense that things could be different and better.

In the summer of 2003 I took an American undergraduate with me to Nigeria to work on a project with my Nigerian colleagues. I had done my best to try to prepare her for the first experiences, including roadside checkpoints. On our way from the airport in Port Harcourt to Aba, the birthplace of the Bakassi Boys, we waited in a line of cars and public buses stopped at a police checkpoint. When the driver of a *danfoe* (minibus) handed the policeman a crunched-up naira note, and the policeman slyly, but obviously pocketed the money required for the bus to proceed, my student asked, "Why, if everyone knows what is happening, do the driver and the policeman half-heartedly try to conceal it?" In retrospect, I believe this simple question incisively penetrates to the very heart of what we must understand in order to make sense of the context of inequality and corruption in Nigeria, and of the contradictions that surface in analyzing the case of the Bakassi Boys.

Explanations for poverty and inequality, both as they are articulated in popular Nigerian discourse and as we must frame them as social scientists, are to be found, at least in part, in the complex intertwining of patron-clientism and the modern Nigerian state. The crux of the matter is that the intersection of the apparatus of a modern state with a more traditional system of patron-clientism, rooted in notions of kinship and reciprocity, has created a situation in which the elite are able to manipulate and pervert the ideal versions of each system to their own benefit. In other words, the massive inequalities in Nigeria are only possible because the structures, trappings, and discourses of the state enable patrimonial patron-clientism to flourish in ways that produce levels of inequality and a lack of accountability that would not be possible were patronage more tightly regulated through kinship and local community structures. On the other side of the same coin, patron-client structures and values provide a means and rationale for looting the state and for undermining ideals of bureaucratic transparency and accountability. Numerous analysts have identified such processes in Nigeria and in other parts of Africa (e.g., Chabal and Daloz 1999; and Joseph 1987). What has received less attention is that the intertwining of these two systems has produced a profound ambivalence on the part of common people. Observation of everyday political discourse in Nigeria reveals that ordinary people deploy idioms of accountability that derive from both systems (Gore and Pratten 2003). Nigerians utilize expectations about reciprocal patron-clientism to criticize the failures of the modern state, but they also employ ideals of democracy and bureaucratic accountability to condemn the corruption of patrimonial patron-clientism. The tragedy is that in many ways both systems are failing to meet their promises to ordinary Nigerians, and the intertwining of the two enables elites to extend and maintain inequality and obscure the processes by which inequities are perpetuated.

The rise of the Bakassi Boys and their impressive initial popularity must be understood in the context of their promise of incorruptibility in the face of such intractable corruption. With their supposed supernatural powers, they seemingly transcended the corruption of the state and the patron-client politics that controls it. Their demise came as they were slowly revealed to be both political and corrupt. To understand the gradual change in popular sentiment about the Bakassi Boys that made federal government intervention politically feasible, one needs to examine the perpetration of everyday violence by the Bakassi Boys on the very public that had supported them. They imposed "protection" levies on the populations they were supposed to protect; they intimidated and roughed up innocent citizens; they intervened in local disputes, siding with the highest bidder; they took innocent prisoners and released them for ransom; and, allegedly, they were paid to assassinate the political opponents of their patrons. Though they invoked and relied on an idiom of accountability tied to the supernatural, the Bakassi Boys' legitimacy was ultimately undermined by their involvement in the very corruption and crime they ostensibly fought.

Indeed, the idiom of accountability tied to the supernatural is itself multivalent. Supernatural powers have long been understood in Nigeria, and throughout Africa, as potentially good or evil. The same might be said of what might variously be called Western, neoliberal, or democratic idioms of accountability. Most Nigerians embrace notions of democracy and human rights. In many contexts they deploy these notions in their relations with the state and in their interpretations of the world. I suggest that rather than viewing neoliberal notions of democracy, civil society, and human rights as unsuitable for Nigerian contexts (an argument I think Harnischfeger [2003] comes close to making in his account of the Bakassi Boys), it is more illuminating to examine the ways that Nigerians play different idioms of accountability off one another. The Bakassi Boys were both celebrated as heroes and suspected as criminals based on the same repertoire of ideas about secrecy and the supernatural. Similarly, they were both hailed as an indigenous alternative to a failed democratic state and condemned for violating some of the rights people ascribe to themselves based, in part, on those same democratic principles. It is the intertwining of these idioms, rather than the final privileging of one over the other, that is salient for understanding popular responses to the Bakassi Boys.

The popularity of violent vigilantism in Nigeria must be understood as part of a complex interweaving of people's experiences of everyday violence and the particular political structures and symbolic systems that both produce this violence and provide the means to interpret it. Vigilantism in Nigeria responded to public perceptions of injustice that projected onto violent crime popular understandings of the roots of poverty and inequality. Ironically, the symbolic construction of vigilantism obscured its entanglements with the state and with political processes that reproduce the inequality and injustices that gave rise to the Bakassi Boys. The way in which discourses of democracy were deployed both in public interpretations and in politicians' manipulation of vigilantism should give pause to any simplistic conclusions about the relationship between civil society and the state in Nigeria's postmilitary democracy. The Bakassi Boys were both antagonistic to the state and co-opted by it. Their ambiguous relationship to the state mirrors a dualism that characterizes Nigerians' experiences of politics. Ordinary Nigerians are simultaneously conciliatory and antagonistic to the state (Gore and Pratten 2003,

218–19), a stance that reflects the dynamics of patrimonial patron-clientism (Joseph 1987; Smith 2001). The deep entanglements of patron-clientism and the state produce tremendous ambivalence, creating a climate in which competing idioms of accountability simultaneously contradict and complement each other.

Notes

I gratefully acknowledge the support of the Wenner-Gren Foundation for Anthropological Research, the National Science Foundation, and the National Institutes of Health for my research in Nigeria. I would like to thank Caroline Archambualt, Nicolas Argenti, Philip Leis, Mary Moran, Nicholas Townsend, and Bruce Whitehouse for their helpful, critical comments on earlier versions of this essay. In addition, thanks to Edna Bay and Donald Donham for organizing the conference "Africa and Violence: Identities, Histories, and Representations," where this essay was initially presented, and to all the participants for their constructive suggestions.

1. I had a difficult time uncovering the origin of the name Bakassi Boys. The Bakassi peninsula is a geographical area between Nigeria and Cameroon that has been the object of a long dispute over sovereignty. Most people I asked could not explain why an Aba-based Igbo vigilante group would bear the name of a region that is distinctly non-Igbo. A few people told me that the name Bakassi connoted armed combat and a readiness to fight, projecting onto the Bakassi Boys a military prowess. However, the most compelling explanation for the name came from a police report reproduced in a Nigerian weekly magazine, in which the original patron of the Bakassi Boys, the president of the traders' association, was questioned about the group. He said that the shoe market from which the vigilante group first emerged was newly located and "situated at the boundary to Osisioma Local Government Area and Aba North Local Government Area which most time cause conflict between the two local government mentioned above hence the name Bakassi" (*Insider Weekly* 2001, 28). In other words, the Bakassi Boys got their name from the market from which they originally emerged, which got its name from a local border dispute. Johannes Harnischfeger (2003) asserts that the Bakassi Boys were named for a section of the market that, like the Bakassi peninsula, was swampy. I find this explanation for the derivation less convincing.

References

Abrahams, Ray. 1996. Vigilantism: Order and Disorder on the Frontiers of the State. In *Inside and Outside the Law: Anthropological Studies of Authority and Ambiguity,* edited by Olivia Harris, 41–55. New York: Routledge.

———. 1998. *Vigilant Citizens: Vigilantism and the State.* Cambridge: Polity Press.

Anderson, David. 2002. Vigilantes, Violence, and the Politics of Public Order in Kenya. *African Affairs* 101:531–55.

Argenti, Nicolas. 1998. Air Youth: Performance, Violence, and the State in Cameroon. *Journal of the Royal Anthropological Institute* 4 (4): 753–82.

Baker, Bruce. 2002a. Living with Non-state Policing in South Africa: The Issues and Dilemmas. *Journal of Modern African Studies* 40 (1): 29–53.

———. 2002b. When the Bakassi Boys Came: Eastern Nigeria Confronts Vigilantism. *Journal of Contemporary African Studies* 20 (2): 223–44.

Bastian, Misty. 2000. "Buried beneath Six Feet of Crude Oil": State-Sponsored Death and the Absent Body of Ken Saro-Wiwa. In *Ken Saro-Wiwa: Writer and Political Activist,* edited by Craig McLuckie and Aubrey McPhail, 127–52. Boulder, CO: Lynne Rienner.

———. 2001. Vulture Men, Campus Cultists, and Teenaged Witches. In *Magical Interpretations, Material Realities: Modernity, Witchcraft, and the Occult in Postcolonial Africa,* edited by Henrietta Moore and Todd Sanders, 71–96. New York: Routledge.

Bayart, Jean-François. 1993. *The State in Africa: The Politics of the Belly.* London: Longman.

Chabal, Patrick, and Jean-Pascal Daloz. 1999. *Africa Works: Disorder as Political Instrument.* Oxford: James Currey for the International African Institute.

Comaroff, John, and Jean Comaroff. 1999. Introd. to *Civil Society and the Political Imagination in Africa,* edited by John Comaroff and Jean Comaroff, 1–43. Chicago: University of Chicago Press.

Edike, Tony. 2000. Anambra Residents Restive of FG Order on Bakassi Boys. *Vanguard,* 29 July, 1.

Ekeh, Peter. 1975. Colonialism and the Two Publics in Africa: A Theoretical Statement. *Comparative Journal of Society and History* 17 (1): 91–112.

Geschiere, Peter. 1997. *The Modernity of Witchcraft: Politics and the Occult in Postcolonial Africa.* Charlottesville: University of Virginia Press.

Gore, Charles, and David Pratten. 2003. The Politics of Plunder: The Rhetorics of Order and Disorder in Southern Nigeria. *African Affairs* 102:211–40.

Harnischfeger, Johannes. 2003. The Bakassi Boys: Fighting Crime in Nigeria. *Journal of Modern African Studies* 41 (1): 23–49.

Haysom, N. 1990. Vigilantism and the Policing of South African Townships: Manufacturing Violent Stability. In *Towards Justice? Crime and State Control in South Africa.* edited by D. Hansson and D. van Zyl Smit. Cape Town: Oxford University Press.

Human Rights Watch. 2002. *The Bakassi Boys: The Legitimization of Murder and Torture.* New York.

———. 2003. *The O'odua People's Congress: Fighting Violence with Violence.* New York.

Insider Weekly. 2001. The Police Report on the Umuahia Murders. 16 July, 18–28.

Joseph, Richard. 1987. *Democracy and Prebendal Politics in Nigeria.* Cambridge: Cambridge University Press.

Marenin, Otwin. 1987. The Anini Saga: Armed Robbery and the Reproduction of Ideology in Nigeria. *Journal of Modern African Studies* 25 (2): 259–81.

Mbembe, Achille. 1992. Notes from the Postcolony. *Africa* 62 (1): 3–38.

McLuckie, Craig, and Aubrey McPhail, eds. 2000. *Ken Saro-Wiwa: Writer and Political Activist.* Boulder, CO: Lynne Rienner.

Momoh, Abubakar. 2000. Youth Culture and Area Boys in Lagos. In *Identity Transformation and Identity Politics under Structural Adjustment in Nigeria,* edited by Attahiru Jega, 181–203. Uppsala: Nordiska Afrikainstitutet.

Onwubiko, Emmanual. 2000. Obasanjo Forgives NAU Students, Okays Bakassi Boys. *Guardian,* 28 August.

Rabwoni, Okwir. 2002. Reflections on Youth and Militarism in Contemporary Africa. In *Young Africa: Realizing the Rights of Children and Youth,* edited by Alex de Waal and Nicolas Argenti, 155–70. Trenton, NJ: Africa World Press.

Richards, Paul. 1996. *Fighting for the Rainforest: War Youth and Resources in Sierra Leone.* Oxford: International African Institute.

Smith, Daniel Jordan. 2001. Kinship and Corruption in Contemporary Nigeria. *Ethnos* 66 (3): 320–43.

———. 2004. The Bakassi Boys: Vigilantism, Violence, and Political Imagination in Nigeria. *Cultural Anthropology* 19 (3): 429–55.

Vanguard. 2000. FG Asks Police to Flush Bakassi Boys. July 27: 1.

Mans is ma soe

Ganging Practices in Manenberg, South Africa, and the Ideologies of Masculinity, Gender, and Generational Relations

ELAINE SALO

T HIS essay draws on an ethnographic study of masculinity, race, and community in the Cape Flats townships of Cape Town, South Africa. In this study of young, colored, working-class male gang members in Manenberg, a township on the Cape Flats, I indicate that gang practices and colored men's gendered identities cannot be divorced from the historical factors of racial and economic dispossession that the residents of Manenberg experienced in the 1960s. More importantly, I indicate that these gangs are central to the cultural grammar and reproduction of community and person-hood in this marginal population. The structuralist analyses of gangs in ur-ban African contexts by social scientists such as Don Pinnock (1984) and B. E. Owumi (1994) have indicated that this subculture is often an expression of and resistance to the dominant political economy of African societies in the 1980s, such as South Africa under apartheid and Nigeria under structural adjustment and military dictatorship. Social historians such as Glaser (2000) have indicated that gang subculture is also a finer cultural expression of the divide between the aspirant middle and working classes in townships, as well as a manifestation of the alienation of working-class urban African youth from their elders. The analysis that follows indicates that gangs are also an ex-pression of social cohesion in peripheral communities. They exist within, and are an integral aspect of, both the cultural and the economic reproduction of personhood in a township community.

Structuralist analyses of South African township gangs by authors such as Pinnock (1984), and of gangs in the Nigerian city of Lagos, known as area boys (Ifaturoti 1994; Olutayo 1994; Owumi 1994), are important contributions to our understanding of this urban subculture because they indicate how this phenomenon is linked to structural political and economic features in society. However, they only partly explain the existence of gangs in the complex social landscape of urban African townships. Such analyses, which foreground male gangs as artifacts of resistance and survival, do not offer satisfactory analyses of the rich social texts of cultural reproduction within the social and physical spaces of the township. These analyses do not explain the complex social and cultural relationships between the gang and its individual members, on the one hand, and the gang members' social relations within households and in the wider local community, on the other. Gang members have other gendered identities that are embedded within the generational continuity of a household and woven into the richly textured social expanse of the township's communal relationships and networks. They are also sons, brothers, husbands, fathers, lovers, friends, and social mentors. These other gendered identities overlap, sometimes articulate, sometimes conflict with, and ultimately shape their identities as gang members. Gangs are not just the social expression of young men's social alienation from and resistance to their elders (Glaser 2000) or to mainstream society. They are also one of the means through which gendered personhood is affirmed and through which communities are forged and reproduced. They provide some of the social and economic capital through which households are sustained, and they uphold the informal system of township justice. They embody the structural bond between the dominant social center and its peripheral communities, and they are the expression of the cultural and economic contradictions between the two.

In this study I build upon and continue the work of other social scientists who have mapped the relationship between gang formation in black South African townships and the wider socioeconomic and political structures (see, inter alia, Breckenridge 1990; Glaser 2000; La Hause 1990; Mokwena 1991; and Pinnock 1984).[1] However, while these studies have contributed a great deal to our knowledge of South African gangs, they tend to explain gangs only in terms of their resistance to or complicity in the dominant political economic system. These analysts argue that township gangs are formed in resistance to an oppressive apartheid state (Austen 1987; Pinnock 1984); as antisocial predators on fellow township dwellers (Glaser 2000; Goodhew 1990); or as the site for reactionary growth of ethnic chauvinism (Bonner 1993). Pinnock's study of Cape Town gangs in the 1980s, for example, is grounded in a political and economic theoretical framework. He argues that colored gangs exist as a means of survival within and in resistance to the socioeconomic and political contexts that reproduce poverty in the racial ghettos of the Cape Flats: "Ganging is primarily a survival technique, and it is obvious that as long as the city is part of the socio-economic system which reproduces poverty, no amount of policing will stop the ghetto brotherhoods" (1984, 99).

I argue that while the dominant structural factors of racial and economic marginalization are important, one has to look beyond these factors and examine the gendered and generational relationships within the gang, as well as between the gang and the community they reside in, if one is going to obtain a more textured picture of ganging practices on the Cape Flats. The gang does not only exist as a means of resistance and economic survival for its members. Through the rites and practices of ganging these men create and offer one another alternative means and resources to assert their gendered identities as heterosexual men. These young men do not possess the dominant material and symbolic capital to affirm their heterosexual masculinity, such as a professional education, a permanent job, or the economic ability to support a wife and dependents. I show that in the context of the township, where men have limited access to the key resources that define a dominant heterosexual masculine identity, and younger men even less access, gang members use physical violence as an alternative way to assert their heterosexual masculinity and their personhood in the local context. I also indicate that an ambivalent relationship exists between the gang and the other community residents that can only be understood if we embed the gang within the social relationships in a community. I indicate how colored males' violent ganging practices in Manenberg township not only facilitate the cultural production of personhood and community, but also assert a subordinate masculinity, while providing these men with the means to make sense of their location on the socioeconomic margins of the township and of South African society.

Racializing Space, Gendering Race during Apartheid

Male gangs in the colored townships of Cape Town are notorious for violent bloody deeds that include severe physical assault, murder, and rape. They are often cited as the reason why Cape Town bears the sobriquet "murder capital of the world." At first the gangs' violent practices may appear to be irrational and incomprehensible. I argue that we need to locate these male gang members within the social and historical context of the colored townships, as well as within the cultural notions of gendered personhood that have evolved within the township spaces, in order to comprehend why violence is an important aspect of ganging there.

Colored townships, such as Manenberg on the Cape Flats, were created through the racialized legislative processes of the apartheid era. These townships and the processes of racial classification and forced relocation that created them imbued the racial category "colored" with unique political, physical, spatial, and socioeconomic meaning. While apartheid legislation such as the Population Registration Act of 1950 defined who "the coloreds" were,[2] the Group Areas Act of 1950 designated that they should be allowed to live on the outskirts of cities, away from the central business districts and other well-resourced amenities.[3] Yet while coloreds were discriminated against vis-à-vis the white population, they were also relatively privileged vis-à-vis those classified African. Further legislation, such as the Colored Labour Preference Policy, simultaneously created a hierarchy of deprivation in the Western Cape, in which coloreds were given job preference over Africans and defined as a ready, cheap labor force for the clothing, textile, canning, and farming industries there.[4]

First, the spatial meanings that informed coloredness were informed by the group's relocation to the Cape Flats, while its gendered meanings were shaped by the specific location and redefinition of adult colored women within the apartheid bureaucracy, through welfare and housing regulations. Within the hierarchy of black deprivation, coloreds were given preferential access to social-security grants, such as the child-welfare and disability grants, over Africans (see Salo 2001, 2004). In addition, more public housing was provided for coloreds than for Africans in the urban Western Cape. This was done in order to create a stable racialized working class and to prevent the permanent settlement of a large urban African population in this region. Colored women became the unintended beneficiaries of this racial legislation and were thus strategically located as the power brokers for their communities within the apartheid social structure.

The gendering of the racial category "colored" occurred in two ways, namely, through the bureaucratic assumptions about family formation that informed the state social-security program and through the specific feminization of the industrial workforce in the Western Cape urban economy (Salo 2001, 2004). In the first case, the apartheid state assumed that all households conformed to the Western two-parent family norm, in which fathers and mothers fulfilled stereotypical gender roles. Consequently, child-welfare grants were only payable to women as mothers, and public housing was only provided to families with women and children.

Second, within the economic sphere, the feminization of the labor force in the textile industry, together with the impact of the Coloured Labour Preference Policy in the Western Cape, resulted in colored women being the preferred workers. Until the early 1990s adult women were relatively powerful within these townships as the conduits to scarce economic resources and to shelter. These women's cultural status as power brokers still holds in the townships to this day, even though their economic power has diminished somewhat, as many were removed from their jobs in the clothing, textile, and canning industries. These women embodied, and continue to embody, the bridge between the national notions of coloreds as nonpersons and of colored personhood in the local context of the township. In Manenberg their relatively privileged economic status in relation to men's is reconfigured to emphasize their social and moral obligation to their households and to the local community. Through the recognition of their social ties to individuals within their households and in the local community they ensure the physical survival of, as well as the recognition of, other individuals as persons.

In Manenberg residents become persons through the adult women, who epitomize local respectability and morality. Adult women in Manenberg embody personhood through the extension and the efflorescence of their economic and social mothering roles beyond the private domain. They mediate relations between the workplace, the state institutions, and the local community. They also mediate conflict between individuals within the local community. Finally, they signify and police the individual's moral standing within the community (Salo 2004).

The individual's conscientious observation of, or failure to abide by, the local moral code is only meaningful when it is recognized, affirmed, or condemned by the adult women, in the first instance, and then by others who know him or her intimately. Identifying and recognizing the individual as a person is only possible and, indeed, meaningful in the context of a small community, where reputation is shaped through the minute webs of intimate, personal knowledge, gossip, and visible performance. I argue that while women's economic activities and moral judgments imbue coloredness with gendered meaning in the local context, it is the ganging practices of the men that define the boundaries of the local community in which these meanings matter.

Men Defining Community

In a township with a population estimated to number between 46,000 and 80,000 people, who constitutes the local community, and how is it defined?

For the outsider Manenberg appears to be a homogeneous racial township, a single geographic and social unit. Certainly it is discursively described as such in newspaper reports and city planners' maps. However, for the residents of Manenberg, sociospatial boundaries criss-cross the apparently continuous geographic unit, dividing it into multiple small communities. Although persons are identified through and by adult women, it is the men who embody and define the social and the spatial boundaries of the community in which the women's opinions count. Men claim their agency in this local context by asserting the primacy of their definition of community over that imposed by the city and state town planners, for it is within the confines of male-defined boundaries that alternative meanings of personhood, gender, style, and community are created.

The adult women's opinions about and actions on behalf of others are recognized as significant by the local residents, within the male-defined boundaries of the local community. This community is ultimately the primary social arena in which the individual is acknowledged to be a person. To define the local community, the men resort to actions that are secretive, threatening, and often violent. However, as will be seen later, these actions also disrupt the work of civil institutions such as schools and clinics, whose origins are situated within a national notion of community and thus serve populations across locally defined boundaries. Finally, the men's actions underscore the contradictory nature of women's roles as they live across these boundaries.

Community, Masculinity

In his book *Masculinities,* R. W. Connell (1995) argues that a hegemonic masculinity exists and that some men dominate other men. The local notions of masculinity in Manenberg are historically rooted in the apartheid era and are mutually imbricated with the familial trope that informed Afrikaner nationalism and racialized masculinity.

During this period national personhood was embodied in the white Afrikaner patriarch. Later this prestige was expanded to include all white men, regardless of ethnic origins. In contrast, African men personified the brutish, infantile primitive who required the white patriarchs' guidance to nationhood,[5] whereas coloreds were officially included within the white South African geopolitical unit as an inferior nation in the making. During the apartheid era, men who belonged to the "inferior" black racial categories could not, therefore, be regarded as part of the dominant masculinity. Even in the contemporary period they remain largely outside the discourse and practices of dominant masculinity. In the postapartheid era the definition of dominant masculinity has shifted from the emphasis on racial membership to an emphasis on men's economic roles as breadwinners in the family and protectors of their communities. Most colored men in Manenberg do not have access to employment and cannot claim to be breadwinners in their families. According to 1996 census data, unemployment in the area is officially 30 percent (Statistics South Africa 1996). In addition, men can only obtain housing if they demonstrate that they have a dependent wife and children. In this context a huge proportion of colored men spend much of their adulthood in prison (Steinberg 2004). Factors such as long absences from the household during imprisonment and unemployment prevent these men from providing for their families through legitimate means. Consequently, relations between men and women are often fraught, and relationships are fragile and easily fractured. Working-class colored men quickly learn that they have to develop an emotional carapace in order to withstand the corrosive acid of structural violence and marginalization. The everyday accretions of social and economic emasculation inform the cultural valorization of emotional toughness among township men. This process of emotional toughening, colloquially referred to as "making strong bones," in Manenberg can be traced in the life histories of adult men in Grande Street, such as Uncle Buks.

Strong Bones: Making a Working-Class Colored Man

A wet afternoon in June 1998 found me sitting in Aunt Dopie's house talking to Uncle Buks and a few of his friends. The four men were quietly welcoming home a friend who had just completed a prison term. When I first began working in Manenberg, I feared Uncle Buks. His neck, forearms, and torso were covered with tattoos, the trademark of a gangster. His forearms were marked with the number "28," the insignia of the feared prison gang. When I encountered him in the street, he appeared to be either morose or drugged. Initially, I would greet him apprehensively.

My curiosity about Uncle Buks grew after he assisted in neutralizing the tensions between the Young Dixie Boys and the Naughty Boys. He had fearlessly confronted the armed men who threatened Paul. A few days after the gang fight was averted, I asked him about the incident, inquiring whether he felt threatened by the Naughty Boys, who were armed. "I am not afraid of that lot!" he said contemptuously, waving his arm in the air to brush away any suggestion of fear.[6] "They're a bunch of kids. I've served two 'Blou Baadjie' prison terms. They know nothing about prison life," he growled, emphasizing his experiences of being toughened up and surviving in prison, the institution that marked many working-class colored youths' path to manhood.[7]

"They're still green. I go where I want, even when there is a gang war. I am not afraid of that lot," he said.

These were no idle words. Earlier, I had learned from Aunt Dopie that Uncle Buks earned his living as an itinerant one-man security force for organizations in the area. At the time, he was safeguarding a marquee being used by a traveling evangelist who was visiting the area for a week. His responsibilities included patrolling the outer perimeter of the marquee grounds through the night. Before that, he was employed as a security guard at the local primary school after school hours. There he was expected to deter local gangsters from writing gang graffiti on the walls to mark their turf. He was respected and feared by most local residents in Manenberg.

Uncle Buks, who was in his fifties, was married to Aunt Dopie. He recalled growing up "amongst white people" in Aberdeen Street in Woodstock: "That time we lived alongside decent people. We lived in a big house. When we were married in the early 1960s Dopie and I were given our own room in the house. Then shortly after that we were forcibly evicted and made to move here. My first job was at the Docks. But it was always a situation where there'd be work for a few weeks and then there'd not be work."[8]

Uncle Buks became a member of the Mongrels, a gang from the nearby township Hanover Park. The gang had a long association with his extended family. During his tenure as a gang member, he burgled a number of houses, "just in white areas; we stole from the rich." He was arrested for housebreaking and theft and jailed for eight years. After he was released, he rejoined the gang immediately, and was arrested soon after for burglary. He was found guilty, and this time he was given a sentence of thirteen years. During both prison terms, he was an active member of the notorious "numbers gangs" in prison. During his first term he was initiated into the 28's, the gang notorious for using rape as an exercise of power over fellow prisoners. When I asked him why he had become a member of the prison gangs, he replied, "You have to learn to survive in prison. There the rule of either you or me holds." He said that when he entered prison for a second time, his eldest daughter, Bridget, was only eight years old. When he was released, she was twenty-one years old and had a son of her own.

At this point in the interview, Buks stared intently at a small brass vase on the battered display cabinet in his living room. He rose, picked it up, and said to me, "This thing, this thing has value. I paid for this thing with my life." The vase, which he had stolen during a burglary, represented his long years in prison.

For older men like Uncle Buks, emasculation is a process of gendered, economic, and racial denigration. Their displays of manhood find expression in their proud though poignant narrations of their emotional and physical ability to withstand denigration. The cycle of emasculation began in the early 1960s, just as they were entering adulthood, when they were evicted from their homes in the newly declared white areas. Thereafter, their lives were marked by the continuous search for secure employment and the means to support their families. On the jobs they were able to find, as unskilled laborers in the dockyards, on fishing vessels, or on building sites, they were called "boy," the peculiar term that is used to refer to unskilled laborers, who are usually black. Ironically, as many adult men attempted to meet the demands of dominant manhood by supporting their families, albeit through illegal informal activities such as burglary, they were convicted and subjected to a seemingly endless cycle of imprisonment. Individuals like Uncle Buks became men through a lifelong process of being toughened up. They learned to bury emotional sensitivity in self-deprecating humor and to withstand the everyday erosion of dignity and respect.

There is a subordinate masculinity in Manenberg. It is constructed through and upholds the dominant racial and economic notions of masculinity that gained purchase during the apartheid era. The dominant notions of masculinity were embodied in white, Afrikaner control of the state apparatus, and upper-class, mainly white men's control of the economy in the public sphere, as well as their easy access to employment, which ensured their ability to support a dependent wife and children in the private home. A small class of privileged black men, often petit bourgeois businessmen, were able to fulfill the goals of the dominant masculinity. However, their racial classification limited their economic and social ambitions. Men in Grande Street, as elsewhere in Manenberg, could not realize this vision of masculinity during the apartheid era. Discriminatory racial policies, such as job reservation, trapped them in seasonal, unskilled, low-paying jobs as laborers in the fishing, construction, and services industries. The dominance of feminized industries in the Western Cape locked them out of the few opportunities for permanent employment.

This emasculation continues in the postapartheid period as the dominant definition of masculinity shifts to one that emphasizes men's economic roles. These township men continue to be excluded from the labor market because of their low level of education and their lack of appropriate cultural capital. They still cannot become breadwinners in their families. In the local context, women remain the economic mainstays of the household and the community, and alternative ideologies of masculinity have had to be found.

Adult men and women, acting in concert, have actively constructed an alternative ideology of masculinity that emphasizes these working-class colored men's economic and social marginality. At the same time, they have cordoned off the local social and moral sphere in which they are recognized as persons of worth. Yet, while the alternative ideology of masculinity originated in and reverberated from the dominant notion of white, nationalist personhood in the old apartheid era, it has been reconfigured in the context of Manenberg. These different definitions of masculinity also inform ganging practices and validate some men's authority and agency as gang leaders.

Respectable Men and Skollies

Paul is the leader of the Young Dixie Boys, a small gang located on Grande Street. While other young men were curious about me and willingly included me in their conversations, Paul kept a respectful distance. When I arrived on the street in late 1997, I would spy him standing at the window of the first-floor apartment he shared with his aged mother, Aunt Gwen, and the extended family, or squatting on his haunches at the bottom of the staircase. He would nod in acknowledgment to my overenthusiastic greeting. I first befriended the younger members of the Young Dixie Boys as discrete individuals: Ziempie, Loppa, Lippe, Zahir, and Markie, a group of adolescent boys who often frequented Morieda's postage-stamp front yard, playing marbles or just sharing a cigarette. They appeared to be caught somewhere between the innocent pastimes of boys and the activities of tough young men. During my first visits these boys were on the margins of my circle of acquaintances on Grande Street. I was interested in befriending the adolescent girls, intent on discovering their world and issues that were important to them. These issues turned out to be relationships with the very boys whom I initially regarded as peripheral to my inquiry.

One afternoon when we were engaged in idle conversation on the sidewalk the girls spoke of the current conflict between the local gang, the Young Dixie Boys, and the gang located on the adjacent street. The Naughty Boys had accused Zahir, a Young Dixie Boy, of stealing wheels from a car that belonged to one of their members. The Naughty Boys had vowed that they would exact revenge for the theft. That very afternoon, an ominous group of young men sauntered down the road and congregated in front of Paul's house. "Here they come," the girls whispered as they glared at the approaching group with lowered eyes. One of the men ascended the concrete stairs to Auntie Gwen's apartment, knocked on the door, and was let in. As we waited with bated breath, Zellie pointed out that most of these men stood with one hand thrust down the front of their pants. This was a sure sign that they were armed, their weapons concealed. They wore baseball caps and dark glasses, through which it seemed they surveyed everyone balefully.

The lazy afternoon had changed to one pregnant with ominous apprehension. Even the afternoon sunlight, which had seemed soothingly warm, now appeared to sting my skin. "Uncle Buks and Auntie Dopie have come," Nadia said with relief. By then, a number of older women, colloquially known as "moeders," or "mothers," and a few men, all wearing a determined expression, had approached the group. Uncle Buks was part of this group. He was known to be fearless, having spent two *blou baadjie* terms in prison for theft. During his imprisonment, he had been a member of the notoriously violent prison gang, the 28's. Before that, he had been a member of the Mongrels in Hanover Park, an adjacent township.

"Go inside Elaine," Aunt Mary said to me meaningfully, as she descended the stairs to join the group. Her tone made it clear that this was no place for me or for any other younger people. All the other girls had disappeared into Morieda's living room by this time. I ascended the stairs obediently though reluctantly, torn between curiosity about the discussion that was now taking place below and concern about my safety. I chose to take up a position in Aunt Mary's doorway, where I could survey the proceedings in the street below yet access the sanctuary of the living room if any trouble occurred. About ten minutes later the leader of the strange group reappeared and descended the stairs to the street. Paul followed, holding in his arms his four-month-old son, wrapped in a cotton blanket. I shook my head at his apparent lack of concern for the safety of his little boy, yet was overawed by his determined display of caring, loving fatherhood. He lovingly embraced the little infant's body, apparently communicating to all that watched from the street below, through cracked doorways or apartment windows, that fatherhood took primacy over all else.

As Paul approached the menacing group, the older women residents and the few men surrounded him in tight, protective formation. Soon everyone was gesticulating and talking earnestly. Fingers and hands rose and fell in concert with voices, and facial expressions were taut. Fragmented bits of conversation drifted up to me like verbal shrapnel. The harsh voices kept me rooted to the doorway, and I became increasingly frustrated at not being able to hear what was being said. But Aunt Mary's command prevented me from descending the stairs. After a long while, the bodies of those in the group below relaxed, the talking hands and fingers now quietly at their sides. Their faces regained composure, and the voices became more fluid. Soon the circle loosened, and the group of strangers separated away from the residents and moved away from Paul. The leader shook Paul's hand, and the Naughty Boys all turned and walked away. It was clear that an agreement had been reached that was acceptable to all parties.

Aunt Mary ascended the stairs, and I stepped aside for her to enter, eager to hear about the discussion. "What happened, Aunty Mary?" I asked, unable to contain my curiosity. She pointedly ignored my question, bustled through the door, and loudly demanded, "Turn on the TV, its time for *Bold.*" Then, "Marlene, make some tea please!" silenced any further inquiries about the averted crisis. As Chantal hurried to turn on the television, Aunt Mary sat down in the nearest couch with ease, and rapidly became engrossed in the images that flickered across the screen. She had just assisted in defusing a menacing gang conflict, perhaps preventing a chain of retributive violence that could have stretched over a few weeks and traumatized every resident, yet she did not appear to be drained by the effort. I was amazed at Aunt Mary's ability to orchestrate the day's activities back into the routine pattern, actively shutting out the trouble that had threatened to disrupt everyone's lives in a bloody gang war.

It was six o'clock in the evening, a time when everyone ordinarily watched the schmaltzy American soap opera *The Bold and the Beautiful,* sipping restorative cups of tea before preparing the main meal of the day. A palpable calm reigned over the small living room as we became absorbed in the characters' endless struggle for true love. I realized that I would have to wait until the next day to hear what had happened in the street below from one of the adolescent girls who would be able to eavesdrop on the adults' conversation in an overcrowded bedroom that night. For now, there was nothing else to do but watch and wait.

The next afternoon I returned to Manenberg, where I encountered a despondent group of young men leaning against the corrugated iron fence that separated Morieda's front yard from her neighbors. Their eyes wore the hooded look that I had learned to associate with repressed anger. Some mumbled a greeting; others ignored me and stared moodily onto the street. I entered Morieda's house and slumped down into a chair. It seemed as though the angry, hostile faces I had encountered in the yard had burned up my initial eagerness to see the residents of Grande Street. I berated myself for only wanting to satisfy my curiosity about yesterday's events. The young men's faces spoke volumes about a solution that had been reached after my departure. Clearly this solution had angered them, even though it had warded off a potentially ugly gang conflict. Zellie and Nadia, who were watching Simunye's youth program on TV, also seemed subdued. I gave Marel some money to buy soda, bread, cold meat, and cigarettes for the little group. Nadia made some sandwiches, poured the soda, and offered some to the young men outside. Soon everyone was in a more relaxed mood and began chatting about the TV program. Suddenly Zahir winced visibly, his torso contorted in pain. "What's happened to you?" I asked. A wary silence descended on the room as everyone looked at Zahir. "Nothing, Elaine," he mumbled with downcast eyes. "He's just a little sore, Elaine," Zellie said cagily. I had unwittingly touched upon an issue that had made everyone uncomfortable. "Why are you walking crookedly?" I persisted. "They've beaten him up because he burgled a car belonging to the Naughty Boys gang. Speak up, you lot!" Piesang said, looking at the others defiantly, apparently daring them to ostracize her for breaking a community code of silence. "Who beat him up?" I asked. "Paul—them and the other Dixies. Yesterday," Claudette responded tentatively.

They were soon telling me about the events that had followed the tense meeting in the road. After the standoff, Paul and the senior members of the Young Dixie Boys had interrogated the younger members to establish who had participated in the burglary. All the other members had then punished the guilty party, Zahir. I was perplexed by Zahir's punishment. "Why would you beat up your brother and then sit here and pretend as though it was nothing?" I demanded of the other young men. Loppa, who seemed to smirk at my middle-class notions of justice, said laconically, "Elaine, you would not understand." At that, the young men all walked out into the backyard. "They had to do it, Elaine," Piesang explained. "Paul is their leader and what he says is the law." "But why did they have to beat him up so badly? He is their brother!" I said plaintively.

Sara moved slowly in her chair, seeking a more comfortable position. It was as if she were preparing to provide a long, patient explanation to me, the naive, privileged newcomer, who knew little about tough discipline in the township. "Yes, but he knows that you don't steal from your own people. The Naughty Boys would be forced to take revenge on all the Young Dixie Boys if Paul did not punish Zahir himself. When he [Zahir] became a member of the Dixies, he knew that he would have to have tough bones."

I tried to make sense of my initial perception of Paul in light of the one that was now emerging. He had appeared to be modest, almost shy, and I had usually seen him squatting on his haunches, by himself, at the bottom of the concrete steps, scrunching his eyes against the harsh sunlight as he surveyed the action on the street. Now he seemed to be a wise gang leader who was clearly capable of carrying out severe physical assault. I laughed inwardly at my own naiveté and my benign reading of character. I was dismayed by the severe punishment meted out to Zahir. Yet Piesang's patient explanation had clearly spelled out the local cultural grammar of community and unacceptable crime. I now understood Paul's reasons for the beating. He had decided to beat up the individual who was guilty of the crime and thereby avert a more serious threat to the overall well-being of the Grande Street residents.

Zahir had put the lives of his fellow gang members and the other residents at risk and nearly caused a gang war through his rash actions.

Residents preferred the gang's kangaroo-style court to a formal investigation by the police. The police might have investigated the car theft, but they would also have learned of other, often illegal economic activities that the impoverished township residents necessarily rely on to survive. The Grande Street community was under no illusions about its right to seek protection from the police. The "Boere," or "Boers," as the police were commonly called in the township, were considered to be part and parcel of the township communities' systematic denigration. Most residents acknowledged that theft was immoral. However, they made a moral distinction between theft committed against the local poor, who could ill afford any material loss, and the nameless wealthy, who were safely insulated from the ravages of poverty and who seemed to care very little about the less fortunate township dwellers. Theft from township residents was considered to be morally reprehensible, while theft from the wealthy, who probably possessed insurance against the ravages of crime, was considered to be an unpleasant but necessary aspect of survival.

Paul had displayed the leadership expected of a male gang leader when he exercised his authority over the younger gang members and decided that Zahir must be punished. His actions implicitly reinforced three important communal rules about local justice. First, Paul had advised the Naughty Boys that he was in control of his turf and that he would appease their call for revenge. In doing so he had reinforced the locally constructed physical and social boundaries between communities and also averted a gang war. Second, he had informed the younger men and the other gang members that he would not tolerate any rash actions that could endanger other Grande residents. In doing so he had taught the younger men from whom one could steal and from whom one could not. This is important knowledge one needs in order to survive in a poor community such as Manenberg. Finally, Paul's actions had affirmed his role as a fair judge who upholds the local values of morality and crime. In doing so he had affirmed his own and his gang's loyalty to the Grande Street community.

In contrast, I was blundering my way through the unspoken, subtle web of protocol expected during situations like these. I had underestimated the extent to which the older men and women in Grande Street had supported Paul's actions. "Come," I said to Zahir, "I'm taking you to Jooste." "Jooste" was the G. F. Jooste Hospital, located on the outskirts of the township. "I'm going along!" Markie, another member of the Young Dixie Boys, piped up, eager, I supposed, for a break in the monotony of his day. "Me too," said

Lippe. Soon I found my little car filled with teenage boys, their lanky, bony limbs stretched into all available space. "Where are you going with that lot?" Aunty Gwen screeched from her perch. "I'm taking Zahir to the hospital," I shouted back. She shook her head grimly and replied, "You're wasting your time, he's not worth it, he's just a skollie. He deserved his beating!"[9] Then she looked into the distance, ignoring me. She had deliberately used the informal, direct Afrikaans form of address, "Djy," instead of the formal, third-person form of address, which connotes respect. Moreover, she had defined Zahir as a "skollie," a worthless man. In doing so, Auntie Gwen had communicated her strong disapproval of my actions. I was assisting someone who had broken the cardinal rules of the local community by stealing from a local resident. Through his actions he had defined himself as worthless, a potential traitor to those who supported him. I drove off, angry at myself for breaking ranks with the many residents who felt that Zahir had deserved his punishment and deserved no sympathy. In addition, I had forgotten that in order to reach the hospital I had to drive through Naughty Boy turf. Paul had appeased the Naughty Boys by punishing Zahir. In contrast, I appeared to be approving of his actions by seeking medical assistance for his injuries. I was endangering the others and myself by driving through enemy territory with a carload of Young Dixie Boys.

Gendered Boundaries, Gendered Persons

The local notions of masculinity are anchored in men's actions, as they simultaneously embody and define the sociospatial boundaries that frame the local community. It is *within* the confines of the local community that men can be recognized as, and perform the duties of, men. And it is within these confines that the adult women identify and ultimately control the ideological means whereby men become persons. Men define the boundaries of the local social and moral community, by embodying the markings of the gangster, the nonperson.

The insular local moral community is considered to be a sphere of loyalty in which everyone is connected in a fine web of actual or imagined kinship. This is the community in which moral and social obligations to others take precedence over crude economic instrumentalism. Here, values such as loyalty, inter- and intragenerational ties, mutual respect, and assistance shape relationships and are valorized. It is the community within which the adult women's power is exercised and the person is identified. Consequently, men anxiously guard and defend the women's continued membership in the local community.

Persons within the community are defined in opposition to the nonpersons, who exist outside its boundaries and can only be identified by those who are not community members. Nonpersons are considered to be antisocial strangers, those who have no visible social ties to adult women's households in the area or who threaten local men's ties to the women. In addition, they are also those who place economic gain over and above the survival of the community, acting out of self-interest, and who commit acts that are immoral and shameful in the eyes of the local residents. The gangster identity is equated with the nonperson. Therefore, members of the local community would not be able to define another member as a gangster. If they did so, they would be classifying them as social strangers.

Paradoxically, in order to identify the boundaries beyond which the nonperson, the gangster, exists, local residents also have to be very familiar with the gangs' activities. Consequently, men embody the nonperson identity and police the boundaries that set the person apart from the nonperson. However, men are not nonpersons only by virtue of being men. They have to be particular men, namely, gangsters, those who simultaneously embody the nonperson and police the boundaries of the local social and moral community. The rite of passage whereby they become particular men is widely considered to be secret, even though local residents, when pressed, reluctantly admit that they know the details. Residents cannot openly admit that they know of the gang's activities; if they did so, they would be perceived to be associating with social strangers.

A Lesson in Defining Community

During the first planning stages of research in Manenberg I relied heavily on my older brother, Bertram Salo, for his insight into the social issues in the area. He was the rector of the area's aptly named Anglican church, the Church of Reconciliation. During a visit to his home in November 1997, I told him of my plans to conduct ethnographic research in Manenberg. He reached for a map rolled up on a bookshelf in his cramped study. "You have to be aware of the gang turf in the area," he said. "Work in a single gang turf. Don't work across gang turfs; you could endanger your life unnecessarily."

He unfurled the map and spread it out on the tabletop. On the now-familiar map, produced by the city council's planning unit, Manenberg township had been divided into eleven discrete units. "This is the map we (the church members) use to locate parishioners and to predict which communities would be caught in gang violence, when gang war erupts," he said.

He had used felt markers in different colors to demarcate the boundaries of the geographic units in which particular gangs dominated. He pointed out the turfs of the different gangs: the Hard Livings and the Americans controlled the largest areas. The remaining area was divided among the smaller gangs, namely, the Young Dixie Boys, the Clever Kids, the Naughty Boys, the Junky Funky Kids, the Respectable Peacefuls, the Wonder Kids, the School Boys, the Scorpions, and the Yuru Cats. He explained that young men who resided within the boundaries of a gang's turf would be identified by rival gangs on the outside as members of the local gang even if they did not actively associate with gang members. Young men living within each community marked its boundaries with the peculiar graffiti associated with their gang. HL$ stood for the Hard Livings; YDB$, the Young Dixie Boys; WK$, the Wonder Kids; SB$, the School Boys; JFK$, the Junky Funky Kids; RPF$, the Respectable Peacefuls; CT$, the Cape Town Scorpions; and YC$, the Yuru Cats. I had befriended the young residents of Grande Street, the single street controlled by the Young Dixie Boys (YDB$).

In Manenberg, graffiti is scrawled on almost every perimeter wall, building, and road sign. The graffiti I had seen scribbled on these surfaces around the township now took on new meaning. For the uninitiated outsider the arbitrary letters along with the cryptic yet ubiquitous dollar sign, seem benign, nothing more than mindless, meaningless vandalism in a township ghetto. The scribble's apparent meaninglessness also seemed to be confirmed by Sharlien, a Grande Street resident, who in answer to a question by me dismissed it with a wave of her hand, saying, "Oh, it's just the lads who write their gangs' names."

The meaning of graffiti takes on new significance when it becomes clear that, unlike other urban media such as company advertisements splashed on huge billboards, it is intended for a select audience. The graffiti's message, though recognized by all in Manenberg, is commonly understood to hold significance for a select few, namely, the members of the individual gang and its rivals. This peculiar discourse actively confers meaning on place and person. Not only does it mark off the boundaries of the local community, but it confers both gender and identity upon the young men residing outside its borders. This process of conferring identity and gender upon individuals, as well as maintaining the boundaries of local communities, is especially pronounced during gang warfare.

Gang Warfare, Gender, and Boundaries

During my initial visits to Grande Street, in November 1997, these local boundaries seemed insignificant and did not affect the round of daily life.

Indeed, except for the occasional reference to "the lads," no one spoke of the gangs or of their territory. The notorious gang members were all but invisible. I had befriended Zahir and his adolescent friends, and they appeared to be just another group of young men from impoverished homes who were at loose ends, undecided about whether to return to school or get on with the endless search for a job.

Then, during February 1998, a gang war erupted between the Hard Livings and the Clever Kids. The war, like so many others, ostensibly had erupted over turf expansion and control over the fairly lucrative local drug trade (*Cape Times,* 25 February 1998). One Sunday, senior members of the Hard Livings abducted three teenage members of the Clever Kids from a *shebeen* (tavern) situated in a neutral zone. According to local rumor, as well as newspaper reports, the three were taken to the Hard Livings headquarters, Die Hok (The Cage), where they were beaten and tortured. All three were later shot and killed. This incident sparked a major conflict between the Hard Livings and the Clever Kids.

During the days that followed the killings, two smaller gangs, the Young Dixie Boys and the Wonder Kids, had become embroiled in the conflict, each siding with a primary antagonist. The Young Dixie Boys had formed an alliance with the Clever Kids and so were now in opposition to the Hard Livings and their allies, the Wonder Kids. These two small gangs occupied adjoining turf—the Young Dixie Boys lived on Grande Street, while the Wonder Kids could be found on Grande Walk. Tensions rose on Grande Street during this time, and the young men spoke fearfully of crossing Wonder Kids or Hard Livings turf.

Boy, an eighteen-year-old homeless member of the Young Dixie Boys, was especially anxious about crossing Wonder Kids territory, where he would be at risk of being beaten or shot by the gang's members. He relied heavily upon the older women for food and shelter. In return, he ran errands for them on a daily basis, purchasing electricity or groceries at the local mall, Nyanga Junction. Each day, women like Auntie Gwen and Auntie Mary would set aside a plate of food for him, allow him to use their bathrooms, or provide him with bed linen and a bed in their backyard shacks. He was provided with this assistance in the most discrete manner, so that he could retain his dignity as a person.

On his daily round of errands, Boy usually walked to the shopping center, situated about a kilometer away from Grande Street. On foot, his route took him across the turfs of the Wonder Kids and the Clever Kids. Usually the boundaries were insignificant and he was able to navigate his way across these areas without incident, except for the occasional hand sign from a member of another gang, to indicate turf possession. Now, his identity as a gang member living in the Young Dixie Boys' territory was significant. His errand run had become dangerous.

During the gang conflict, Boy would take me aside, out of earshot of the other youth, and pester me to run the errands in my car or to drive him to the mall. Most days, I would accede to his requests. However, on one occasion, when I was feeling tired and irritable, I crossly asked him why he couldn't take another route himself. "But if I'm with you, they [members of the opposing gangs] won't touch me," he said. When I asked why, he responded, "Because you're a woman and they usually leave the women alone and, besides, we're driving." "How would they know that you were a member of the Young Dixies Boys?" I asked. "Because I wear the mark [tattoo]," he shot back.

It quickly became clear that the policing and maintenance of local boundaries was men's work. These boundaries were marked by the tattoos on the men's bodies. Unlike women, the elderly, and children, who were allowed access to any local community, for men who resided outside the community and who did not have the appropriate gang tattoo, local boundaries became impermeable during gang conflict. These were particular types of men, namely, those who had been made into *die jongens* (lads), members of gangs.

Gang practices not only define the boundaries of local communities, but also provide a rite of passage into manhood for adolescent youths who, like Boy, find themselves in a liminal state, between the local markers of childhood and those of adulthood. These youth are usually high-school dropouts, having rejected the dependency status that is associated with students, but without the resources, such as jobs, that, within the dominant ideology of masculinity, would define them as men.

Making a *Jong:* Gang Rites of Passage

After Boy told me about the *tjappie,* or tattoo, that marked gang membership, I asked the other young men about their tattoos and how they had acquired them. However, when I did so, during an afternoon visit in March 1998, Zahir, Ziempie, and the other young men met my questions with smirks and expressions of outright contempt. "No, we can't tell Elaine. Elaine's not a member of the Young Dixie Boys!" Ziempie growled. Clearly, only the exclusive group of gang members—the brotherhood, in Pinnock's (1984) phrase—could have access to this knowledge. Secrecy was the hallmark of the brotherhood. I had to look elsewhere for an explanation.

At the time, a fellow researcher, William Ellis, and I were also attending counseling sessions for adolescents at the Community Counselling and

Training Centre (CCATC) nearby. The group being counseled was made up of both men and women, but young men constituted the majority. Their schoolteachers and parents had referred them to the Centre as a last attempt to save them from expulsion from school. These youth were considered to be at risk of joining local gangs and dropping out of the education system. During these counseling sessions Geraldine, the counselor, would begin by sketching a scenario that incorporated all the elements of the dilemmas that these young people faced on a daily basis in the township. The group members would then express their own opinions about the situation and the choices that the protagonists made. At this particular time, the group discussion focused on the current intergang conflict.

It was during one such session that we befriended fifteen-year-old Ashley, who had been a member of the Junky Funky Kids. That day, Geraldine had told of a case where a young man had been shot and killed by a rival gang. His teenaged friend had discovered his body and was faced with the dilemma of whether to avenge his friend's death by taking the life of one of the rival gang's members, or to report the murder to the police and let justice take its course. Most of the young men argued vociferously for avenging the death, while a minority, that included a few men and all the women, argued that the matter should be left to the police and the justice system. The debate became quite heated, and Ashley angrily led the case for vengeance. As the noise level rose and the debate became disorderly, he stood up and shouted, "That is his blood brother! He has to show that he has strong bones! It is his duty; he must stand by his brother!" At this point, he defiantly rolled up his sleeve to display a tattoo on his biceps.

Later, we asked Ashley about the tattoo. He became defensive and told us that his mother had warned him constantly about the dangers of gang membership. In 1998 he had entered his first year at the local high school, where he had befriended the members of the Junky Funky Kids. They had enthralled him with tales of their gang activities and then invited him to join them. When he agreed, he was invited to meet all the members one Sunday evening at The Greens, the only soccer field in Manenberg, where he would be initiated into the gang. On a Sunday evening, the field would be deserted and they would not be disturbed as they carried out the initiation ceremony. He said that the members were armed with leather belts, wooden clubs, and planks. They stood in two parallel lines, facing each other. The leader then instructed him to run through the gauntlet of gang members, who beat him with their assorted weapons. He had to do this because, "You must demonstrate that you have strong bones. You have to display your ability to stand by your man. When your brother is in trouble, you must be able to assist him."

He said that after his initiation he and the rest of the gang would confront commuters at the Athlone train station and demand their wallets and jewelry. They would also harass young women outside their gang turf. "We never stole from Manenberg residents," he said.

Ashley quit school and began to frequent the JFK$ hangout. The school authorities informed his parents of his absence from school. His mother then confronted him about his activities and demanded that he undress so that she could inspect his body for the telltale tattoo. When her fears were confirmed, she told him that he had to either leave the gang or leave home. His mother demanded that he accompany her to school to meet with the school principal. The principal indicated that he would allow Ashley to return to school if he agreed to attend the counseling sessions at the CCATC.

William Ellis and I later met with Ashley's mother, Auntie Charlotte. We informed her of our discussion with Ashley and asked her about Ashley's actions. She said that she was afraid that Ashley's gang membership would lead him to prison. "I know that they [the young men] are mischievous. Often the rumors that people spread about them are not true. When the school principal called me about his absence from school, as a mother I had to accompany him to the school to meet with the authorities. I told the principal that Ashley comes from a good home and that I did not want him to find himself in trouble."

The making of men in the township through gang rites of passage is a process that marks the start of the journey into the wider world of gendered adulthood. As in other rites of passage, men are encouraged to take on the values and responsibilities that signify manhood within their communities. In Manenberg, toughness and loyalty, first to local men and then to other members of the local community, are the quintessential characteristics of masculinity. Individuals who want to be recognized as men are expected to display their ability to withstand the emotional and physical privation that will mark their lives. More than that, they have to display their potential loyalty to the gang, measured by their ability to withstand the severe beating and painful tattooing without flinching, for the gang has to be sure that in future conflicts a gang member will display enormous courage and the ability to defend his brother's life.

The process of becoming a gangster not only reflects a local rite of passage into manhood, but also signifies a man's embodiment of the contradictory meanings of race, class, and gender. During the apartheid period, men were at once members of the dominant gender and of a subject race and class. However, subtle changes in ganging practice also indicate the shifting meanings of masculinity in the contemporary period.

Ganging in the Postapartheid Era

In the postapartheid period, young Manenberg men are the newly created citizens of a recent democracy and members of the dominant gender. How are the new national persons being imagined, and how do these persons compare with the impoverished reality of the Manenberg youth?

The "new" South African youth is depicted on television, in local soap operas such as *Backstage,* and in the image of the announcers on the trendy Channel One. Manenberg youth are avid fans of both programs. In an effort to emphasize the work of nation building that its programs wish to communicate, Channel One is also known by its isi-Xhosa label, *Simunye,* which means "We are one." Its television hosts tend to be young adults, who work in multiracial pairs. They are usually dressed in designer clothes that display the Nike, Fubu, or Levis label. *Backstage* is a soap opera about young people who attend a local drama school, and the nightly episodes usually focus on their efforts to break into acting, dancing, or broadcasting careers. Whereas dramas in the past usually employed all-white casts, the *Backstage* cast includes actors from all the local racial groups. The racial representation sends a powerful message to all South African youth that the racial segregation of the past is gone and that they too can be part of this prosperous, new, trendy nation. All these TV personalities display the accoutrements of the economically prosperous middle class, as evidenced by their fashionable clothes and their seemingly leisurely, independent lifestyles. The programs communicate the message that in the new South Africa all young people can acquire the style and image that will make them equal. All one needs is access to the financial resources that will enable him or her to purchase the exorbitantly expensive fashionable clothes.

Yet despite this promise of the postapartheid era, implementation of the Growth, Employment and Redistribution Programme (GEAR), which began in 1996, has led to increased privatization of state services (Bond 2002). This program, together with the increased retrenchments and job insecurity in the textile and other industries (Bond 2002), has led to the increased economic marginality of the working poor of all races. Through the process of democratization, coloreds and, by extension, women, no longer have privileged access to social security and housing. Bond (2000) indicates that the gap between rich and poor South Africans has widened and that township residents have become increasingly impoverished. The poor populations who reside in the old apartheid townships, such as colored youth in Manenberg, seem to be trapped in a web of deepening poverty.

The adult women in the area can no longer ensure the physical survival of these youths, and the acquisition of the style of the new South Africans can only be imagined. At the same time, gangs are now able to increase their income as they are incorporated into the global drug trade (*Cape Times,* 3 March 2000). The globalization of the gangs has changed the meaning of the gangs of local communities such as Grande Street. In the past, the gangsters demarcated the boundaries of the local communities in which an individual's personhood was identified. In addition, they performed a policing function within these communities. In the contemporary period, the gangs are being redefined primarily as economic units whose core business is illegal drug trafficking and smuggling scarce marine resources. These men are now able to obtain substantial economic resources without the assistance of the adult women. Consequently, the gendered and generational relationships within these local communities have been reconfigured.

Conflict and Change in the Local Context

The expansion of the local gangs within the Cape Town metropolis and within the international context has been made possible by their access to more sophisticated communications technology, such as the cell phone, and the burgeoning taxi industry. Irvin Kinnes, a conflict mediator in Manenberg, indicates that gang leaders are now able to access drug networks as far afield as Venezuela via cell phone (Kinnes 2000). Consequently, local gang leaders, such as Rashied Staggie, leader of the Hard Livings, have become wealthy drug lords and own homes in the township as well as in the more sought-after areas on the Atlantic coast, such as Seapoint. These drug lords now lure adolescent youths, both boys and girls, into joining the gangs, with the promise of clothes sponsorships and housing in the more cosmopolitan areas of the city. In this manner, young men as well as young women gain access to the resources that include them in the new images of national personhood— the designer clothes and access to the wealthier, multiracial suburbs.

Gang members find themselves increasingly at odds with the older generation, as well as with the state authorities in the local context. In the past, the gangster identity provided a young man, at the end of his school career, with a recognized role in the community. Now, high-school students are known to be gang members. When asked about this, Uncle Buks shook his head in contempt and said, "This lot today . . . they're not gangsters. If you want to become a gangster you have to have wisdom and maturity. But them . . . they attend school in the mornings and in the afternoon they are gangsters. They shoot with guns . . . they hide behind the buildings and shoot. That is why they kill innocent people."

Wisdom and courage, characteristics once associated with the gangster identity, no longer seem to be prerequisites for becoming a gang member. According to aging gangsters like Uncle Buks, the cultural meaning of the male gangs has changed, and the familiar path to maturity in the male life cycle in Manenburg has grown murkier. Uncle Buks believes that violence in the area has increased as a result. He argues that in the past the old gangs carried out warfare in a more ritualized, carefully planned fashion. Gang leaders challenged each other to warfare at an appointed time, at night, on open fields beyond the residential perimeter, in order to prevent injury to innocent residents. He blames the killings of innocent people on the new gangsters' lack of wisdom and their immaturity.

Buks also calls attention to the change in the technology of violence, which has reduced the need for the skill, wisdom, and courage that were required when warfare was conducted with knives and clubs. He seems bewildered by the youths' acquisition of seemingly conflicting identities, namely, those of the immature student, on the one hand, and the mature gangster, on the other. He blames this change on the shift in weaponry.

The youths' acquisition of multiple, conflicting identities has also put state institutions, such as schools, at odds with the gangs. Increasingly, school authorities are asserting their control over the youths by cordoning off school-yards with electric fencing and labeling the student gangsters as "youth at risk." These youths are then expelled or referred to special counseling programs, such as those offered by the CCATC.

The gangs' ability to control youths of both genders without the restraining effects of the adult women's moral authority has increased the gendered tensions between the women and the gang leaders. Whereas in the past women did not recognize the police system's legitimate control over the gangs, and looked to the gang leaders for policing functions, these days women stage marches to the police to ask them to stop the gangs from operating in the area. In retaliation, local gangs are targeting attacks on more women residents within the local community.

Conclusion

I have argued that the making of men in Manenberg through gang rites of passage is a process that marks a young working-class colored man's journey into the world of gendered adulthood. As in other rites of passage into manhood, male youths in Manenberg are encouraged to take on the dominant values and responsibilities that signify manhood within the local community. The values that define masculinity in Manenberg are opposite to, yet anchored in, the dominant ideology of masculinity that held sway during the apartheid era, and that still reverberates in the contemporary period of transition.

During the ganging rite, violent beatings and the painful tattooing process mark men's bodies with the signs of toughness, courage, and loyalty. The initiates are also expected to display the stoicism with which they must confront the challenges of racial marginalization, unemployment, and impoverishment. The initiation rite not only epitomizes the dominant definition of colored, working-class men as subaltern racial and economic masculinities. It also marks men's bodies as the physical boundaries of the local community, an alternative social and moral space in which apparently different notions of personhood, gender, and style dominate.

These alternative notions of personhood are anchored in women's roles as the economic mainstays of the local community. Colored women's important economic roles are reconfigured in the context of the local community, through the "moeder" identity, to epitomize the core characteristics of local personhood, namely, morality and respectability. While women identify the persons in the local context, men as gangsters define the boundaries of the local community within which persons are identified.

Recent changes in ganging practices reflect the reconfiguring of national personhood in the new South Africa and the decline in colored adult women's economic status. Local gangs have become incorporated into the global drug trade and have increased their economic resources as a result. Adult women's ability to ensure the physical survival of the local community is declining, as is their power to identify or make persons in the local context. The meaning of the gang in the local context has been reconfigured owing to its access to greater economic resources and more efficient, sophisticated weaponry, as well as to the expansion of gang networks across the Cape Town metropolis. Men's identities as gangsters have flourished in the local community. These men are challenging the adult women's position as the anchors of local personhood.

Numerous anthropological studies of physical violence have shown that violence is not an arbitrary action, "devoid of historicity, meaning or reflexivity" (Schmidt and Schroder 2001, 18). At the local level, violence has been shown to be an inherently social act, expressing a relationship between the perpetrators and the victims, as well as the witnesses or the observers, and conveying meaning to the actors involved. In Manenberg, gang violence is not a gratuitous, empty expression of male aggression: it not only symbolizes these men's marginal position of masculinity within the social structure, but also creates and reproduces the meanings of personhood and community in the local context.

Notes

Mans is ma soe can be translated as "Men are like that."

1. I use "black" here in the inclusive sense to include state-designated racial groups—coloreds, Indians, and Africans.

2. The Population Registration Act divided the people of South Africa into three main racial groups, White Indians, Africans, and coloreds. Coloreds and Africans were further divided into subgroups. Africans were subdivided into ethnic groups based upon linguistic differences. Coloreds were subdivided into seven subgroups even though *colored* was defined negatively as "those who cannot be defined as either white or African" (Western 1996; Wilson and Ramphele 1989).

3. The Group Areas Act legislated race-based residential segregation in 1950 and caused the forced removal of approximately 750,000 people in urban areas from the 1960s to the 1980s.

4. The Coloured Labour Preference Policy legislated that colored labor be given work preference over Africans in the Western Cape. In this way, Africans were denied residence in the Western Cape and the urbanization of Africans was contained until 1985 (Goldin 1987), when the pass laws were removed from the statute books.

5. See Alexander 1984. Alexander quotes the speech to the parliament by Minister of Education Hendrik Verwoerd in the early 1960s. Verwoerd characterized the African population as children who were fit to become nothing but hewers of wood and drawers of water.

6. All quotations from the interviews are from Salo 1998–99.

7. *Blou baadjie,* literally "blue jacket," is long-term imprisonment, ranging from eight to fifteen years.

8. "The Docks" is a colloquial reference to Cape Town harbor, where many black men are employed as unskilled laborers.

9. "Skollie" is Afrikaans slang, derivative from the Old Dutch term *schoelje,* meaning "scavenger." Dutch sailors shouted "Schoelje!" at the seagulls that snatched the ship's offal from the waters of Table Bay. Later, the word was used to describe vagrants who survived from the pickings off dumpsites or from begging on the street (Pinnock 1984, 24).

References

Primary Sources

Cape Times. November 1997–August 1998.

City of Cape Town. 1996. Urban Policy Unit Census '96 Community Profile Manenberg.

Salo, E. 1998–99. Manenberg field notes.

Secondary Sources

Alexander, N. 1984. Race, Ethnicity, and Nationalism in Social Science in Southern Africa. Paper presented at the fifteenth conference of the Association of Sociologists in Southern Africa, University of the Witwatersrand, Johannesburg.

Austen, R. A. 1987. *African Economic History: Internal Development and External Dependency.* London: James Currey.

Bond, P. 2002. *Unsustainable South Africa: Environment, Development, and Social Protest.* London: Merlin.

Bonner, P. 1993. The Russians on the Reef, 1947–57: Urbanisation, Gang Warfare, and Ethnic Mobilisation. In *Apartheid's Genesis, 1935–1962,* edited by P. Bonner, P. Delius, and D. Posel. Johannesburg: Witwatersrand University Press.

Breckenridge, K. 1990. Migrancy, Crime, and Faction Fighting: The Role of the Isitshozi in the Development of Ethnic Organisations in the Compounds. *Journal of Southern African Studies* 16 (1): 55–78.

Connell, R. W. 1995. *Masculinities.* Cambridge: Polity Press.

Feldman, A. 1991. *Formations of Violence: The Narrative of the Body and Political Terror in Northern Ireland.* Chicago: University of Chicago Press.

George, K. 1996. *Showing Signs of Violence: The Cultural Politics of a Twentieth Century Headhunting Ritual.* Berkeley: University of California Press.

Glaser, C. 2000. *Bo-tsotsi: The Youth Gangs of Soweto, 1935–1976.* Portsmouth, NH: Heinemann.

Goldin, I. 1987. *Making Race the Politics and Economics of Coloured Identity in South Africa.* London: Longman.

Goodhew, D. 1990. *Between the Devil and the Deep Blue Sea: Crime, Policing, and the Western Areas of Johannesburg.* Johannesburg: University of the Witwatersrand History Workshop.

Ifaturoti, T. O. 1994. Delinquent Subcultures and Violence in Nigerian Universities. In *Urban Management and Urban Violence in Africa,* edited by A. O. Albert, J. Adisa, T. Agbola, and G. Hérault, vol. 2. Ibadan: IFRA.

Kinnes, I. 2000. *From Urban Street Gangs to Criminal Empires: The Changing Face of Gangs in the Western Cape.* Pretoria: Institute for Security Studies.

Kynoch, G. 1998. From Ninevite to Comstotsi: Township Gangs, Divided Communities, and Urban Violence in Twentieth Century South Africa. Seminar paper. Johannesburg: Institute for Advanced Social Research, University of the Witwatersrand.

La Hause, P. 1990. "The Cows of Nongoloza": Youth, Crime, and Amalaita Gangs in Durban, 1900–1936. *Journal of Southern African Studies* 16 (1): 79–111.

Mokwena, S. 1991. The Era of Jackrollers: Contextualising the Rise of Youth Gangs in Soweto. Seminar paper, Project for the Study of Violence, University of the Witwatersrand.

Olutayo, A. O. 1994. Youth in Urban Violence. In *Urban Management and Urban Violence in Africa,* edited by A. O. Albert, J. Adisa, T. Agbola, and G. Hérault, vol. 2. Ibadan: IFRA.

Owumi, B. E. 1994. New Trends and Attitudes towards Crime: The Phenomenon of Area

Boys in Nigeria. In *Urban Management and Urban Violence in Africa,* edited by I. O. Albert, J. Adisa, T. Agbola, and G. Hérault, vol. 2. Ibadan: IFRA.

Pinnock, D. 1984. *The Brotherhoods: Street Gangs and State Control in Cape Town.* Cape Town: David Philip.

Salo, E. 2001. "Moeders vannie Manenberg": Gender, Identity, and Personhood in Manenberg. Seminar paper, Anthropology Seminar Series, University of Cape Town and University of Western Cape.

———. 2004. Respectable Mothers, Tough Men, and Good Daughters: Making Persons in Manenberg Township, South Africa. PhD diss., Emory University.

Schmidt, B., and I. Schroder. 2001. *Anthropology of Violence and Conflict.* London: Routledge.

Statistics South Africa. 1996. *The People of South Africa: Census 1996.* Report 03-01-25. Pretoria.

Steinberg, J. 2004. *The Number: One Man's Search for Identity in the Cape Underworld and Prison Gangs.* Johannesburg: Jonathan Ball.

Western, J. 1996. *Outcast Cape Town.* Berkeley and Los Angeles: University of California Press.

Wilson, F., and M. Ramphele. 1989. *Uprooting Poverty: The South African Challenge.* Cape Town: David Philip.

The Social Construction of Forgetting and
Remembering Violence

Memory, Forgetting, and the Alexandra Rebellion of 1986

BELINDA BOZZOLI

OCIETIES that have experienced extreme trauma and violence are today thought to require a kind of Freudian rebirthing in order to "come to terms with" what has happened. Our contemporary culture of confession and catharsis expects us to treat social trauma much as it attempts to treat personal trauma, that is, with "counseling," writ large. This, it is believed, will somehow permit those whose historical experiences have included various degrees of horror to "work through" their anger, "face up" to the "truth" about what has happened, and move "beyond" it.

This kind of belief in the redeeming power of confession and of the outpouring of the "truth," infused with a powerfully Christian discourse, shaped the design of the South African Truth and Reconciliation Commission (TRC). Society, it was believed, would be healed from the traumas suffered under apartheid by the holding of public hearings in which what had "really" happened would be stated, recorded, and remembered. Former enemies would be brought face to face, and forgiveness would be sought in exchange for confession.

Skeptics realized that the establishment of this commission was in fact the result of a deal in the early 1990s between the incoming African National Congress (ANC) and the outgoing National Party, in which the ANC had sought to buy the ruling National Party's cooperation in the transition to

ANC rule in exchange for guarantees of nonprosecution of those who confessed to apartheid crimes. Without this deal, the transition might never have
taken place at all. Subsequent criticisms of the TRC have always to be read
skeptically in light of this. Nevertheless, the evidence provided by the commission hearings does provide us with an opportunity to test its assumptions,
and by extension the assumptions of contemporary commentary on the question of social trauma.

In this essay I reflect on the processes of catharsis and memory construction that took place in the period leading up to the creation of the TRC and
during some of its hearings in South Africa, with particular reference to a
single small, but politically central rebellion in the Johannesburg black township of Alexandra in 1986. I examine the immediate aftermath of the rebellion and the process of memory construction in two subsequent trials, and
then examine the commission's proceedings themselves, assessing what they
offered to participants. I contrast the narratives that emerged in the trials
and in the TRC hearings with our knowledge of what "actually happened"
during the rebellion. (Of course, the latter interpretation will always itself be
subject to revision. Here, it is presented as my version of the truth, derived
from empirical research into the events of the time.) I ask how the beliefs
emerging from the acts of catharsis, confession, and redemption related to
preexisting beliefs about the trauma concerned. And I suggest that we need to
move away from any notion that the patterns of memory emerging from the
TRC hearings actually replaced older conceptions, thus liberating the victims
and perpetrators from the traps of binary thinking about their hatred and resentment of their respective enemies. Instead, I suggest, new ideas came into
being in a complex relationship with older ones, deeply influenced by the
rising tide of nationalism in the culture at large. Some new ideas may simply
have been superimposed upon older ones, but others entailed the silencing
of existing beliefs rather than their replacement. And the new ideas about the
rebellion were by no means a serendipitous result of what emerged during the
hearings. They had already been profoundly shaped by the discourses of the
press and of the trials, as well as by the powerful emerging forces of nationalism at the time. The binary assumptions of the "Christian" confessional discourse concerning social trauma are clearly unable to cope with this kind of
complexity.

Besides setting out to debunk these naive versions of "truth-telling," the
essay also seeks to understand the topography of the said complexity. What
kinds of storytelling did the trials and the commission entail? How did these
stories construct memory? And by what inner and outer visions of the social
and personal world were they themselves shaped? I ask not only *whether*, but

also *how,* nationalism somehow manages so often to triumph over other versions of history.

Background

Alexandra Township, in Johannesburg, epitomizes the kinds of society in which the worlds and subworlds of the poor remain uncaptured and authority is unstable. For the past one hundred years, townships such as this have provided important dramaturgical arenas within which social movements and collective action have been developed and nurtured. But their spatial boundedness permits them to be controlled, at least minimally, even by quite weak states. From a purely economic point of view those living or employed in such townships may be predominantly of the working classes. But socially and culturally these are social strata whose worlds do not resemble those of workers where industrialization is highly advanced and states are well developed.

In the Alexandra of the 1980s the very presence but also the disruption of this complex private and spatially distinct realm—indeed the weakening of the state itself that the apartheid modernizers of that period unintentionally brought about—was to provide unprecedented opportunities for collective action, as well as a new set of motives for undertaking it. Two social processes were at work here. First, a free-floating stratum of young people was created. Slow economic growth failed to draw this stratum into employment, and the networks that had drawn most earlier youths into township society—through schooling, age hierarchies, family influence, patronage systems, and cultural forms—were substantially weakened. The humiliations and degradations their parents and elders experienced as a result of apartheid's laws, which themselves were invasive of the previously private realm, added to the weakening of adult legitimacy in the eyes of the young.

The processes at work here reflected the syncretism of the culture. The cleavage between the generations had been a defining feature of traditional African societies, but it had been regulated by a variety of social mechanisms. It now became exaggerated and highly politicized. The social disruptiveness of the modernizing thrust of the state was typical of early capitalism. The state moved rapidly and uncompromisingly, oblivious of the complexities of the social worlds it sought to transform and the unintended consequences it was likely to generate.

Second, by the 1980s the modernizing imperatives of the state had reinforced and exaggerated the *spatial* significance of township society on a number of levels. Segregation had itself been highly spatial, socially excluding

and controlling, but always somewhat at a distance, using paternalistic inter-
mediaries. But now the ambitious state was bidding for greater power, and it
sought to enter into and further control the private world of the ghetto. And
one of the defining features of apartheid was that space came to be used in
extreme ways as a means of ordering society. But while space may be a useful
source of power, it is an unstable basis for authority. This paradox of space
was revealed by subsequent events. While even newly extended spatial control
did to some extent acquire a veneer of normality that lent it some legitimacy,
it was but a poor substitute for the older, paternalistic systems of authority
that had been undercut. The National Party established local power brokers
within townships to try to recreate the stability of earlier times, but activists
saw that these were weak and vulnerable, lacking an economic base from
which to dispense anything that might change power into authority.

In the eyes of the newly free-floating stratum of youth in most townships,
the spatial order had the potential to be turned to other purposes. It could
become a target through which they could attack a state that embodied their
own and their parents' degradation, and whose oppressiveness they felt in an
increasingly unmediated fashion; in addition, it could be a useful and powerful resource for new forms of collective mobilization. In Alexandra the potential for rebellion was realized in a startlingly extreme way.

In February 1986 the events known as the Six-Day War shattered the veneer of normality in Alexandra, opening the way for the development of
a revolutionary climate within the township. The processes—not necessarily consciously planned—through which the veneer was shattered involved
hundreds of random acts of violence throughout the six days, day and night,
by both youths and their chief opponents, the police: ganglike behavior by
groups of youths; the spreading out of violent and invasive acts so that every
physical space came to be thought of by residents as vulnerable and therefore
unpredictable; random and more directed shootings, many fatal, of residents
and youths by police; more directed acts of violence and murder by youths
against police and local councilors, many of whom fled, thus directly weakening the tangible sources of power in the township; the gathering and sometimes spectacular and brutal acts of uncontrollable mobs; the formation of
larger, more controllable crowds for more ritualized purposes; and others.

The effect of this short, brutal period upon the minds of the inhabitants of Alexandra was profound. The already weakened legitimacy within
the township was destroyed. The state's immediate response was to subject
Alexandra to what amounted to occupation by the military, a force far more
experienced in combining control with persuasion than were the police. It developed a longer-term response only after the township had experienced fur-

ther profound changes. This military occupation, plus the reassertion of their presence by the police, and the experiences of the Six-Day War itself caused residents to question the moral universe that had previously seemed normal to them. The population of Alexandra as a whole, and not simply the younger generation, came to see things in new ways and to make themselves available to new ideas. The Six-Day War changed the meaning of the township's space. Old styles of existence, even of protest, were disrupted. The whole of Alexandra came to be redefined as a theater for new genres of collective action.

Even as the Six-Day War raged, new, more sustained forms of mobilization, some already nascent, were envisaged and planned much more systematically by emerging or consolidating groups. These began to take distinct but overlapping forms. Three "frames" of mobilization could be discerned. It is important to note, from the point of view of the later construction of memory, that none of these resulted from ANC strategy in a straightforward manner. ANC discourse had penetrated the township, some ANC cadres were indeed present, streets came to be renamed after ANC militants and leaders, and some members of each grouping were in fact ANC members. Nevertheless, mobilization in Alexandra was created by residents out of a range of resources. These may have included these ANC ideological, cultural, even military and political resources where available, but they undoubtedly also included a huge repertoire of others.

The first of these three frames was the evolving millenarianism or utopianism of the militant, revolutionary youths, who sought an overturning of all authority and the creation of a better world. Alongside of this there emerged a second, adult-based "popular democratic" genre of opposition. Both had their structural roots in the immediate past history of the society and the township, both remained confined to the private realm of the township, and both took a strikingly radical form. Each had recourse to distinct (but again overlapping) sets of intellectuals, ideas, popular support, and resources; and each attempted to implement its own plans for the revolutionary metamorphosis of Alexandra, sometimes in opposition to the other and sometimes alongside or even in cooperation with it. The third frame, that of the more conventional versions of African nationalism, was more public. This frame had far deeper historical roots in the township and in the society at large, and far wider resources, which it could use to mobilize. The youth and adult groupings were combative; African nationalism was defensive. This dislocation between nationalism and the more private rebellion was a fact that the state, when later mounting trials of rebels, failed to perceive.

The utopians were mainly youths aged sixteen to about twenty-five from extremely poor families, unemployed or partially employed, with some expe-

rience of the narrow-minded, racist apartheid educational system known as
Bantu Education, and of resistance to it. They were clearly divided by gender.
The young men drew upon male networks in soccer, schooling, activism,
gangs, church groups, even choirs, and ideas of age cohorts inherited from
African traditionalism. They lived and moved in a ganglike world in which
violence and authoritarianism, both in their personal lives and in their experience of the wider world, played an integral part. These mainly male youths—
"comrades"—saw the township as a degenerate and degraded place. They believed that their parents' generation had naively pursued the path of respectability, had been the unresisting victims of the horrors of high apartheid, or
had unforgivably sunk into degradation themselves. This, they believed, was
why the older generation had failed to deliver political liberation or social
dignity. They believed that a better future was imminent and were driven by
a passionate idealism. They sought to constitute their minirevolution so that
it simultaneously tackled everything they perceived to have caused their and
their parents' suffering—the problems of capitalism and apartheid, the need
for new concepts of self-hood (the "ideal comrade"), and the social decay and
moral weakness within their own world.

Building upon the spatial war they had already waged, and using older,
deep-rooted gang traditions of territorial belonging, they established youth
groups to control precisely defined territories, at times patrolling the streets
to find and disarm, or beat, criminals or those carrying weapons. All physical
landmarks, streets and schools in particular, were evocatively renamed. Over
time, they constituted "People's Courts" in tin shacks at some of their headquarters. In each court was constructed a newly ordered dramaturgical space
that inverted the age-based authority systems they had grown up with and
thus parodied the traditional courts, or *lekgotla,* by placing them, the youth,
at the pinnacle of a reformed moral universe. Here the ideals of good behavior
(not drinking, not abandoning one's family, being a good comrade, not fighting, not committing crimes, paying maintenance to divorced wives) could be
induced within—or imposed upon—adults and young people alike.

Their abrogated position at the moral pinnacle, as well as their high level
of militaristic organization and brutality, gave the utopian youths an increasing sense of their rights and power over adults, whose failures they had self-
righteously proclaimed. Their highly symbolic as well as militaristic revolution seared itself upon the minds and memories of the adults. The township
public found the theatrical imagery and symbolic moments of the period
unforgettable.

Because the "rule of the comrades" drew so extensively on repertoires of
older, gang behavior, it was not surprising that the ideal comrade proved a

difficult part for militant young men to play consistently. They came to be feared for the ways they patrolled and controlled the streets, wielding sjamboks and destroying the meager possessions of shoppers who had broken the consumer boycott, or herding the unwilling to meetings. Some took part in spectacular mob burnings and necklacings of those whom they believed were witches and informers; the line between the two forms of accusation was a fine one. Some groups of youths became so distinctively criminal that they came to be labeled *com-tsotsis* (comrade-criminals), perceived as bad elements masquerading as comrades. The presence of a mass of unemployed and socially uncaptured youths perhaps rendered this decay into criminality inevitable. But comrade-ness did achieve some legitimacy within the township and was perceived by all as a distinctive, new form of behavior. Furthermore, there were those among the adults who found it useful to have comrades, at least those who professed to be idealistic, as allies. Older women in particular found that the comrades' ideals of good behavior sometimes coincided with their own need to strike back at the sexist men in their lives. Adults would bring "cases" to the people's courts, sometimes requesting even harsher punishments than those visualized by the youths. Adults would sometimes participate with zeal in burnings or necklacings. Few people minded that criminals were disarmed or beaten, and most were not averse to having a militant and militaristic force of young men within the township when it came to coping with the despised and feared occupying army or police force.

However, this implicit adult-comrade alliance did not preclude the continuation of a separate adult movement. Adult intellectuals, networks, repertoires, and ideologies were different from those of younger people, clearly manifesting generationally stratified politics. They drew upon trade-union traditions of participatory democracy, which for many reasons were particularly significant in Alexandra; local memories of older resistance movements, revived by the "people's history" movement then active among the white intelligentsia; as well as the more common organizational forms that adults throughout the country were using at the time—lobbying and mobilizing committees, workshops, and large peaceful meetings. Their networks developed in churches, trade unions, youth and political organizations, yards themselves, shebeens, sporting teams and clubs, and at work.

A set of unusually powerful leaders, some but not all more highly educated than the youth, one with a national and international reputation, and all with organizational experience gained from these and other social and political activities, sought to create institutions through which residents could take part in the regulation of the private realm of township life. These activists drew upon the ideas of the burgeoning left-wing culture of the time—nonracial-

ism, feminism, Marxism, democracy, and answerability. Their style was practical rather than utopian or theatrical, peaceful rather than violent, patient
rather than impulsive, seeking to mobilize around peoples' experiences rather
than their own moral outrage, and participatory rather than tyrannical. The
ideas of respectability, which had long prevailed among the older generation,
permeated their culture even as they rebelled. The adults worried about and
tried to control the "indiscipline" of the youth. Like the youth, they sought
to impose a spatial template upon the township, but theirs was based upon
the yards, blocks, and streets where ordinary residents' experiences of life were
located. Like the youth, they created people's courts as an aid to reforming
the perceived decadence of the culture of the township, but adults remained
in charge within them, and their methods were conciliatory rather than punitive. Significant as these developments were for the evolution of a democratic
culture, authoritarianism was far from absent. Democratic participation at
the grassroots level did not preclude a powerful impulse toward organizational centralism at the top. Instead of ganglike violence and the rule of fear,
these leaders promulgated an ideology of consensus but ensured their own
hegemony within it.

These two forms of mobilization overlapped. Some participants in the
world of "adults" were in fact extremely young. Youth experiences of organizing and mobilizing were brought to bear in adult groups. At times the
two kinds of people's courts were hardly distinguishable. Adult ideas of yard,
block, and street organizing were rapidly appropriated by youths. Furthermore, adult leaders, in their search for a centralized consensus, incorporated
and tried to tame youth initiatives through repeated attempts at forging
structural unity among the disparate interest groups of youths, adults, men,
women, school pupils, and others that had emerged in Alexandra during recent years. For a short while, they were successful.

There was a dislocation between these two highly original forms of mobilization and the third, nationalist, repertoire, which was the most extensive,
theatrical, and symbolic. African nationalist mobilization had long been suppressed by apartheid laws, but had revived in the climate of reform, particularly after the establishment in 1983 of the lawful United Democratic Front
(UDF), effectively a front, but one with its own social roots and momentum,
for the still-banned ANC. The revived forms of nationalism, which had been
disrupted rather than displaced during the Six-Day War, came to flourish
alongside the new repertoires. Established religious, UDF, and other leaders
from within and outside the township saw their constituency in this case as
the mass of the people, but both the more revolutionary-minded groups—
youths and adults—contributed to and drew from the growth of nationalism,

with varying degrees of skepticism. Some of them saw it as a conservative force, but none could afford to disregard it.

The nationalist repertoire embraced several central motifs, including the people, the church, the nation, suffering, and martyrdom. Women and symbols of martyred or suffering womanhood were central. These motifs appeared at huge, emotionally charged funerals, marches, and mass meetings, which were redolent with the passionate symbolism of nationalism and highly ritualized. National rather than township leaders led songs, prayers, speeches, and hymns. Flags, uniforms, banners, coffins, and many other symbolic forms were used. Both adults and youths attempted to introduce their "frames" into these occasions. Adult organizations would bid for supporters; militant youths would dance the *toyi-toyi,* display posters with specific local meanings, and loudly express their resentment of what they saw as the conservatism of national leaders. But when journalists ensured that these events gained considerable publicity, both nationally and internationally, it was to the readily available and more familiar symbolism that they turned, perhaps finding it difficult and sometimes politically awkward to cope with the complexities of Alexandra's multilayered struggle.

The overlay of nationalism was extremely powerful. Its power lay in several factors: it was public; it was opportunistic; it was of long standing; it could capture the syncretism that underpinned the private world of township residents; and it was widely appealing, not only to township residents but also to those millions all over the world who supported the ending of apartheid. Nationalism in general has the capacity to triumph over other forms of mobilization because of its skill in tapping into human passion. Thus, to an extent nationalism appropriated the public version of what had been happening in the township. The very open, much publicized nationalist activities, such as large funerals and peaceful marches, plus its overwhelming emphasis on martyrdom, contributed to the fiction, promoted by some, that public nationalism constituted most of what was happening in Alexandra, permitting the private realm of activities to remain mysterious to outsiders.

The cauldron of mobilization and oppositional ideas could not survive in the South Africa of 1986, however much the state may have been weakened over time. But the ending of the rebellion was not a simple affair. Because the state was internally divided, the township was subjected to the ambiguous forces of both the reformism advocated by some and the repression that others attempted to sustain. Both the municipal and the national police resented being driven out by the youth. Encouraged by the growing right-wing vigilantism throughout the country, which was reinforced by pro-repression forces within the state itself, the police launched an anonymous vigilante attack upon the township one fateful night in April. The murderousness of those posing as a township gang, the Makabasas, later to become prominent in TRC testimonies, was unprecedented. Activists were killed, their homes destroyed. People's courts were burned. There followed a period of renewed war reminiscent of the Six-Day War. Trenches were dug, barricades were mounted, and youth were more militarized than ever, determined to defend and resurrect their alternative institutions. This they did with partial success for a time, although the sliding into criminality continued. Adults still claimed that they ruled the township. The appointment of a new township administrator to replace the discredited and destroyed local council was the state's "reformist" reply to this claim.

The arrest five months after the Six-Day War of two separate groups of key activists—one group of nine youths and one of five adults—and the bringing of charges of treason and/or sedition and a series of others against them spelled the end of the revolt. While previous detentions of activists had been short term and had tended to enhance their radical reputations in Alexandra, these serious charges, when combined with the assault upon the township by police, proved crippling. The rebellion ground to a halt. By August it was widely agreed that normality had returned. The dramatic performance of the revolt had come to an end, and the briefly imagined theater of revolutionary scenes and nationalist spectacle within which it had been staged, the township itself, reverted to the mundane.

Narrative and Memory: From Trials to Truth Commission

The weakening apartheid state of the 1980s had led to a disruption and finally an eruption of the secluded, private realm in township life. In what ways did officially sanctioned narratives construct the revolt, both as a private experience and as a public occurrence? Did the three frames of collective action survive to constitute three frames of memory?

The recording and remembering of the rebellion had begun before the flames died down. Academic theses, memoirs, and newspaper reports flourished. It was not long before it became clear that everyone wanted this to have been a nationalistic uprising, and most press reports tended to reproduce the public nationalist narrative, treating other events in the township as exceptional. The ANC propaganda machine was part of the nationalist appropriation of events. To the ANC the rebellion had been "the consequence of a grand revolutionary conspiracy" to replace the apartheid government, created and guided by themselves (Carter 1991a, 6). In its journal *Sechaba,* for example, the ANC's main propagandist, Mzala, wrote: "Even the least attentive study of the situation in South Africa will show that taking place almost simultaneously with ungovernability is the creation of a new type of governability, that which is exercised by the people. Places like Port Alfred, Lingelihle, KwaNobuhle, Mamelodi, Alexandra and others . . . provide the ground for the growth and development of our people's army and for the escalation of our people's war." The "organs of people's power" had emerged not only as a result of subjective momentary conditions "but also by the objective level of our revolution towards seizure of power by the people. . . . Let the racist magistrates and lawyers shout their lungs out in scorn of the 'necklace' method of punishing collaborators, let them call the people's courts 'kangaroo courts' if they want to, but we shall always reply to them by saying: when we say power to the people, we also mean the right to suppress the enemies of the people, we also mean the country's administration and control by the ordinary people." He likened these "liberated districts" to the Paris Commune (Mzala 1986, 12).

Additional narratives of the revolt came to be constructed within two other worlds, both of which took a theatrical form: the courtroom, where in 1986–87 the key treason trials involving activists were held; and the TRC hearings, where ten years later a different memory of the township more broadly and of the revolt in particular was evoked.

Constructing the Trials

The two trials took place while the old state continued to display an ambiguous approach toward reform, as well as a frightening capacity for repression (see Supreme Court of South Africa 1987a, 1987b). The trials stand as imperfect monuments to the rebellion and also reflect these conflicts within the state. During the actual trials and the mounting of the cases significant shaping of memory took place. For one thing, the thirteen accused from the two trials were held in the same communal cell. And then the lawyers, particularly for the adult case (called, after its chief accused, the Mayekiso trial), some of whom had been trained at the University of the Witwatersrand, where Marxist and Gramscian academic discourses were prevalent, sought to cast the whole event in a sociological light, using sociologists, including me, as expert witnesses. We portrayed the rebellion as a form of collective action resulting from the structural situation in which the inhabitants of the township found themselves, and argued strongly against the state's assertions that it had been the result of a conspiracy by township folk, a plot hatched by the ANC, or simply treasonous and illegal activity. The lawyers spent hours going over the case and attempting to give meaning to it. Thus, trial evidence was shaped not only by factors such as fear and state manipulation, but also by a narrative of the revolt that reflected contemporary academic concerns about resistance, collective action, and popular consciousness. This narrative came to infuse the evidence given by the accused.

The portrayal of the revolt was rehearsed and meticulously constructed. As Mzwanele Mayekiso said: "The preparations with the lawyers were rigorous. Like an actor who learned the role, I knew what to expect" (Mayekiso 1996, 34). Most of the violence was blamed on "wayward youth." The adults, by contrast, were portrayed as sensible seekers after justice for their people, idealists with a broader vision than that of the "disreputable" and "uncontrollable" young. The reasons given for the rebellion were broader social as well as economic factors, and a sense of the nature and existence of the private social world of the township was conveyed in the defense argument. The judge was not unsympathetic to this approach, and at times a relatively cozy atmosphere of clever jokiness pervaded the courtroom. It was difficult for the state to sustain a case of treasonous or seditious activity in the face of evidence of the adults' patently constructive activities and the unclear relationship between the ANC and adult ideology. The state itself had not penetrated the private world of the township sufficiently to distinguish between adult democracy, youth utopianism, and the more generally pervasive nationalism.

By contrast, in the youth trial the prosecution emphasized the brutality, randomness, and willfulness of the youths' anticrime, people's court, and consumer boycott activities. Their own community, it was argued, had suffered most, although their aims had also coincided with those of the ANC's strategies of ungovernability and peoples' war. The defense relied on exposing contradictions and weaknesses in, or simply disputing, prosecution evidence, as well as portrayals of the youths' lives of hardship and suffering in the poverty-stricken township. Moments of aggression and disbelief on the part of the prosecutor were met with hostility or angry withdrawal on the part of the accused. Although the defense did try to deflect onto others responsibility for the better documented of the more vicious youth activities, this strategy was difficult to sustain, and anybody who followed the trial knew that its evidence could not be embraced within a sanitized version of what had happened. Not surprisingly, the trial was barely reported publicly and remains little known.

It was the adult trial that occupied the public stage. It became something of a cause célèbre, both nationally and internationally. For a time the activities of adults appropriated the "public" ground. International support, said one of the accused, was "crucial." The United Auto Workers, in the United States, took a particularly active role in mounting an international campaign, as did many other trade unions, while the then U.S. ambassador attended the trial frequently. The trial was widely reported in the South African and occasionally in the international press. In Britain, support for the Mayekiso trial was in fact divided, with the Anti-Apartheid Movement (through the South African Congress of Trade Unions, or SACTU, the ANC union movement, which the chief defendant, Moses "Moss" Mayekiso, had not supported) deciding "not to take our case seriously, using the argument that the Mayekiso treason trial promoted personality cults. There were also allegations that Moss was a workerist, and yet the rest of us came from the Congress of South African Students and other groups from the Congress tradition, which always held the Freedom Charter banner very high" (City of London Anti-Apartheid Group 1986). This was a hint as to the difficulties that later emerged in constructing a valid ANC-sanctioned memory of the rebellion through the TRC. The then controversial "City of London" antiapartheid breakaway group, as well as the then British ambassador, provided the main nonunion support in England for the trial.

The two trials ended differently. While the youths were acquitted of treason, they were found guilty of sedition, and most of them were imprisoned.[1] Few knew of their plight. On the other hand, none of the adults were found guilty. The prosecution, it was found, had failed to prove that the accused had been responsible for the establishment of street committees and other alternative structures, or that there had been a conspiracy with the ANC to render the township ungovernable, and the five adult activists were released to great public acclaim in April 1989. The "sociological defense" had worked.

The overall effect of the two trials was that the contributions to the revolt of the main rebellious groupings were startlingly misremembered. The adults came to be thought of as victors on behalf of public nationalism, whereas in fact they had pursued their struggle to a certain degree independently of the nationalist frame. Even greater distortion accompanied the construction of the story of the less palatable actions of the youths, who became profoundly marginalized in the public and private memory. Youths who had taken part in brutality and violence were portrayed as the other. Although their actions may not have been forgotten entirely, increasingly the youths came to be thought of as outside of the virtuous realm the adults claimed for themselves. The fact that the "sensible" revolution had depended upon the youth movement was downplayed. Instead a working misunderstanding was cultivated concerning the respective roles of these two strata.

Together, the press and the trials had engendered powerful public myths about the township and its people, to add to those that already existed. Even today the story of oppression and resistance in the township is frequently told as part of the litany of African nationalism—Africa's civil religion. It is also embodied in numerous published writings, as well as in unpublished theses and dissertations (Bozzoli 1998, 2000a, 2000b, 2004; Carter 1991a, 1991b, 1991c; Jochelson, 1988a, 1988b, 1990). By the time the TRC was established, the public myth went something like this:

THE PUBLIC MYTH OF ALEXANDRA BEFORE THE TRC
Alexandra has always been a sadly neglected township, and for this reason, and because it was unlit, was called "Dark City." However, it had always had a strong sense of its own "community" and of belonging, in spite of the fact that violent and criminal youth gangs had often plagued the township. This "community" was at times indistinguishable from the "nation"—belonging to the community meant belonging to the nation. And the nation, in turn, was often indistinguishable from the ANC. Indeed, prominent and famous ANC figures, including Nelson Mandela, had actually lived in Alexandra. Alexandra's residents had suffered but were very brave. They had constantly experienced poverty, crime and hardship, and yet took part in courageous bus boycotts and squatter movements in the 40s and 50s. They resisted government attempts to remove them more than once. They, guided by the ANC and their own local leaders, and in the face of terrible repression and provocation, about which numerous tales abounded, mounted a local revolution in the mid eighties, followed by a famous treason trial in which the accused were victorious. This was followed by the tragic conflict between the ANC and the Inkatha Freedom Party (IFP) in the late 80s and early 90s, and the appalling overcrowding and rising social tensions as thousands more squatters, including "foreigners," moved in after the ANC was unbanned. The ANC's ascent to power in 1994 was in part due to the heroic struggle of Alexandrans, and although today they continue to live in great poverty, plans will soon be under way to rebuild and upgrade the township. The people are cynical of such plans, but hopeful that they will come to fruition.

The TRC: A New Public Myth?

When in 1996 the TRC held a special hearing on Alexandra Township, a different configuration of narrative and memory emerged, through a different series of processes. A great deal had happened since the trials had ended. The main activists had moved on, some into key government positions and others into professional jobs. Some remained active in grassroots politics, while still others remained marginalized and unemployed, as did most of the population of the township.

But most importantly, the country had been liberated, and a new government had come to power. Alexandra itself had voted overwhelmingly for the ANC in the 1994 election. Nationally and in local contexts the ANC rapidly sought to establish itself as the legitimate, hegemonic party, using history as part of its comprehensive bid for power. Public nationalism was rapidly appropriated to this end. The rebellion had not been forgotten, but gradually came to be thought of as part of the public history that the now ascendant nationalists sought to construct.

The TRC had three committees, dealing with human-rights violations, amnesty, and reparation and rehabilitation. Together they were, in the words of the Commission itself, to "reveal the truth about the political conflicts of the past." Their ultimate aim was to develop a "culture of human rights in our country, so that the suffering and injustices of the past never occur again" (TRC, n.d.).

The TRC took thousands of statements from victims of apartheid, hundreds of them residents of Johannesburg's townships. People were asked to come forward if they or their kin had been killed, abducted, tortured, or severely ill treated for political reasons. The commission defined such experiences as gross human-rights violations and undertook to investigate them through its Investigative Unit, aiming to discover who had been responsible and how and why the violations had occurred; and to hold public hearings. The Committee on Reparation and Rehabilitation would receive the information thus derived, consult with "communities," and make policy recommendations to the South African president for appropriate reparations to victims. So far, a minute proportion of these reparations have been paid, discrediting the entire process quite fundamentally. Even so, the importance of the hearings should not be discounted, as they played a part in shaping subsequent perceptions of the events of the rebellion.

Twenty-two Alexandran residents were invited to present their testimonies concerning resistance in the township from the 1960s to the late 1980s. The commission chose to use the method of cultural ritual rather than that of legal procedure to achieve its purpose. How were the already established myths and narratives embedded in the ritual? What definition of community did the ritual embrace? What did it allow to be said, and what silences did it permit? And what patterns and types of storytelling accompanied it? The patterns of ritual clearly would have had profound psychological effects upon the participant who sought catharsis. They also would have had significant *social* effects upon the longer-term meanings given to the crucial period of the mid-1980s. In order to understand the ways in which the personal experience of each participant extended into the broader social realm, some discussion of the nature of ritual is required.

Émile Durkheim divided religion into belief and ritual, the latter including actions, cults, rites, ceremonies, and practices (Durkheim 1915, 24). Hidden in these, he said, are realities of the greatest significance. Durkheim rejected simple psychologism and saw ritual as *social and symbolic,* asserting that "behind these outward and apparently unreasonable movements" lay "a mental mechanism which gives them a meaning and a moral significance" (Pickering 1984, 128). In ritual, the worshipper is brought face to face not just with himself but also with his society. The TRC hearings tended to resemble what Durkheim called "the piacular rite," which has an ambiguous nature. Normally embodied in such occasions as funerals, the marking of drought or plague, or the occasion of a poor harvest, the piacular rite is both positive and negative. It is negative in that it permits the separation of the sacred from the profane and of the individual from the collective. Most importantly for our purposes, it allows for *the replacement of individual representations by collective beliefs.* But it is also positive in that it allows the worshipper to bridge the gap between himself and the object of his cult by encouraging recall and the construction of myths. It allows expiation but also brings to the fore "sentiments of sorrow or fear" about "every misfortune, everything of ill omen" (Pickering 1984, 339ff.).

In order to bridge the gap between the personal and the social, rituals require the use of sacred ground, the gathering together of an "assembly," and the definition of a purpose: "the gathering of people seeking the same goal and vibrating with the same emotions" (Pickering 1984, 324). In this respect, Durkheim rejected what he saw as "psychological reductionism." He did not view the assembly as being primarily concerned with the giving up of individuality by those taking part. Rather it was a deeply *social* institution that created and recreated beliefs and sentiments, caused new beliefs to come into existence, and strengthened existing ones. Rites remake individuals and groups morally and therefore have power over things, he said. "They have a profound effect on the participants as individuals and as a group, intellectually and emotionally." Participants take away a feeling of well-being. "Men are confident because they feel themselves stronger, and they really are stronger" (Pickering 1984, 338).

It is not difficult to see the connections between some of these observations, the ritualized events at many TRC hearings, and the "public myths" that surrounded such events as the Alexandra rebellion.[2] The physical elements of the TRC ritual embodied the commission's function as a bridge between the public and the private. The ceremonial form of the hearing was protoreligious, adding to the emotion it evoked, and was constructed around a variety of carefully chosen collective representations. Order was emphasized, and a sense of a peaceful oasis conveyed, amid the undoubted chaos that is Alexandra.

Each session opened with a prayer conducted by a religious figure from the community, who would then light a candle to symbolize the bringing of the truth. The national anthem followed. Tears would flow, hidden pain would be revealed, and terrible stories would be told. But the symbolic calm of the hall would both permit and control these things, and render them social as well as personal. Ritual could bridge the realms of the personal and the social. On the individual level, the TRC undoubtedly wished to see its rituals, in Durkheim's words, "make men stronger" throughout the land. It set out to allow people to participate in rites of confession, mourning, and making public their private pain and anger. It opted for an expiational and healing approach rather than a punitive one. It sought to transform stances of individuals and assemblies of individuals from resentment, anger, hatred, and guilt to acceptance, wholeness, forgiveness, and confession. It was hoped that these transformations would then take place in the society as a whole, freeing it from the burdens of unspoken passions and from a possible future age of retribution. This twofold purpose was not always articulated as such, and the gap between the personal or private and the social or public was bridged, I shall argue, in ways that had their own effects upon memory.

The ostensible aim of the TRC was to bring to the fore the stories of those who had been silenced in the past. But would that simply reinforce the existing myths? To what extent would the real complexities of the situation come through? And to what extent would it create new myths?

One aspect of the initial mythmaking was the way in which the ritual itself referred implicitly and often quite explicitly to an abstract notion of community, thus precluding any reference to the divided nature of the rebellion. Key speakers were included in the hearings, not as witnesses to specific abuses but as "community representatives." Thus, a person clearly designated as a spokesperson for the township, Patience Phasha, opened the proceedings by welcoming the commission "on behalf of the community of Alex." The commission, she said, was there to hear not just the individual witnesses—who in a purely legal setting would be individuals before the law—but an entity thought of as "the community," of which the witnesses were representative in some way. The "community" came to resemble a congregation: the truth would be spoken from and about it, as well as from and about individuals who were part of it.

Phasha's welcome concerned the task of the commission to heal. She sketched the "community" experiences that she believed Alexandra residents considered to be the central motifs of their suffering under apartheid. Sure enough, the existing myths resurfaced. She included the bus boycotts of the forties and fifties, the gangsterism of the fifties, the removals and upheavals of the sixties, the Six-Day War of the mid-eighties, and the orchestrated conflict between the ANC and the IFP and the plight of displaced people of the nineties. Clearly, Phasha was invoking a story that encapsulated key moments and perceptions of the township's suffering, to which the audience clearly related. She concluded by linking community, the TRC, God, and the nation, arguing that the TRC was there to act as a national lifeline, in a context in which South Africans could express their need for one another and their capacity to work together. People said "we did not know," but that was not true, she said. This was a time for sorrow, but God would give them strength.

The following day, the stories of two others, Benjamin Lekalakala and Obed Bapela, were presented to the commission as testimonies "for the community" rather than for themselves.[3] Both indeed claimed to speak on behalf of the community. Obed Bapela had been a major figure in Alexandra politics from the 1976 township uprisings onwards, as well as a leading participant in the revolutionary events of 1986, and was by 1996 an ANC provincial councillor. He was one of the accused in the "Mayekiso" treason trial. Detained more than once, he displayed wide knowledge of the recent history of resistance and state repression in the township and gave the hearings a certain weight. He spoke of the need for forgiveness and reconciliation. Bapela often referred to examples of human-rights abuses inflicted, not upon him but upon others, reinforcing the impression that he was spokesman for the community.

A second aspect of the TRC's mythmaking was, as already indicated in Phasha's speech, that it elided community and nation while it permitted the ANC to claim to represent both. Witness selection itself was part of this. As commissioners did for all TRC cases, the commissioners charged with handling Alexandra had held preliminary hearings with witnesses. All had been interviewed and prepared. Many had already had a chance to express their feelings and wishes. Initial interviews were often accompanied by weeping, for example. From the group of witnesses who testified in the preliminary hearings a smaller group was selected to appear at the main hearings.[4]

The selection of witnesses to represent the "community" was heavily influenced by the ANC. Obed Bapela, together with his wife, Connie, assisted the commission in finding its witnesses. And as the hearings proceeded, the impression was given that Bapela and his wife were the hosts of the occasion. Thus, they were thanked in the opening speeches for their help and cooperation, and even though he gave evidence (but of a very particular sort, as we shall see), Bapela did not sit with the rest of the witnesses. I do not mean to imply that efforts were not made to include non-ANC witnesses who had experienced human-rights abuses, nor that the ANC was not a key, highly significant player in the events experienced by Alexandra residents. But the identification of the ANC with the public telling of the story of Alexandra's past—with the very definition of community—was surprisingly central and to an extent built into the hearing from the start.

A third aspect of TRC mythmaking was the way in which the existing public myths were modified. Bapela, for example, restated the existing public myth, but with a strong slant toward the ANC. Thus, he stated that during the struggles of the early 1980s the leaders of the ANC-linked UDF had been detained, and he asked why the leaders of the rival liberation movement, the Azanian People's Organisation (Azapo), had not, implying a close collaboration between Azapo and the authorities and clearly distancing himself from non-ANC Alexandrans. He talked of the many leaders of UDF-aligned organizations who had been killed, several of them close friends of his. He said that violence had been sponsored by the state, which had set up joint management councils, run by the military, throughout the country to try to manage the townships. Winning the hearts and minds of Alexandra residents had also been tried. One Steve Burger had come forward, on behalf of the authorities, with plans to install electricity and sewerage and to paint roofs. Plans had been made to "indoctrinate the youth, through clubs, and camps and choirs." And "the strategy worked," at least for a time, not least because all the resistance leaders had been jailed.

Bapela then spoke of the Six-Day War and the subsequent adult treason trial. Following quite closely the accepted narrative of the time, he said that it had all started in June 1985. A lot of townships were aflame. There was a lot of activity. "People" established street committees. There was also a consumer boycott. In January 1986 things had started to take off in Alexandra. Shooting at "Jazz Stores," in which a young man was killed, had "provoked the whole situation." After the young man's funeral at Alexandra stadium, his parents' home had been tear-gassed, provoking the youth. The police became targets. Alexandra was aflame for six days, and ninety people died. No suggestion was made that the rebellion was anything other than a united uprising by the community, led by ANC-linked leaders.

Bapela's own role and that of other adults was put at the forefront. "How did the Street Committees start?" Bapela was asked. "They began in the Eastern Cape," he said. He had traveled a lot and seen how they worked. He had shared the idea with other comrades, who tried to get support. They started yard and block committees, and the idea "spread." They moved from street to street. Asked whether the consumer and rent boycotts had been violent, particularly in light of the fact that the police had said that they were responding to the violence of the day, Bapela answered that they had not been violent. The police had had legal means to respond to consumer and rent boycotts that did not involve killing and attacking.

When Bapela was asked about people's courts, he took the opportunity—the only one given during the hearings—to describe the youths' activities. They came across as having started off "well" and then deteriorated into more dubious practices. The idea of people's courts had arisen in 1985, he said. They were started by the youth, who formed anticrime patrol groups that physically removed youths and told them not to drink, fight, and so on. Crime went down to zero. The patrol groups confiscated many knives and weapons. People began to have confidence in these groups and brought cases to them. They would get the complainant and the perpetrator together and give advice. The courts spread. There was no sjambokking at this time, but after the Six-Day War, when youths "got excited" and started to hold trials and prosecutions, there was sentencing and sjambokking. Bapela distanced himself from these activities, saying that he had not been personally responsible for the sjambokking.

While Bapela claimed that the "sensible adults" had been important to the rebellion, he portrayed Moses Mayekiso as having been less important than him. Bapela thus presented quite a different picture from the one given in the Mayekiso treason trial, in which Mayekiso had been seen as the leader and the solid trade unionist, keeping the unruly youth under control. Was this because by the time of the TRC hearings Mayekiso had been publicly revealed as a member of the Communist Party and perhaps therefore found less suitable as a key figure to give evidence of community worthiness and folk nationalism? Asked whether the strategy of the 1980s had been to form an alternative government, Bapela answered, in contradistinction to the "sociological" defense of the trial, that the intention had indeed been to undermine the government and to make Alexandra, and indeed the whole society, ungovernable—an admission that could have seen him found guilty in the trial. This had been a just war and a just struggle. "Now we are liberated," Bapela said.

Bapela's evidence combined and interwove both the "adult" and the "nationalist" narratives, co-opted them into an ANC version of history, and negated the part played by the youth. In distancing himself from the more dubious and brutal actions of the youth, Bapela followed the line of defense taken at the Mayekiso treason trial. There was to be no admission, not even indirectly, of responsibility for violent and overtly revolutionary behavior at the TRC hearings. The youth were portrayed as the architects of their own descent into a sort of depravity. The commissioners reinforced this portrayal by asking only if the rent and consumer boycotts had been violent, thus allowing Bapela neatly to sidestep the question whether there had been other forms of violence at the time.[5]

The significance of this double marginalization of the story of the experience of the youth—first in the trials and then in the TRC hearings—cannot be underestimated. They had been the key actors in the entire revolt, both in Alexandra and throughout the country, yet these versions of the past obfuscated their role and any direct or indirect connections there may have been between the youth and the ANC or its surrogates.

Bapela's telling of the story of the revolt gave weight and coherence to the occasion. He had created a new central "myth" to which the more personal and fragmented stories of those who were not leaders of "the community" could be connected.

The TRC's "Private" Stories: Good and Evil within the Community

With the remaining witnesses the commission undertook a far more difficult task: to make public the much more private versions of events of ordinary people who did not "represent" the "community." An elaborate process was developed. Witnesses were accorded a dignified welcome. Each was told that his or her testimony was very important and then asked several pointed questions. Most testimonies reached a dramatic point when the witness recalled his or her greatest suffering, and many broke down. When witnesses wept, women would come forward to hold and comfort them—the women were clearly there for precisely that purpose—but the witnesses were encouraged to carry on, sometimes quite relentlessly. Thus, those called "witnesses" behaved more like witnesses to God than like witnesses in a court. This was an occasion upon which both collective and individual memories and experiences were drawn upon, and emotional displays were common. A strong relationship developed between witnesses and their audience, and between witnesses and their questioners.

After testifying, each witness was then ceremoniously thanked by the chairperson, who summed up important elements of the testimony and indirectly praised the witness. The chairperson would speak of, say, the "kind of son you had," "what was in your heart," "your sad story," your "gratitude for survival," or "your spirit of reconciliation."

While the TRC defined human-rights abuses as mainly concerned with deeply personal tragedies, there was room in the hearings for broader issues to be raised, as the discussions of Bapela and Phasha have already indicated. And although they were not the centerpieces of any story, social and cultural matters were clearly part of the generalized experience of apartheid, as well as part of the discourses within which such experiences were retold. In fact, so powerful were these social and cultural matters that they often "burst through" an individual's story even when they were not specifically requested by the commissioners. The residents of Alexandra, like most witnesses in the TRC hearings, were cast as mere victims. Their extraordinarily courageous, unique, and imaginative struggle was almost entirely ignored. The gross unfairness of apartheid; the ways in which whites and blacks were regarded as enemies at worst, or alienated from one another at best; the presence of, and appalling behavior of, hated officialdom; ignorance; poverty; the uncared-for children and youth; poor education—these things all appeared in the stories of the witnesses. Witnesses were not familiar with the workings of courts, police stations, mortuaries, and the other institutions with which they had to interact in their moments of suffering. They felt that the police were not only violent and murderous, but also deceitful. Guns and bullets were ubiquitous; violence was common. The eighties were a time in which the "people," portrayed as poor and humble, —were cast against the police in all their power and might. As Jabu Malinga said, "We fought the police with stones and dustbin lids."

The emphasis was on the oppressive actions of the police during the revolt, and the vigilantes who ended it. The community, it was felt, had been invaded by the forces of the state. Irene March said that Alexandra was a "battlefield," a term also used by others. Dorah Mkihele described a day when the streets were blockaded and people were stopped from going to work.

Obed Bapela also told the story of the Makabasas, with the greater perspective that he brought more generally to the occasion: "During that period the police wanted to identify a group to use against us. In April when they could not find a local group they themselves dressed up and called themselves 'Amakabasa' [after a local gangster]. They dressed up like them with uniforms on, though they pulled their shirts out. They came from Wynberg; they entered Alex and attacked all meeting places and houses. They retreated back to Wynberg."

The Alexandra police, seen as invading, deceitful, and violent people, were also heartless, said witnesses. When Jabu Malinga was beaten until his teeth were loose, he asked who could help him; he was told, "Go to Mandela." When the house of Linda Twala, a community leader, was burned down, the fire service would not extinguish the fire. Nkosana Mngadi said that when he had had his leg amputated, a doctor from South America working in the hospital had referred to him as "Mandela's terrorist."

Good and evil were personified in many testimonies. The names of famous local people who had been directly or indirectly involved in the rebellion were included in the testimonies as points of reference for "goodness" and, in most cases, "victimhood." "Jingles," Ace Hlongwane, and Michael Dirading were important figures in the community and, indeed, in the public narratives of the past. It was they, and their harsh experiences, rather than the participants in the revolt, and their courage and imagination, who took center stage.

Jessie Moquae told about her fiancé, "Jingles," the well-known Alexandran "people's poet." He was shot dead: "A white Mazda had passed three times. They shot Jingles." Subsequently, moreover, "whites disturbed us from preparing for the funeral. . . . Teachers and comrades were not allowed in Jingles' funeral." At first the funeral was arranged by the police, which made the comrades so angry that they "collected his body again" (i.e., removed it from the mortuary). Then the police showed up at Nineteenth Avenue, looking for his body; they threatened to shoot, and there was tear gas. The funeral did not go well. "The police took the corpse and threw it into a hearse," said Moquae, weeping. "They stopped the people from going to graveyard. I am proud of him. They had to bury him. At graveyard the reverend came, but people were absent. They took the body, threw it, like any rubbish, and threw soil on top of it. The 'body was abused.'"

Another witness, Montshentshe Matjila, remembered that when the police, posing as the Makabasas, arrived, their faces were painted black and they were wearing berets. People were scared. They were told to go inside the house, but instead they tried to leave. The police threw canisters. "One landed in front of me. I tried to run away. I fell inside a drum." Two black policemen, including the notorious "Mothibe," and four white policemen "kicked me. They hit me with batons. I lost consciousness. I found myself in hospital. My arm was broken. My teeth were out."

Some policemen, such as the above-mentioned Mothibe, personified evil. Mothibe's sin was that he was both of and yet against the community. He epitomized the traitor. Maria Malakoane said that she had seen Mothibe, whom she knew, among the police. He had even tried to warn her, saying, "I know you. Get away. We are going to cause damage." But she was nevertheless injured. She had a bullet "in her bones."

Bodies, Souls, and Spaces

In this stark world of good and evil, how was suffering to be defined? Unlike the ideologues of nationalism, the ordinary witnesses in the TRC hearings did not cast their memories in terms of larger images of community, nation, or social movement, but rather on a more intimate, though no less socially constructed scale, where the body, the soul, and personal space were the main markers of suffering. Bodies, for example, were attacked, brutalized, and abandoned. Dorah Mkihele told of how her son Jabulani, a nineteen-year-old with a Standard Two (fourth-grade) education, "who delivered papers for Allied," was shot after leaving home very early to go to work. But "before he reached the bus stop, he came across white police at Twelfth Avenue and was shot by them." Three people who had been with him ran away and climbed a tree; they "were shot at until they fell." Others ran into a shack but were pulled out. One Sizakele called an ambulance, but when it arrived the "police would not allow it." The police "finished the rest." Dorah did not discover what had happened until the next morning; she found Jabulani's body in the government mortuary.

Margaret Madlana's story of physical abuse was brilliantly told. It combined place, event, and time, conjuring up a visual image of the events, apportioning blame, and situating the tale within the known narratives about Alex. Like many of the stories told at the commission, it was almost biblical in its force and impact. She appeared in front of the commission with her daughter to talk about her son, Bongani.

It was February 1986; Monday the seventeenth. I was at home. There were some youths who came to my house. They were telling us to get out of the house. My twelve-year-old son went with the youth. After a while I got worried. I had had no breakfast. I needed to go to my sister, at Fifth Avenue. When I passed Twenty-fourth Avenue, I found a child shot in the yard. They were pulling him. They were white police. He was not dead. They pulled him up and hit him against a rock. They chased us away. I looked back. More police arrived. Mothibe was there. . . . I passed the place. I told my sister they had killed a young child. She said don't worry, relax. I said how could that happen. Bongani would not do that. I went home. He was not there. I told them I saw the police. I woke up at 5 AM. Still no Bongani. I went to the Alex Clinic, and then home. Then I went to Bramley police station. The police didn't listen. I looked at their records. He was still not there. Some had been hit by bullets. They said go to Khotso House; go to the mortuary. I went to his father's work. I explained about the hippos [armored police or army vehicles]. I took a taxi, and went to the mortuary, not to Khotso house. The taxi passengers agreed. There was a queue at the mortuary. "Mama," they said, "we have seen one child. He came alone and was carried in a hippo." . . . They took me into the mortuary. There were bodies lying on the ground. Bongani was there. I cried, "Bongani, you have left me behind." . . . They gave me letters for the police and myself. I went and told his father. Mothibe took the letter. He said the child was killed at number twenty-four—the one I had seen they had photos of him holding a half jack which was a petrol bomb. Therefore the police knew him and knew me—yet they took him to the mortuary alone because they knew me. Most children disappeared and parents could not find them.

Later, the commissioners ask her to give more details of his death: "They hit him with irons," she answered. "He may have survived but his head was hit against a rock. He was swollen."

Searching for a loved one and finally finding his or her body in the clinic or mortuary was a horror that several experienced. Of course, such experiences were interpreted as examples of the callousness of the police. But parents also saw them as a reflection of the waywardness of their children—echoing the way in which youth rebelliousness was marginalized in the public version of events. Lesoro Mohlomi's son Reuben had been shot in the eye in 1985, his eyesight permanently damaged; a year later, he was shot dead. His mother had tried to stop him from taking part in rebellious events, but to no avail.

Reuben was a comrade.. . . It was the Friday before Michael Dirading's funeral; Reuben wanted to go—but I advised him not to go because he couldn't see clearly and couldn't run. He went but denied it. I was selling alcohol—I asked him to stay home and sell for me. When we heard there were police and bullets I closed the business. Reuben could go. They came and told me he was shot, suspected dead. At the clinic all the bodies were lying in the hall. I tried to drag him out. I tried to talk to him. I took off his shoes, a key and a letter to the President. A nurse came in and said he was dead. They refused to let us into the mortuary. The priests of Alex helped us get the bodies of our children, but only after five weeks.

The phrase "our children" suggests that what Reuben's mother was experiencing was so common as to have become a part of the collective memory of the township. Thus, Dorah Mkihele spoke of "a big ambulance" that went around the township calling people to come and identify bodies. Reuben was, like many others, buried at a mass funeral, and the family's mourning became part of a communal process. Maria Makaloane remembered that "They were buried—that is many people, seven at a time, though nine were advertised. They were all shot." Like Reuben's mother, she too remembers the time lapse: "They were buried after 4 weeks," she said.

The virtual imposition of the mass-funeral format upon families meant that women's stories of a child's or husband's death inevitably became part of the wider story of the suffering of the community. Martha Smiles, whose husband was shot in the Six-Day War, was drawn into this: "After three days

I realized he must be dead. I found him in the mortuary. He had to be buried with the children who had died, because 'he died for his country.'"

The denial, manipulation, or control of burial rites was a further abuse—of the body, of the soul, and of the bereaved. We have already seen this in the case of the poet "Jingles." Matsiliso Monageng also suffered greatly in this respect. She said that "Boers harassed us every day" before her son Jacob's funeral, at which the number of attendees was limited by law to only twenty-five, and which was held with "police all around the graveyard." No buses were allowed, people were stopped from attending, and some were arrested in the church. Those at the subsequent night vigil were tear-gassed, as was frequently the case. Irene March, too, reported that night vigils were "very difficult to attend," and that the burial of her son was "disturbed by teargas." Similarly, the Reverend Snoeki Mzamo expressed his outrage at the fact that after "dozens of young people were killed in the Six-Day War of 1986, the magistrate refused permission to bury them in a mass funeral."

Personal spaces were unforgivably attacked. The destruction of homes and possessions was also desperately deeply felt by witnesses. Linda Twala, a local businessman and community big man, spoke bitterly of his losses: "My home and cars were destroyed; my furniture, my clothes, everything when my house was bombed. My children were inside—but my three daughters went into the dog's kennel and were saved. The fire brigade came but had been instructed not to put out the fire." His neighbor's house was also burned down. "I saw my house was on fire," said Mabusane Moquae. "It was the police. Children were inside. A neighbor came and helped us try to put on water. A cop came and asked whose house it was. Linda Twala's and mine was the reply. The cop said he had wanted that. We found the children—but had nothing left." Moquae wept at the memory. "I worked very hard for my clothes, my furniture," he said. "Everything was burnt to ashes. It was very cold. It was winter. If you lose your home you are destitute."

Daisy Mashego described the violence and conflict in the street when she was shot in the back while looking for her children in the mayhem following Michael Dirading's funeral. People were crying, looking for their children. She was in the hospital for two to three months afterwards. She was left completely helpless and depended on the Red Cross and on her disability pension. Maria Malakoane, shot in 1986, lived with a bullet in her body for several months until she finally had it removed. But she had suffered from constant headaches and was no longer healthy. Sekitla Mogano attributed her loss of health to the deaths of her two sons. "I lost strength," she said.

Two of the witnesses implied that the loss of a child was so great a tragedy for parents that they died subsequently. The link is indirect; however, their statements are surely an indication that whatever suffering occurred in those times was thought of as part of a generally oppressive experience.

Thus, the stories convey a sense that the community of Alexandra had been insulted, invaded, damaged, and cheated. The people had been cast in opposition to the evil state, embodied in the police. The idea of the community as a spatial and symbolic entity deeply interwoven with the experience of apartheid was an integral part of the memories of the witnesses. The TRC stories were not quite the same as the public myth of Alexandra's story, described above, in which the community was always portrayed as a united social force rather than a series of spaces and places, but some overlap clearly did exist.

The Forgotten Rebellion

One unintended consequence of this particular way of constructing the narrative of Alexandra's suffering under apartheid was to exclude the story of the actual revolt that took place in 1985–86. The witnesses described a cohesive community of mainly older parents and somewhat wayward youth who were surrounded by a series of set rituals, such as funerals, over which they had no control, and subjected to unbearable brutality. Many of their loved ones died, their homes were burned, and their lives were overturned. And, of course, that is how it was. But this version precluded the telling of another story, in which intrepid youths manned the barricades, reconstructed social and cultural relations, and tried to create alternatives to the governance of the township; in which adults sought to control this uprising and turn it into an example of civic-mindedness; and in which nationalists came to claim the rebellion as part of their teleological march to glory.

Additional ritualized processes within the hearings attempted, not entirely successfully, to transform what have so far been portrayed simply as private experiences into a more stable public myth. On the personal level, what it meant to be a victim of a human-rights abuse was defined by the occasion. But as witnesses gave their testimonies, their lives and stories came to carry meanings beyond the personal. A public sphere was constructed, within which private experiences could become the property of all. It often seemed as if many of the witnesses were speaking their lives for the first time, at least in public. Experiences such as theirs had been hidden, or only partially brought to light. Oral historians are conscious of the ways in which they take part in processes of this sort. However, for an institution as morally and politically charged as a truth commission, the complexities are multiplied.

A subtle and complex social process took place. The stories of the witnesses were recalled in ways meant to transform their memories and their persons. Their stories were meant to be transposed from the private to the public sphere; the profane was meant to be transformed into the sacred. Did their personal stories come to be emblematic of a wider experience? If they did, through what processes of meaning construction did this occur?

The hearings contained within them what could be called "rites of closure." By this I do not refer only to the closure of the ceremony of evidence taking—for example, the ritual thanking of witnesses and concluding of each one's story. There was also evidence that the hearing set out to achieve a sense of psychological closure in the witnesses themselves and succeeded in doing so. This in turn affected both the audience in attendance and the "imagined" audience, the general public who would read press reports, watch television, or perhaps ultimately read the commission's report itself. Such a conclusion was meant to occur through the witnesses' reaching a stance of closure, such as forgiveness. Yasmin Sooka, who chaired the hearing on the first day, expressed this intention in her welcoming statement. She pointed out that the TRC sought to listen, to create a record of what had happened, and to discover what kinds of reparations victims wanted. The commission could not, however, itself offer forgiveness, she said, telling the witnesses that that "is up to you." As we shall see, this turned out to be an extremely complex process.

In order to reach an understanding of the concluding stances of the witnesses, it is useful to examine first what their opening stances were. How did the witnesses think of themselves in relation to their own possible transformation as they took the witness stand? Two possible opening stances can be described broadly as the "weak stance" and the "strong stance." Of interest to the sociologist is how these stances reflect how the witnesses remembered apartheid, what they thought the purpose of the commission was, and their own personal life stances.

One type of weak stance was often unsuccessful from the transformative point of view. This was the stance of witnesses who appeared mystified by what had happened to them, who, indeed, seemed lost in a sea of tragedy. In this case, their "weakness" may have been a function of their inability to find concepts to help them make sense of their memories and experiences. Dorah Mkihele, whose son had been shot, gave a deeply incoherent tale of the subsequent proceedings in court, a tale that seemed to go nowhere. Her brother had to intervene to help convey her message. And Sekitla Mogano seemed unable to explain why "the police came and looked for him [her son]"; she said that "he taught others to write on walls." He was a leader of the comrades.

Fear was another weak stance. Commissioners found this hard to deal with. Ntombizodwa Sidzumo would not name the people suspected of driving her son away from his home, in spite of being pushed hard by the commissioners. "God would reveal" them, she said. She appeared to be deeply traumatized and to find giving evidence extremely difficult. She could hardly answer when asked whether her son had been killed or had committed suicide, saying she did not feel free to do so.

The other most common weak stance, weeping, was perhaps the most transformative. Witnesses who wept were the most malleable. Often, they at first demonstrated reluctance to expose themselves, and they were gently pressured in order to reach the truth. However, the listeners were not psychologists, and more was at stake than freeing the individual psyche from the torment of unacknowledged suffering. Often they were pressured so that the community would feel through their suffering. Perhaps their suffering was thus turned into martyrdom, their weakness into catharsis.

A stance of "strength" was transformative in a different way. The coping, strong witness was the witness who could most easily forgive. Common themes were those of dignity, the strong woman, God's protection, the benign presence of Mandela, and the good fortune of having a strong family. Irene March, who had lost all three of her sons, showed no self-pity at all. She had survived, she said, because of her strong family, the gift of love, her neighbors, and the presence of Mandela.

Another strong stance was that of indignation and anger. Linda Twala's fury was evident as he read out a statement: "My rights have been violated by the police in the previous government. My home and cars were destroyed. My furniture, clothes, everything. Who were they and who instructed them?" Many witnesses cast the relationship between victim and perpetrator in clearly binary terms. Innocence stood opposed to guilt. This stance was encouraged by the mandate of the commission itself, which did not seek out ambiguity. Witnesses frequently felt it necessary to proclaim their own moral innocence. Linda Twala and his neighbor were both keen to emphasize that they were Christians, Catholics, who were attending church when their homes were attacked. Obed Bapela's testimony was interlaced with frequent emphases on his innocence and on that of his colleagues and, at first, the youth. Dorah Mkihele's son Jabulani had been with comrades who were "just sitting there" when they were attacked by police.

From the strong and the weak witness various forms of closure emerged. The weeping, weak witness reached, it has been suggested, a sort of catharsis, and his or her weeping helped the audience attain this state. Other forms of closure included strong statements about the desire for truth and a belief in its healing power. "Everyone must come forward," said Jabu Malinga, "even the Kabasas." "Have the commission call all the people to ask for forgiveness—or maybe they want us to point them out," said the Reverend Snoekie Mzamo. After recalling his house being surrounded by police, he asked, "Where are those police? Why don't they come out? They must come and confess, confess they were Makabasas. This should be part of the commission. I can understand why they did it. They were driven out, isolated, they could not drink in our shebeens, they could not fall in love with our women, they could not buy in Alex. If they come forward and confess, the community will be very happy."

In his opening speech Obed Bapela had made enthusiastic claims about the healing power of truth. But this had elicited less than positive responses from the audience present. He named five policemen who owed the commission both information and an apology, including Sergeant Mothibe, who was now, Bapela said, a preacher and repentant. "What about Erasmus and Ndaba and the informers—what will your attitude be when you know them?" the commissioners asked. To which Bapela replied, "Some I meet—I am friends already. But they must come and repent to the whole community." Asked whether the community shared these feelings of reconciliation, Bapela stated, "If they come back the community will welcome them." But the audience jeered at this response. They knew better, perhaps. Sergeant Mothibe had indeed attempted to visit Alexandra in recent months, but had been "almost killed," according to one informant. Another said he had been stoned.

Some witnesses said they would forgive. Often these were witnesses who took a stance of strength. In their view, truth telling and repentance would lead to forgiveness. Thus, Martha Susan Smiles claimed to speak on behalf of everyone when she said, "People who hurt the people of Alex should come forth, like de Kock, and tell the truth and maybe we will forgive them. I would like to forgive them, because if I do not forgive them the Lord will not forgive us."

Many witnesses would not, however, contemplate forgiveness, as the example of Mothibe seems to suggest. It could be said that these witnesses did not achieve "closure" at all. Linda Twala would not "forgive or reconcile." When asked by a commissioner whether he held out any hope, he answered, "We need something to motivate us. We had it in the old days. Now we don't." Jessie Moquae rhetorically asked, "Will I ever forgive white people?" Margaret Madlana, mother of Bongani, was at first passionately unforgiving: "I apologize before God, but I will poison the white man's children," she cried. "I will never forgive in this case. What will make me to forgive is if Sindane and Mothibe come and confess and say sorry to the parents . . . they killed children of the wars. How can Mothibe be a minister now? Which children is he preaching to? I will never forgive, I will never forgive, I will never forgive, I will never forgive, I will never forgive." And later she said, "We work for them [whites], raise their children for them, cook for them, but they still kill us like dogs or baboons." She continued by blaming the ANC government as well: "I can't forgive for at the moment the government is doing nothing for us." However, she contradicted herself by saying that she would forgive, but only if "Sindane and Mothibe confess and come and say sorry to the parents."

A more common form of closure than forgiveness was an expressed desire for reparations. Most demands were extraordinarily modest. Linda Twala suggested that the "children who died in Tanzania" must be brought back and buried at home. He said that the government should give families tombstones for the dead. More ambitiously, he suggested that the government should "create jobs for the school dropouts now unemployed." Similarly, Jessie Moquae wanted the government to "help us through education." Obed Bapela, in his more nationalistic style, said, "We must honor the victims of the Makabasa attack as heroes and heroines on the 85th anniversary [it was not clear whether he meant of the ANC or of the founding of Alexandra itself] next year." He said that the government would or should "declare Alex a presidential project in honor of its people who have carried the flag of freedom since 1912." Martha Smiles said that the people of Alexandra should make tombstones for those killed during the Six-Day War. Daisy Mashego wanted a bullet removed from her body—and a house of her own. Very few of these requests were met in the subsequent years.

Some chose to enact closure through apology. Tlale said to his family: "I am sorry I burnt the church down." Obed Bapela rendered an apology on behalf of the community: "I must say that in the conduct of the struggle there were things that went wrong. But these were not planned. We sometimes succeeded in stopping it, but not always. People's Courts were not set up by us as leaders, but by members of the community. People demanded and wanted them. But unfortunately people got excited. There was great anger after the Six-Day War. Wrongs were committed." Kenneth Manana was now a Christian. "You have changed, repented," a commissioner said to him, "but from what?" He answered, "To show that in all that had happened, I now realize that some of those things were mistakes. I had the heart to forgive."

Some used the occasion to make a general statement. It is not clear whether these qualify as "closure," however. Many of these statements raised more questions than they resolved. Irene March spoke about the need for crime to end and "policemen to do the job" of securing South Africa as a home for both blacks and whites. Linda Twala was even clearer about this: "Most of the youth are loitering around the streets. They are our future leaders and must be assisted. We must groom our leaders of tomorrow." Interrupted by applause from the audience, he continued: "Youth were 'nice' in those days when they were fighting for the struggle. But today, in these times of drugs, liquor and unemployment, youth are no longer nice." This was followed by further applause. Others contrasted the Alexandra of 1996, with its high crime rate, with the Alexandra of the past. As Margaret Madlana put it, "Now they, the youth, are with the criminals." The audience muttered agreement.

Because such statements were outside the terms of reference, the discourse, of the commission, they were perhaps not "heard" as readily as the main forms of closure. However, it was these statements that received the greatest support from those present.

Conclusion

The Alexandra hearings of the TRC provided a vehicle for the events of the mid-1980s to become part of a newly imagined past. The Six-Day War and its aftermath featured prominently in the hearings. The commission's chief task had been to uncover "private" stories rather than to repeat public ones. Numerous private stories of suffering in the period of the revolt were brought to light, giving great insight into the meanings attributed to the past by ordinary Alexandran residents, as well as permitting some catharsis to take place. But another dynamic was at work at the same time: the presence of an already powerful public myth of the period, retold in highly nationalist terms during the commission's hearing by one of the main accused in the adult treason trial; the stark opposition the hearing posed between oppressor and oppressed; the way in which the commission cast ordinary people as victims rather than actors; the numerous silences in the hearing, in particular silences about the role of the youth; and the only partial ability of the hearing to achieve closure in its witnesses—all together, these meant that the private stories were only briefly brought to the public view and then re-sequestered. The perhaps unintended consequence of the hearings was a new narrative version of the revolt that involved an even lesser role for the youth and also downplayed the adult role to the extreme.

The new public myth of Alexandra, articulated by Bapela and by the very shape and form taken by the Alexandra hearings, placed the ANC firmly and purposively in the lead of a just war. It cast the organically defined and united community, identified clearly with the ANC, in opposition to the apartheid state. It reluctantly acknowledged the role of the youth insofar as they were "good," but attempted to marginalize their "bad" behavior. It sought closure through articulating how peace and liberation had been attained and where forgiveness needed to be granted.

The private narratives of the witnesses were much less seamless but did, it has been argued, form something of a statement. In these narratives, "community" was sometimes absent altogether. Instead, the township was thought to comprise a series of geographical and ritual markers around and upon which resistance occurred. It was also thought of as an entity subjected to wickedness, insult, or deceit; the forces of evil were often personified through the image of, say, the Kabasas, or Mothibe. The experiences of the witnesses were not so much those of participants in a just war as they were those of a suffering people subjected to loss, abuse, and social oppression.

Like the public TRC narrative, the private ones also tend to marginalize the role of the youth. How the youth behaved in the 1980s is only indirectly referred to. The fact is that the youth of Alexandra organized and led a revolt whose main contours hardly appeared at all in the hearings. No mention is made, except in the most anodyne of terms, of the marches, the street committees, the youth groups and their "headquarters," the mass meetings, the *com-tsotsis,* the banners, the placards, the songs, the renaming of parks, schools, and streets, the setting up of barricades, the hounding out of local town councilors, the boycotts of police stations, the petrol bombs, the neck-lacings, or the people's courts. The most well-known spectacular necklacing, of one Theresa, accused (correctly, it later emerged) by the youth of being an informer, was not mentioned. When I asked Obed Bapela why it had not been mentioned, he answered, "Theresa had been told to leave the township." Thus, the youth were the absent witnesses to what actually happened in 1986. We do not know how they felt about what they did. We do not know whether they felt they had won major victories or lost. Almost the only way in which their experiences were recounted in the hearing was at second hand, through the tragic stories of parents who had lost their children. Thus, what the youth were actually doing at the time they were shot or attacked was side-stepped. This both demeaned the youth and let them off the hook.

If the youths were demeaned or excused, their parents were portrayed as the victims of the brutality of the system. Indeed, the motif of "the victim" prevailed, which is not surprising, perhaps, in a commission designed mainly to uncover the truth about suffering. Africans became passive rather than active in the memories of this era. Young people were spoken of critically, or in the worried tone of the parent whose child has acted waywardly. Closure in these narratives was only partially achieved. It was hindered by problematic links to the difficult present, by an unwillingness to forgive, or by an uncertainty about precisely how much "truth" was going to be told by the perpetrators.

Although the hearings allowed these disparate private narratives to be brought into the public realm, it was the much more coherent public narrative that prevailed. It was increasingly formalized, and had already begun to be sanctioned more broadly in the society, or even promulgated by the state. Press reports of the hearings reflected this. Even so, the public narrative only partially succeeded in appropriating the private stories, which remained focused upon the myriad tragic experiences of ordinary people. The private stories were not usually heroic. They often reflected a sense of helplessness and marginality. A new sequestration of the experiences of ordinary Alexandrans was the result.

The rebellion has never been forgotten in Alexandra. Together with a hundred other uprisings in the town and the countryside, it contributed to the eventual demise of apartheid because it made clear that the establishment of legitimate authority was not feasible. Power had to rest with the army and the police, a situation that was impossible to sustain as a long-term form of governance. However, memories of the rebellion are ambiguous. One survey, done in 1997, shows that of the dates that Alexandrans thought should be commemorated, the Six-Day War and the massacre together were the first choice of almost 20 percent of respondents, and the second choice of 17 percent (Isserow and Everatt 1998, 95). The rebellion left a legacy of pride and a memory of tragedy. A sense of ownership of the space had existed for a brief moment, and this was indeed a source of pride for residents. The rebellion, however, in its turning upside down of many of the features of normality, has also left a heritage of normlessness that adults still to some extent regret. Youth are said to still be out of control, even more so now that the "new South Africa" has come into being and the more noble cause for which the youth of the 1980s fought has given way to crime and social decay. The older generation feels a sense of anomie, particularly strongly now that Alexandra has become a center for vast immigration by rural dwellers, who have built shacks in every minute space that was vacant, and "foreigners," who have created their own little ethnic spaces and who have been the target of vicious, sometimes murderous, xenophobic attacks by residents. In the TRC hearings on the rebellion, some older residents even expressed a certain nostalgia for the days before the rebellion, when, they felt, youths had been more well behaved, adult authority had not been questioned, and the aims of the struggle had been clearer.

Notes

I would like to thank the Ernest Oppenheimer Trust for funding research time, which enabled me to write a large portion of this essay; Lincoln College Oxford for hosting me during some of that time; and Gavin Williams and Stanley Trapido for their support in Oxford. I would also like to thank the commission itself, and particularly Hugh Lewin and Fazel Randera, for making my attendance at the Alexandra hearings possible and for their help and interest in my work. They are, of course, in no way responsible for the views expressed here.

1. Ashwell Zwane, aged 22; Vusi Ngwenya, 22; David Mafutha, 21; and Piet Mogano, 25, were sentenced to eight years' imprisonment, of which four years' imprisonment was conditionally suspended for five years. Andrew Mafutha, aged 24; Arthur Vilakazi, 22; and Albert Sebola, 24, each received six years, with three years suspended. Philemon "Chicks" Phalongwane, who could not be named during most of the trial proceedings as he was under 18, was given a four-year sentence, wholly suspended. Those imprisoned were only released after the first amnesty granted to political prisoners, after 1994.

2. I attended the Alexandra hearings, and what follows is taken from my verbatim notes of the hearings, not from the official TRC transcripts.

3. Himself a member of the ANC youth league, Lekalakala used a series of academic books, theses, and articles on the events of the 1980s for his research and was to give a major portrayal of the revolt of 1986. He arrived late and discovered that his findings had been covered by Bapela, a much more central participant in the events.

4. Further research is needed on the selection of witnesses, which appears to have involved important processes of community construction and sanctioning of existing narratives.

5. Like Lekalakala, Bapela had prepared his evidence using published documents and dissertations (some gleaned from academic theses borrowed from me, reinforcing the argument that academics played an important, if indirect, role in constructing the TRC's narratives), as well as the evidence he had given in the treason trial and his own memories.

References

Bozzoli, B. 1998. Public Ritual and Private Transition: The Truth Commission in Alexandra Township, South Africa, 1996. *African Studies* 57 (2).

———. 2000a. Space, Power, and Identity in an "Enclosed" Rebellion: Alexandra, South Africa, 1986. *Political Power and Social Theory* 14.

———. 2000b. Why Were the 1980s "Millenarian": Style, Repertoire, Space, and Authority in South Africa's Black Cities. *Journal of Historical Sociology* 13 (1).

———. 2004. *Theatres of Struggle and the End of Apartheid.* Athens: Ohio University Press.

Carter, C. E. 1991a. Community and Conflict: The Alexandra Rebellion of 1986. *Journal of Southern African Studies* 18.

———. 1991b. Comrades and Community: Politics and the Construction of Hegemony in Alexandra Township, South Africa, 1984–7. PhD thesis, Oxford University.

———. 1991c. "We are the progressives": Alexandra Youth Congress Activists and the Freedom Charter, 1983–85. *Journal of Southern African Studies* 17.

City of London Anti-Apartheid Group. 1986. "Non Stop—Against Apartheid." *Monthly Bulletin.* October.

Durkheim, E. 1915. *The Elementary Forms of the Religious Life: A Study in Religious Sociology.* Translated by J. W. Swain. New York: Macmillan.

Habermas, J. 1989. *The Structural Transformation of the Public Sphere.* Cambridge: MIT Press.

Isserow, M., and D. Everatt. 1998. Determining Our Own Development: A Community-Based Socio-economic Profile of Alexandra. With T. Yanta and M. Schneider for the Community Agency for Social Enquiry. Johannesburg: CASE.

Jochelson, K. 1988a. People's Power and State Reform in Alexandra. *Work in Progress* 56–57.

———. 1988b. Urban Crisis, State Reform, and Popular Reaction: A Case Study of Alexandra. BA honors diss., Department of Sociology, University of the Witwatersrand.

———. 1990. Reform, Repression, and Resistance in South Africa: A Case Study of Alexandra Township, 1979–89. *Journal of Southern African Studies* 16 (1).

Mayekiso, Mzwanele. 1996. *Township Politics: Civic Struggles for a new South Africa.* Edited by Patrick Bond. New York: Monthly Review Press.

Mzala [pseud.]. 1986. Building People's Power. *Sechaba,* September.

Pickering, W. S. F. 1984. *Durkheim's Sociology of Religion: Themes and Theories.* London: Routledge and Kegan Paul.

Supreme Court of South Africa (Witwatersrand Local Division). 1987a. *The State vs. Ashwell M. Zwane, Vusi A. Ngwenya, Andrew Mafutha, David Mafutha, Arthur S. Vilakazi, Albert A. Sebola, Piet Mogano and Phillemon C. Phalongwane, before the Honourable Mr. Justice Grosskopf.* Case No. 50/87. Transcript.

———. *The State vs. Moses J. Mayekiso, Paul N. Tshabalala, Richard M. Mdakane, Obed K. Bapela and Mzwanele Mayekiso, before the Honourable Mr Justice van der Walt.* Case No. 115/87. Transcript.

Truth and Reconciliation Commission (TRC). N.d. *Truth: The Road to Reconciliation.* Johannesburg.

Wilson, Richard A. 2001. *The Politics of Truth and Reconciliation in South Africa: Legitimising the Post-apartheid State.* Cambridge: Cambridge University Press.

Veterans, Violence, and Nationalism in Zimbabwe

JOCELYN ALEXANDER AND
JOANN MCGREGOR

O NE of the most notable aspects of the crisis that so dramatically engulfed Zimbabwe in 2000 was the role played by veterans of the 1970s
liberation war. They led occupations of white-owned farms, acted as
agents of violence on behalf of an increasingly authoritarian government, and
served as central symbols in a politics that sought legitimacy by reference to
the nationalist struggle. Taking on these roles was for many a complicated,
and by no means inevitable or unidirectional, process. It required the remaking of veteran identity and the renegotiation of veterans' relationship to nationalism, violence, and the postcolonial state. For Zimbabwe's aging ruling
party, a reworked nationalism proved to be a powerful tool for legitimating
violence; for veterans it was an important means for advancing economic interests. Its uses were not, however, easily contained within these boundaries:
nationalism was also about claiming rights and accountability and about the
contours of personal identity. Interviews with former guerrillas of the Zimbabwe People's Revolutionary Army (Zipra) underline the diverse ways in which
veterans have acted as symbols of contested versions of nationalism, and of
how these contestations—over history and identity, over political ideology,
authority, and obedience—played into the violent conflicts of independent
Zimbabwe and the changing character of the postcolonial state.

The former Zipra guerrillas on whom our account relies were members of one of two liberation armies that fought for Zimbabwean independence in the 1970s. Zipra was the armed wing of Zapu, the Zimbabwe African People's Union. In 1963 a breakaway group formed the Zimbabwe African National Union (Zanu), and eventually the Zimbabwe African National Liberation Army (Zanla). Zanu went on to win Zimbabwe's first elections in 1980, and, renamed Zanu(PF), for Patriotic Front, has ruled Zimbabwe under Robert Mugabe's leadership ever since. The relationship between the two armies and their political leaders was from the start characterized by violence and suspicion. Their differences were deepened by the regional bases established in the war: Zipra and Zapu came to dominate in the western Matabeleland regions, with their Ndebele-speaking majority, while Zanu and Zanla dominated most of the far larger Shona-speaking areas. Ethnic differences played a central role in the 1980s, when the new Zanu(PF) government launched a war against what it called "dissidents," that is, Zipra guerrillas who had taken up arms again, as well as a far larger group defined in terms of loyalty to Zapu and Ndebele ethnicity. This period of violence resulted in the absorption of Zapu by Zanu(PF) under the Unity Accord of 1987, leaving Zimbabwe with just one inheritor of the nationalist mantle.

It was only after the end of the violence of the 1980s that former guerrillas of both liberation armies joined together under one umbrella, the Zimbabwean National Liberation War Veterans Association (ZNLWVA). The association was acutely critical of what it saw as the Zanu(PF) government's neglect of veterans specifically and the goals of the liberation war more broadly. Its alliance with the government only dates from 1997, when veterans were awarded payouts and pensions. The relationship thus created was central to the much-contested and violent process by which the bureaucratic state, with its claims to civic and developmental legitimacy, was remade as a vehicle for violent political patronage. Veterans' prominence reached its high point during the national elections of 2000 and 2002, and in the land, company, and other "invasions" that started in 2000. Veterans appeared in the national and international media as the leaders of the long-delayed "revolution," defined in terms of finally reclaiming the land stolen by white settlers and defending the nation against a new set of enemies led by the recently formed opposition party, the Movement for Democratic Change (MDC). Veterans' role subsequently declined, as the Zanu(PF) government came to rely increasingly on the newly politicized security arms of the state and the newly constituted youth militias.[1]

Norma Kriger's analysis of the politics of war veterans emphasizes the parallels between this recent alliance with the ruling party and the relationship between Zanla war veterans and the Zanu(PF) of the early 1980s. She argues:

Just as the ruling party used Zanla veterans to win electoral power among the rural majority in 1980 and then to build power in the army, the bureaucracy, and among urban workers in the first seven years of independence, so today it is using veterans (ex-Zanla and ex-Zipra) alongside others to try to preserve its power among these constituencies. Land resettlement, like the cooperative movement, is merely a symbol of the party's revolutionary credentials. . . . Even collaborative attacks on the judiciary by party and veterans are not entirely new. Veterans clearly have their own agendas as they persist in seeking privilege and power, both of which are threatened by a change in regime. The party and veterans collude against the new political opposition . . . and continue to rely on liberation war appeals and on violence and intimidation. (Kriger 2003, 194–95)

Kriger's comparison usefully draws attention to the weaknesses of Zanu(PF) at independence and now, to its need to build support among new constituencies and its use of violence to do so, as well as to the economic and other interests of veterans. However, pointing to the continuities in party and veterans' use of each other does not explain one of the most remarkable aspects of recent politics, given the history of murderous rivalry between the two guerrilla armies and nationalist parties before and after independence. The veterans association has successfully united former Zanla combatants with their Zipra antagonists, including those who became "dissidents" and were so notoriously hunted down in the 1980s (see Ranger 2004b, 166). In that period, the ruling party directed violence against Zipra, Zapu, and "the Ndebele" in the name of a nation from which they were excluded. In the 2000 elections, one-time victims of that violence were prepared to ally themselves with their former persecutors under the rubric of a redefined nation.

The emphasis on continuity also obscures the different dynamics involved in the ruling party's efforts to establish authority after independence, and its efforts to hold on to it in the face of mounting internal opposition some twenty years later. Pointing to continuities in the use of a "war discourse" hides discontinuities in how the war was portrayed, how the boundaries and content of the "nation" and nationalism have been redrawn, and how the state operates. Other commentators have emphasized differences rather than parallels with the early 1980s, drawing a distinction between the nationalism of the past and the ruling party's current use of a "patriotic" discourse rife with violent intolerance (Ranger 2004a). Reference to the liberation war was never absent in Zanu(PF)'s appeals, but in the 1980s it was coupled with the promise of modernizing development delivered by a nonpartisan bureaucracy, democratic representation, and racial toleration. In the "patriotic" versions of history coercively instilled in the young after 2000, nationalism was reduced to the struggle for the land and the heroic acts of a single, unified liberation army.[2] The role of the party and popular nationalism was overlooked, the history of division obscured, while the language of democracy and rights was cast as imperialist. Britain's role as an imperial power and perfidious betrayer of the guerrillas in the negotiations that concluded the liberation war was given pride of place as the nation's "founding moment," placing Britain, not successive Rhodesian regimes, at center stage (see White 2003, 95 and chap. 6). The exclusions of this nationalist discourse narrowed the moral community, not in ethnic terms, nor even in terms of the nationalist divisions of the past, but so as to exclude the urban and educated classes, whites, Asians, and others associated with the MDC and critical civic associations (Raftopoulos 2003).

In this essay we hope to throw light on the social processes, conflicts, and debates that shaped the changing character of nationalism, the shifting uses of liberation war history, and the transformations in authority. The ruling party's promotion of a newly exclusive "patriotism" did not go unchallenged. Critical voices included those of dissenting war veterans and the new political opposition of the MDC, each concerned to foster alternative views of the liberation war, concepts of the nation, and notions of authority. We focus on the ways in which former Zipra guerrillas understood and debated the past and on how they justified taking a range of stances in the violent political milieu of 2000 and after. The repositioning of Zipra guerrillas in relation to Zanu(PF)'s nationalist discourse is of particular interest given their former exclusion from it and their violent persecution by the Zanu(PF) government in the 1980s. For us, it was particularly important to understand why those with whom we had worked closely, and with whose politics and acute marginalization we had sympathized in the mid-1990s, were prepared to embrace a violent and intolerant ruling party that lacked popular support in their home region and that seemed to embody in its uses of the state all that they had so recently denounced.

This essay falls into two parts. In the first, we explore the oral histories and autobiographical accounts of the liberation war that we collected from former Zipra guerrillas and dissidents in the mid-1990s, situating them in terms of the emergence of the unified and outspoken ZNLWVA. In the second part, we follow some of these former guerrillas through the politics of the post-2000 period, exploring how they positioned themselves in relation to the veterans association's alliance with the ruling party, the articulation of new versions of liberation war history, and the remaking of authority in a newly violent mold. These guerrilla accounts further our understanding of the complex politics of recent years and of the diverse and contradictory roles of nationalist ideology used by the government and its critics as both an incentive to violence and the moral critique of it. They also underline the intimate, personal nature of the calculations and justifications that shape individual choices about the use of violence.

Remembering the Liberation War in the Mid-1990s

When we carried out our interviews with former Zipra guerrillas in the mid-1990s, Zimbabwe's ruling party was the subject of burgeoning criticism and protest over corruption and economic hardship, organized in a new, urban-based politics of opposition that would eventually find expression in the MDC. This pattern of opposition emerged in the aftermath of the Unity Accord, in late 1987, which brought about the absorption of Zapu into the ruling Zanu(PF) and a quick end to the extreme repression that had been meted out to regions loyal to Zapu. In this climate, the legacies and history of the liberation war came under renewed scrutiny, as did, for the first time, the violence of the 1980s.[3]

In the 1980s Zanu(PF) had grounded national identity in a particular interpretation of the liberation war. As Kriger (1995) argues, Zanu(PF) sought to institute a hierarchical version of nationalism that privileged the elite, the wealthy, the leadership, over the rank-and-file guerrilla and party members, and that excluded Zapu from the heroic past. It did so publicly and symbolically in the creation of a hierarchy of Heroes' Acres, at which the variously valued fallen fighters and nationalists were buried and memorialized. But with the Unity Accord, and in fact even before it was formally consolidated, this version of the past came under heated attack. Zipra and Zapu had long been angered by their exclusion from nationalist history and by the betrayal of the nationalist goals of rights and democracy evidenced in Zanu(PF) repression. In 1986 the revered Zipra commander Lookout Masuku was denied a place at the national Heroes' Acre. The Zapu leader Joshua Nkomo used the occasion of Masuku's funeral to vociferously condemn the failures of nationalism in Zanu(PF)'s reproduction of violent discrimination, now ethnic and political rather than the racial discrimination of settler rule (Kriger 1995, 153; Werbner 1998, 91–92). Zipra guerrillas also joined with their Zanla counterparts and other critical voices in raising thorny questions about the elite and exclusive nature of Zanu(PF)'s nationalism and the lack of material benefits for wartime sacrifices. The "living heroes," they argued, deserved more.

Ex-combatants, as they were most commonly known, began to mobilize in this context, forming the ZNLWVA in 1989. As Kriger (2002) notes, the shift from the language of "ex-combatants" to that of "war veterans" was significant. The new term implied distance from the immediacy of war and fighting. It was hoped that it would confer respect on a stigmatized group and bring them into an international frame of reference useful in securing state benefits. There followed a complex process of negotiation among ex-guerrillas, their former commanders, and nationalist leaders that both shaped and was shaped by Zanu(PF)'s political insecurity. This process of negotiation, which Luise White (2003, 36) argues was so central to wartime mutiny and authority, applied equally to peacetime.[4] Claims for material compensation at first resulted in a highly corrupt process in which party elites colluded in the "looting" of the War Victims Fund for their own benefit. Public, and violent, protests by veterans followed, in which they insulted party leaders and ministers, heckled Mugabe at his Heroes' Day speech, and occupied the Zanu(PF) headquarters in Harare (see Werbner 1998, 81–82). The veterans were subsequently promised payouts and pensions in 1997, thereby remaking their relationship to political authority, as discussed further below.

Zipra guerrillas were central to the process of organizing veterans, to making material claims, and to challenging Zanu(PF)'s nationalism. Their renewed activism and the public acknowledgment of the 1980s conflict amidst the increase in protest and opposition activity created a context in which they were more willing than ever before to speak about their experiences and in which they spoke with a renewed sense of purpose. Zipra guerrillas wanted to insert their experience into the nation's history and to engage in the widespread reassessment of the meaning of the nationalist struggle. For these guerrillas, telling their life stories was a process of both personal and political redress, at a moment when they had not yet succeeded in making new material claims on the state.[5]

We have discussed the narrative form of these guerrilla accounts at greater length elsewhere (Alexander and McGregor 2004). Here, we are concerned to explore what they say about the relationships between nationalism and violence and between authority and identity. Guerrilla accounts of the 1970s war are not principally stories about violence. They are heroic accounts in which the process of political education sits side by side with the transformation of students, cattle herders, and subordinate "boys" in the employ of whites into "real soldiers." As a result of their passages through time and place and their engagement in military institutions, these men attained a new identity, one that was, in the mid-1990s, counterposed to a caricature of Zanla and Zanu and shaped by the unresolved violence of the 1980s.

Guerrillas' stories begin with their politicization at their homes, usually through encounters with a version of Zapu's nationalism that emphasized the petty cruelties, exploitation, and racist repression of the Rhodesian regime.

They decided to fight because "violence was the only language the colonial-ists could understand" (Nkomo 1996, 6). Those who joined later, when the war was well under way, emphasized simply the "enthusiasm of fighting," the "spirit of war."[6] Joining the struggle involved border crossings and often dif-ficult journeys to Botswana, and then Zambia. Their entrance into the guer-rilla training camps of Zambia was the moment when they literally received a new identity—their war names.

It was in the camps too that guerrillas gained the apparatus and training of soldiers: guns, military knowledge, and survival skills. A great pride in the mastery of new skills and weapons marks many accounts, and was often counterposed to the shoddy training and weaponry of Zanla. Crucially, it was also in the camps that guerrillas' political education was refined. Nationalism was not to be about simply ousting the whites; it was to be about transform-ing a political system. It was not to be about race, but about rights and re-distribution (Nkomo 1996, 13). In many accounts the description of political instruction takes on the quality of an epiphany.

Zipra guerrillas' political education did not, however, make politicians of them. They were at pains to emphasize that they had eschewed the Zanla practice of holding all-night political meetings, or *pungwes*. As one explained, "The men with whom I served were highly trained in both modern warfare and guerrilla warfare, they were soldiers not armed politicians! Therefore, sloganeering and singing was not their appetite."[7] Politicization was left to the civilian party, not soldiers. As soldiers, their primary identity lay in their status as disciplined professionals, highly trained and answerable to a military hierarchy. This was the ideal of the Zipra soldier, and it stood as a critique not only of Zanla in the 1970s but also of Zanu(PF)'s politicization of the army after independence.

Guerrillas' stories of war itself revolved around crucial moments in which they had realized the power of their training. The first "contact" was often described as the last step in their "initiation," through which they finally realized their potential as professional soldiers.[8] Descriptions of the use of violence on the battlefield were couched in the military language of casual-ties, tactics, and operations, not the morally ambiguous language used by civilians, with its focus on the difficulties of controlling young men with guns and the consequences of violence in a divided society.[9] Guerrillas stressed instead the good stead in which their professional training and sophisticated weaponry had stood them.[10]

Guerrilla accounts were not, however, devoid of pathos and horror. For guerrillas the worst events of the war were the Rhodesian bombings of the camps in Zambia and the internecine battles within Zapu and Zipra and against Zanu and Zanla. Those caught up in the ill-fated attempts to unite the two guerrilla armies in Mozambique had been "forced to denounce our party, Zapu, and its leadership"; they were tortured and imprisoned, "just as if we were in Rhodesian captivity" (Nkomo 1996, 17). Guerrillas described the Rhodesian bombing raids on Zipra's Zambian camps, in which so many had died, as "burned into their memory," as haunting.[11] These experiences stood as exemplars of what the disciplined army should not be: it should not be unable to protect its own; it should not be technologically inferior to the enemy; it should not be riven by disunity and disloyalty, rumor and gossip, ethnicity and political ambition. The reality of these weaknesses, and the emphasis guerrillas placed upon them as the most painful aspects of their experience, underlined the moment of recall in mid-1990s Zimbabwe. It emphasized the obligation of leaders to respond to and protect their soldiers, to value their skills and sacrifice, and to recognize that the violence they used or instructed others to use must serve a legitimate political aim.

The camp accounts, alongside the stories of training in foreign lands, also had positive aspects of note. Guerrillas emphasized their cosmopolitan experience. In the camps, they had mixed with people from all over Zimbabwe and found common cause in their commitment to becoming soldiers. They had traveled abroad, within the region as well as much farther afield—to the Soviet Union, Cuba, Algeria, and Libya. They had received the backing of superpowers. Theirs had been a struggle that could be placed side by side with those of freedom fighters from around the world.

Zipra guerrillas in the mid-1990s thus told a tale in which their uses of violence in the liberation war had been justified and heroic, underlining their claims to military proficiency and their membership in a formidable, internationally supported army that was always superior to its Zanla equivalent. For those who had taken up arms again in the 1980s, these claims remained essential to their identity, if difficult to sustain (Alexander 1998; Alexander, McGregor and Ranger 2000, chaps. 8 and 9). The "dissidents" of the 1980s were not accepted by their political or military leaders as engaged in a legitimate struggle. Nor did rural Zapu leaders accept them as equivalent to the Zipra of the 1970s. Instead, they labeled the dissidents *silambe over* (overhungry) or *ozitshwala* (from the Sindebele for the staple, maize porridge), both terms invoking their failure to abide by the moral economy of wartime behavior regarding reasonable demands for food from civilians (Alexander and McGregor 2005). This failure symbolized the rupture between dissidents and the nationalist project of Zapu. They were no longer soldiers; they had become simply armed men who used illegitimate violence.

In their accounts, former Zipra dissidents blame the corruption of nationalism by Zanu(PF) and their abandonment by their leaders for the difficulty in maintaining their status as soldiers. Nationalism had become tribalism. They no longer received international backing.[12] Violence in this context took on a new meaning. It was about survival, and it could not conform to the wartime rules elaborated under the rubric of Zapu's nationalism. As one former dissident put it, "A party constitution, ideology, a court of discipline—those weren't there. It was a tribal war. . . . People were confused, they had no line, they were only trying to survive by carrying a gun to protect their lives."[13] When the Unity Accord was signed and the war drew to a close, Zipra dissidents nonetheless drew great pride from turning themselves in with militarily precise organization, thus proclaiming their status and identity as professional soldiers—even if they belonged to an army that no longer existed.

After the end of the 1980s repression, former dissidents struggled to regain their status as soldiers in the eyes of those among whom they lived, as well as in the eyes of their leaders. They went to great lengths to become something other than "overhungry," but they largely failed. Instead, they, along with many other former Zipra guerrillas, languished in poverty and without recognition. Senior commanders who had been imprisoned and expelled from the army in the 1980s had never resumed careers fitting for men of their education and status; individuals who might have been national political figures instead held minor positions on village development committees, or retired prematurely to family life. Rank-and-file Zipras who had fled persecution stagnated in the villages and townships, reluctant or unable to fill public roles. In the mid-1990s they were unable even to gain the involvement of their political leaders in acts of ritual cleansing. All this changed, however, with the veterans association's successful claims to compensation and pensions. Former guerrillas were suddenly set apart materially and politically from the civilians among whom they lived, who also struggled against the hardships of a declining economy. The change for former "dissidents," who had been among the most comprehensively marginalized socially and economically, was dramatic: they wore new clothes and boots and sunglasses, and they spoke of finally being able to build a good house, and to marry properly.

This transition involved a reinstitutionalization of veterans and a transformation of their relationship to state authority and political leaders. It also made their 1970s military status—their identity as soldiers—crucial to their well-being. The association that represented them undertook rigorous vetting procedures in which the divisions and identities of the 1970s were revisited. War names, camps, and operational areas had all to be verified. Those who had participated in breakaway groups struggled to gain approval as legitimate claimants to the veteran mantle.[14] As Kriger (2003, 192–93) notes, this raised the question of guerrilla authenticity, much as it had been raised in the 1980s. But while veteran identity was once again a "political weapon," the context in which it was invoked and debated had changed dramatically. It was now about claiming the right to challenge political marginalization and to belong to a newly reconstructed group at a time when the ruling party was intent not on instituting its authority but on protecting it from new challenges. In the 1990s former guerrillas were not the victorious, only recently disarmed (if disarmed at all) military wing of a nationalist party. Many of them, especially in the case of Zipra, had been pushed from the political mainstream, and found their lack of education and ex-combatant tag a distinct disadvantage in their search for jobs and social standing. The debates over the "living heroes" underlined their marginal status. For the ruling party, the promise of development, upon which it had relied so heavily for its legitimacy in the 1980s, now looked distinctly tarnished. The inability of Zanu(PF) to draw on this claim to legitimacy in the era of structural adjustment was central to its movement toward a narrow reliance on the legitimacy conferred by the nationalist struggle, the redistributive potential of land, and the politics of patronage and violence.

The process of establishing and contesting guerrilla credentials in the 1990s constituted a new community that cut across the divisions of the 1970s and 1980s. It brought veterans into contact with one another as they had not been since the early 1980s, as they went to meeting after meeting in rural and urban areas all over the country and congregated at the barracks in Harare where their credentials were assessed. Rank-and-file guerrillas were reunited with their former commanders, now essential to validating their past. And they interacted with the local and national leadership of the veterans association, men whose authority lay less in their military achievements than in their political connections and acumen, and in the case of some, such as veteran leader Chenjerai "Hitler" Hunzvi, their medical expertise. Even as veterans queried Hunzvi's war credentials (he had never fought), they valued his political leadership. In the process, a new identity was being formed, one that still emphasized the unity and loyalty, discipline and hierarchy of the soldier, but applied it to guerrillas as a whole and that was now linked to a single, embattled ruling party and a state about to be turned to new purposes.

For Zipra guerrillas, and more so for those who had become dissidents, reincorporation into the political mainstream and recognition for their wartime contribution was an extraordinary reversal of fortune, and it worked to distance them from their grievances against Zanu(PF) over the 1980s repression they had endured alongside civilians. Acknowledgment and compensation for the 1980s violence was publicly discussed, but it was not acted upon. Nationalist referents were once again rooted in the 1970s. The ability of (some) Zipra guerrillas to "forget" the 1980s was the result of a number of factors. First, their 1970s leaders were now leading members of the ruling party, and they had an interest in preventing the rupture of the "unity" that served them so well. Key figures such as the former Zapu leader Joshua Nkomo, once so outspoken in their denunciation of the violence of the 1980s, were now crucial in silencing calls for redress on the grounds that it would undermine "unity" (see Werbner 1998, 96).

Second, former Zipra guerrillas knew all too well the risks of opposing Zanu(PF), risks that would now threaten not only their own lives but also those of their often recently established families. Many guerrillas had married late in life, as a result of their lengthy wartime service and subsequent persecution, or as a result of their poverty, their lack of education and jobs, and their at times unstable personal lives. They did not want to add state repression to the factors that could destabilize their fragile social relationships. Finally, a central component of Zipra veterans' identity was their claim to being soldiers, not politicians. Their emphasis on loyalty, discipline, and hierarchy (however divorced from their experience of the 1970s and 1980s) was reinforced by the making of new bonds with other veterans and with the Zanu(PF) political leadership, which now lionized fighting men as the truest exemplars of the ideals of the struggle for independence.

If Zanu(PF)'s payouts and political appeals worked for many veterans, they had far less purchase on those who could not be subsumed under the rubric of fighting men, and on those who invoked the political education that had gone hand in hand with their transformation into soldiers. Those who had been detained in the nationalist era, or who had aided guerrillas on the battlefield but had not received formal training, struggled to gain access to the privileged category "veteran." They threatened Zanu(PF)'s leaders with revelations about the illegitimate uses of violence—rape and the killing of those wrongly accused of being sellouts—in the 1970s (see Alexander, McGregor, and Ranger 2000, 256). Those former guerrillas who had fallen foul of the divisions within Zanla in the 1970s emerged as some of the most outspoken of critics, forming the Zimbabwe Liberators' Platform and using it to enunciate an alternative vision of liberation war goals that drew on long-suppressed critiques of the ruling Zanu(PF) leaders. Trade unionists angrily denounced the status accorded veterans, stressing that all had suffered in the war. For people born after independence, the "born-frees," the constant references to the liberation war held little attraction. This youthful constituency was important to the MDC,[15] but with the passage of time it was also disconcertingly effectively mobilized by Zanu(PF) through promises of jobs and indoctrination in the newly created youth militias. Among former Zipra guerrillas, the alliance with Zanu(PF) also proved to be far from straightforward as Zanu(PF)'s nationalist discourse took on new forms.

Veterans and Violence in 2000 and After

Our relationships with Zipra guerrillas date from an era when they were struggling to assert their claims on the nation and the state, when they were intent on rewriting a nationalist history that they saw as outrageously partisan and hypocritically exploited by a self-interested, violent, and corrupt leadership. In this latter goal, they were at one with a broader constituency in Matabeleland, and with the increasingly vocal nationwide criticism of the Zanu(PF) government. The context of 2000 and after was decidedly different. It transformed debates over violence, nationalism, and the state, and Zipra veterans' relationship to them. We struggled to understand the politics of this period as we revisited Matabeleland in 2000–2002: How was it that some of those with whom we had worked to document the hidden histories of the 1970s and the repression of the 1980s were now prepared to participate in the violent intolerance and partisan politics of the ruling party? Why were they willing to invoke an idea of nationalism that seemed a travesty of the one they had so recently defended?

The prominence of Zipra veterans within the veterans association and among the vocal advocates of Zanu(PF)'s "patriotism" was notable from the outset. The Zipra medical doctor, "Hitler" Hunzvi, who had been a key player in securing veterans benefits, played a central role in the publicity surrounding the "invasion" of white-owned farms. The state media followed him around the country and broadcast images of him at the head of jubilant groups of veterans, youth, and black smallholders, and in angry confrontations with white farmers. In Matabeleland North, where the occupations were slow to gather pace, for example, Hunzvi "swooped" on a ranch with a group of seventy veterans and a ZBC crew, called in to support local veterans who had been beaten by farmworkers (Alexander and McGregor 2001, 516). Evidence of the violence he and others were prepared to use on the farms, and of incidents of torture at his "surgery" in Harare, accumulated in human-rights reports.

Former dissidents were also among the most prominent and willing agents of political violence. Andrew Ndlovu, for example, threatened the violent overthrow of the MDC and the installation of a military government in the event of an opposition victory in the June 2000 elections. Placing an MDC victory in the same category as Rhodesian rule, he argued that war veterans would never allow the country to go back to Ian Smith (Kriger 2003, 197). In

Nkayi District of Matabeleland North, the former dissidents who dominated local veteran politics were associated with some of the worst violence against civilians and with the subjection of the township to a reign of intermittent terror, including the murder of a headman and others. All over Matabeleland, it was former Zipra guerrillas who headed the small groups of veterans stationed at district centers as unofficial paramilitary forces that spearheaded the expulsion of suspect teachers, nurses, and civil servants from their jobs (McGregor 2002). Veterans were everywhere central both to the violent remaking of the state as a partisan force and to the politics of patronage.

There was a class element in all this. Those who were prepared to play a key role in the Zanu(PF) alliance were disproportionately drawn from the urban and rural poor, people lacking in education and prospects. They owed the satisfaction of their "hunger" to their new role and recently acquired benefits; they relied on patronage and violence, not qualifications and experience, to gain access to civil-service, police, and other jobs. Other former guerrillas chose to have no role in party or veteran politics, opting for identities as businessmen, traders, civil servants, workers, or farmers. Zipra veterans were among those who joined the Zimbabwe Liberators' Platform; others joined the MDC; at least one worked for a prominent human-rights group, documenting the abuses of his erstwhile colleagues. However, peer pressure from veterans, with whom their relationships had been so recently renewed, and the importance for Zanu(PF) of veterans' allegiance, meant that open support for the opposition carried heavy risks. In the course of the June 2000 elections there were significant numbers of cases in which veterans who supported the MDC were aggressively targeted, abducted, and beaten by Zanu(PF)-allied veterans. In one such incident in Dete, Zanu(PF)-allied veterans, angered by the "defection" of one of their number to the MDC camp, abducted him alone among the local MDC campaign team. They took him to their camp on an occupied farm, where they argued with him at length, beating and threatening him before eventually releasing him.[16]

Former Zipra guerrillas who chose to align with the ruling party and the veterans association in 2000 were not, however, always uncritical. Many remained in the alliance despite intense unease and a long-standing hatred for the Zanu(PF) old guard. They justified their stance by stressing the importance of discipline, and of loyalty to former comrades and leaders, particularly to "Hitler" Hunzvi and former Zipra commanders in government, after Joshua Nkomo died in 1999. In Matabeleland the ruling party at the local level incorporated many of the nationalist generation of political leaders with whom they had worked in the 1970s. This long-standing association made it easy for them to speak in a shared language of nationalism and revolution, even if its meaning was hotly contested. Veterans in fact upheld notions of nationalism that both coincided with and increasingly also differed from those articulated by Zanu(PF)'s leaders. Thus, some veterans echoed their leaders in emphasizing the importance of the land issue in the struggle for liberation, or their suspicion of the "white" or "imperialist" backers of the MDC, while also stressing the illegitimacy of partisan violence and patronage politics. Some veterans issued public statements denouncing violence at party rallies, veterans' meetings, and elsewhere. In the context of the June 2000 elections, this strategy was effective in some places, depending on local politics and the status of the individuals concerned (see Alexander and McGregor 2001).

The June 2000 parliamentary elections were overwhelmingly won by the MDC almost everywhere in Matabeleland. This shocked veterans who had campaigned, violently or not, for Zanu(PF), and it sparked a brief period of reflection on nationalism and violence at a time when it was unclear how Zanu(PF) would respond. Thus, the veterans who were so crucial in campaigning for Zanu(PF) in Nkayi District issued a heated denunciation of the Zanu(PF) leadership. They returned, not to the touchstone of the liberation war, but to the violence of the 1980s in explaining why Zanu(PF) had so miserably failed to retain allegiance.[17] In doing so, they echoed local MDC activists who had campaigned so effectively by invoking Zanu(PF)'s murderous past and seeking to disentangle the "good" nationalism of Zapu from its grasp. The brief respite from violence that followed the elections provoked reflection and made some former Zipra guerrillas wonder whether they had been "used" (Alexander and McGregor 2001). This hiatus did not, however, last long; nor did it result in a significant political reorientation of war veterans, for a complex mix of reasons.

Veterans in Matabeleland did not believe that their authority and status could be rehabilitated outside of their alliance with Zanu(PF). Recognition of their standing as soldiers, legitimated by nationalism, would not come from those among whom they lived. They feared their MDC neighbors would take revenge; some had court cases brought against them, some talked of finding refuge on occupied farms. Rural MDC leaders spoke of them derisively as people who could be bought and used. Their standing was too closely tied, politically and materially, to the identity of veterans, and controlling the meaning of that identity in the face of its national mobilization on behalf of Zanu(PF) proved too great a challenge.

It also rapidly became clear that Zanu(PF)'s strategy after the elections would continue to reside in the use of violence, legitimized through reference to the liberation war and involving a thoroughgoing transformation of the bureaucratic state. Zanu(PF) leaders knew that rebuilding the party's power and control over the state would be difficult, and they turned to veterans to do the job. President Mugabe gave them a central role in the "restructuring" of the party after the elections, calling on them to "recall and employ those mobilization and organizational skills we developed and relied upon during the struggle to motivate and rouse our people," and emphasizing that, once again, "Zimbabwe is under attack" (Mugabe, n.d., 70).

The possibility of remaining in an alliance with the ruling party while keeping a distance from violence narrowed dramatically. Some veterans withdrew from a public role as they lost the ability to influence events. Others found that their efforts to control violence led to accusations that they were "sellouts" and "camouflaged" MDC supporters from youth militias and Zanu(PF) politicians. One prominent former Zipra commander was forced to flee into hiding after he tried to control the excesses of militia by arguing that their uses of violence were out of keeping with Zipra's tradition. His colleagues worriedly discussed the case, and in an indication of how dangerous any association with the opposition had become, held that he needed to be "cleared" by senior veterans before they could associate with him again.[18] Another Zipra veteran, whose immediate family members had left the country, worried that any association with MDC membership used to secure entry to the United Kingdom would be enough to provoke accusations and violent attack.[19] While some former guerrillas spoke of their discomfort with the title "veteran" because of its association with violence they deemed illegitimate, they were unwilling to leave the umbrella of Zanu(PF) for fear of becoming subject to violence themselves. Veterans were still heavily involved in political violence, but they were increasingly marginal in its direction as the security arms of the state took on an overtly partisan role.[20] Fear, rumor, and coercion silenced those voices that might have offered a critique.

Zipra veterans also found new ways to justify their continued involvement in the veterans association. As it became clear that the land occupations were not going to end, as some had believed (including some senior former Zapu and Zipra leaders in government), they argued that their continuing involvement in the process was important, though not for the reasons that Zanu(PF) leaders propounded.[21] In Ndebele-speaking Matabeleland, veterans worried that the Zanu(PF) government would seek to give the land to "Shonas." This fear was fed by the widespread circulation of a document of unknown origin that argued that Zanu(PF) had always been a party intent on Shona dominance and called for all land, including in Matabeleland, to go to Shonas. The explicit attacks on the "Ndebele" by the Fifth Brigade in the 1980s made such views all too plausible to many.[22] Thus, senior members of the veterans association justified participation in the National Land Committee on the grounds that their presence could secure land for the Ndebele. At lower levels too, veterans and others such as chiefs justified alignment with Zanu(PF) as necessary to ensuring the just redistribution of land. Zipra veterans also increasingly accommodated Zanu(PF)'s language of racial intolerance. In 2000 there had been distinct unease over the ousting of white farmers; in 2002 their rights were considered irrelevant, the question of ethnic access being more important. Asians came in for attack as well, on the grounds that they owned a disproportionate share of businesses and houses in Bulawayo. Dispossession was no longer controversial; the modalities of "repossession" were the topic of debate.[23] Zipra veterans thus entered into their own, localized versions of the patronage politics promoted by national Zanu(PF) leaders.

It was not only in relation to land that veterans justified their activity in populist terms, with lines of argument that shifted over time. Veterans legitimated their interventions in the workings of local government, labor disputes, and courts as a response to popular grievances. Just as the land occupations brought together a range of actors with diverse interests, so veterans' occupation of businesses was often in response to invitations by disgruntled workers, and was justified by reference to attempts to secure better remuneration and working conditions. In the case of the Hwange Colliery occupations in August 2001, for example, the high-profile veteran Joseph Chinotimba justified his actions on the grounds that he had been invited in by workers and was there to "represent the workers and take up their grievances."[24] Veterans justified their closure of shops in Victoria Falls by arguing that they were defending local consumers against shopkeepers' profiteering, "artificial" price increases, and preferential treatment of Zambian customers.[25] Veterans' involvement in the closure of councils was legitimated by reference to deeply felt and genuine grievances over rises in rates and taxes, corruption, and unpopular development projects (McGregor 2002). Some local veterans justified their purges of teachers, nurses, and other civil servants by including Shona speakers among those they expelled. They argued that Shonas had been given preferential access to public-sector jobs in Matabeleland, again a very widely held belief and a source of bitterness.[26] Veterans' attempts to give their actions at least the appearance of a broad popular appeal was an important aspect of the politics of this period and central to the processes by which the state itself was transformed.

From late 2001, and particularly after the presidential elections in March 2002, drought, food shortages, and hunger meant that it became, quite literally, difficult to eat without an alignment with the ruling party. This changed moral debates over the question of allegiance to Zanu(PF) in the context of the council elections and parliamentary by-elections that took place in this period. Human-rights reports documented the ruling party's use of food as a weapon. Zanu(PF) monopolized food supplies and put veterans, youth militias, and party representatives in control of its distribution at the local level. Zanu(PF)'s control over food deeply undermined the rural MDC's support base and its ability to organize.[27] Unable to provide food, or the conditions under which their supporters could buy food privately or gain access to relief food, MDC candidates were forced to encourage their supporters to vote Zanu(PF) to prevent them from starving. Power and resources, if not authority, could only come from siding with the ruling party. The former dissidents who had once been "overhungry" in their demands for food from civilians now controlled the distribution of food to a starving population. In a context in which dependence on the resources distributed by the Zanu(PF) government had become so extreme, choosing an alternative identity to that of "veteran" and an alternative politics to that of violent patronage had become too costly for many former Zipra guerrillas.

Conclusion

The realignment of Zipra veterans with Zanu(PF)'s violent patriotism drew on an image of the liberation war, an idea of nationalism, and an understanding of authority that differed profoundly from those they had articulated in the mid-1990s. The Zipra narratives of a decade ago took pride in professional training, in the new understandings of national liberation as something more than a war against whites, in the status gained from association with a liberation movement of international standing, of relationships with a civilian leadership that endeavored to contain excessive violence and prevent the politicization of soldiers. They held up Zapu's military strategy and nationalism as a moral standard from which to condemn the Zanu(PF) government's partisan and tribalist uses of violence in the 1980s. As the Zipra dissidents emphasized, and had learned to their cost, it was impossible to retain the status of soldiers without international support and the backing of a popular party.

Many former Zipra guerrillas had suffered persecution and penury since independence. The promise of recognition and compensation offered by the veterans association held, unsurprisingly, a tremendous appeal. They would have the authority and status of soldiers once again; they would finally be able to rebuild their lives. When the veterans were embraced by Zanu(PF), however, they entered a new political terrain at a time of deep social division, economic crisis, and political ferment that would transform them from "forgotten heroes" into the most central symbols of Zanu(PF)'s political legitimacy, and into its agents of violence. The willingness of some Zipra veterans to align themselves with the travesty of 1970s history propounded by Zanu(PF) meant that they too could be fêted at Heroes' Acre, as Hunzvi was on his death in 2001, but it did not gain them recognition among the people with whom they lived. Zipra veterans' alliance with Zanu(PF) was not inevitable, as shown by the many who chose not to involve themselves in Zanu(PF) politics and the moments of real reflection in 2000, but it became exceptionally difficult to avoid.

Our discussion of how Zipra guerrillas justified their path to alliance with the ruling party is not a comforting one. It is perhaps important to distinguish between those who embraced violence wholeheartedly and those who were prepared to support the alliance at a distance from the beatings, abductions, and torture. In the latter group were some of the more senior Zipra figures with whom we had worked. They remained critical of the violence, and fearful and deeply suspicious of Zanu(PF). Nonetheless, they supported the farm and other occupations, maneuvering to get what they could out of the upheavals in 2000 and after both for themselves and for a broader community. Their acceptance of the partisan politics of patronage was central to the demise of the state's civic role. Even where they did not participate directly in violence, they contributed to the narrowing of the public sphere, to the militarization and politicization of the state, and to the justification of intolerance in the name of nationalism. For others, the decision to participate in violence was rooted in a complex of social and political relationships, from obligations to kin to the loyalties of soldiers, and often became the only route away from hunger, real and symbolic. Nationalism as moral standard, as a language with which to hold the government to account, did not disappear in this context, but it was sidelined by the intolerant and violent "patriotism" of an embattled ruling party, symbolized most forcefully by the veteran.

Notes

We owe many thanks for the perceptive comments of participants in the conference, "Africa and Violence: Identities, Histories, and Representations," at Emory University, in Atlanta, 11–14 September 2003, where this paper was first presented. The thoughts of Fred Cooper and Luise White in particular have enlivened our revisions.

1. See Zimbabwe Human Rights NGO Forum 2003. In February 2003, for example, Zimbabwe Republic Police officers appeared to be the principal perpetrators of human-rights abuses. Of course, some veterans have been absorbed into the police, at times in high-ranking positions. From 2000 to 2002 it was useful for the Zanu(PF) government to appear to be responding to veterans, construed as a popular pressure group, rather than for it to be seen to be directing political violence and land occupations. The need to rely ever more heavily on violence and coercion has, it seems, made a quasi-independent

group with its own interests less useful than the formally constituted (and now highly partisan) coercive arms of the state or the more dependent youth militias. The International Crisis Group (2003, 1) considers the patronage links that tie guerrillas and youth militias to the state to have broken down, thus increasing competition between them and exacerbating divisions within the veterans' organization.

2. A collection of President Mugabe's speeches outlining the Third Chimurenga and Zanu(PF)'s political struggle and history in a highly distorted way was used for the purposes of "educating" youth militia. See Mugabe, n.d.

3. On the violence of the 1980s and its legacies, see Alexander, McGregor, and Ranger 2000, chap. 11. The 1980s violence was explored through journalistic investigation from the late 1980s and in an extraordinarily meticulous human-rights report published in Zimbabwe in 1997 (Catholic Commission for Justice and Peace / Legal Resources Foundation 1997).

4. White draws on the important work of Christopher Browning (1998) in making this point.

5. On the earlier history of state and NGO assistance to demobilized guerrillas of the early 1980s, see Kriger 2003, 141–80.

6. See, e.g., interviews, Davison Ndlovu, 17 February 1996, and Robert Zenzo Ncube, February 1995. The former Zipra guerrillas who wrote autobiographies for us or whom we and our co-researchers interviewed in the mid-1990s are referred to by their war names and the date of the interview or autobiography only so as to retain anonymity. For detailed discussions of these sources see Alexander and McGregor 2004; and Alexander, McGregor, and Ranger 2000.

7. Interview, Patson Sikhumbuzo, 28 February 1995.

8. Nkomo 1996, 15; interviews, Melusi Ncube and Cohen Tsambani, 17 February 1996.

9. See Alexander, McGregor, and Ranger 2000, chap. 7. The killing of sellouts and witches, so central to civilian debates over the morality of violence, went entirely unmentioned by guerrillas save in reference to cases in which such killings had become a threat to military discipline and efficacy. See McGregor 1999.

10. Autobiography, Mjoni Mkandla, 18 January 1995, 14.

11. Interview, Gertrude Moyo, 17 February 1995.

12. See, e.g., autobiography of Mawhobo Sibindi, 27 November 1995.

13. Interview, Langford Ndiweni, 10 October 1995.

14. We witnessed these processes while carrying out our fieldwork.

15. Many commentators on the elections have pointed to a generational divide. One mother explained: "The younger generation don't care about the struggle—what father tells his family that each time they drink tea, the children should say 'thank you' and remember that he went out to work? The younger generation are grateful, 'yes, yes you did a good job, but do I have to say so every day?' Born-frees don't care, they want jobs and want to look forwards." Interview, Hwange, 22 July 2000.

16. Discussions with MDC supporters and ZNLWVA officer, Dete Kamativi, 22 and 25 July 2000.

17. See Nkayi District Zanu(PF) Committee 2000, authored by a Zipra veteran.

18. Discussion with former Zipra guerrillas, Bulawayo, August 2002.

19. Discussion with former Zipra commander, Bulawayo, August 2001, and with family members in the United Kingdom on various occasions in 2002.

20. Discussion with former Zipra guerrillas, Bulawayo, August 2002.

21. For an introduction to the politics of land in this period, see Alexander 2003; and Hammar and Raftopoulos 2003.

22. See Progress Review on the 1979 Grand Plan, n.d. This document was familiar to, and heatedly discussed by, people all over Matabeleland.

23. Discussions with former Zipra commanders, Bulawayo and Kezi, 2000 and 2002.

24. Interviews, colliery workers, Hwange, August 2001. Chinotimba's intervention came in the middle of negotiations between management and labor representatives (whom Chinotimba sidelined and tried unsuccessfully to expel), thus dividing the workers and undermining their previously strong bargaining position. A range of accusations, including from the workers who had invited Chinotimba, followed amidst suspicions that the colliery managers had themselves orchestrated veterans' interventions.

25. Interviews, Victoria Falls residents, August 2001.

26. See reports in the regional newspaper, *Indonsakusa Ilanga,* 30 March–12 April 2001; and McGregor 2002.

27. See Zimbabwe Human Rights NGO Forum 2002.

References

Alexander, Jocelyn. 1998. Dissident Perspectives on Zimbabwe's Post-independence War. *Africa* 68 (2): 151–82.

———. 2003. "Squatters," Veterans, and the State in Zimbabwe. In *Zimbabwe's Unfinished Business: Rethinking Land, State, and Nation in the Context of Crisis,* edited by Amanda Hammar, Brian Raftopoulos, and Stig Jensen, 83–118. Harare: Weaver Press.

Alexander, Jocelyn, and JoAnn McGregor. 2001. Elections, Land, and the Politics of Opposition in Matabeleland. *Journal of Agrarian Change* 1 (4): 510–33.

———. 2004. War Stories: Guerrilla Narratives of Zimbabwe's Liberation War. *History Workshop Journal* 57 (1): 79–100.

———. 2005. Hunger, Violence, and the Moral Economy of War in Zimbabwe. In *Violence and Belonging: The Quest for Identity in Post-colonial Africa,* edited by Vigdis Broch-Due, 75–90. London: Routledge.

Alexander, Jocelyn, JoAnn McGregor, and Terence Ranger. 2000. *Violence and Memory: One Hundred Years in the "Dark Forests" of Matabeleland.* Oxford: James Currey.

Browning, Christopher. 1998. *Ordinary Men: Reserve Police Battalion 101 and the Final Solution in Poland.* New York: Harper Perennial.

Catholic Commission for Justice and Peace / Legal Resources Foundation. 1997. *Breaking the Silence, Building True Peace: A Report on the Disturbances in Matabeleland and the Midlands, 1980 to 1988.* Harare.

Hammar, Amanda, and Brian Raftopoulos. 2003. Zimbabwe's Unfinished Business: Rethinking Land, State, and Nation. In *Zimbabwe's Unfinished Business: Rethinking Land, State, and Nation in the Context of Crisis,* edited by Amanda Hammar, Brian Raftopoulos, and Stig Jensen, 1–48. Harare: Weaver Press.

International Crisis Group. 2003. *Zimbabwe: Danger and Opportunity.* Brussels.

Kriger, Norma. 1995. The Politics of Creating National Heroes: The Search for Political Legitimacy and National Identity. In *Soldiers in Zimbabwe's Liberation War,* edited by Terence Ranger and Ngwabi Bhebe, 139–62. London: James Currey.

———. 2002. Political Constructions of War Veterans. Paper presented at the annual meeting of the African Studies Association, Washington, DC, December.

———. 2003. *Guerrilla Veterans in Post-war Zimbabwe: Symbolic and Violent Politics, 1980–1987.* Cambridge: Cambridge University Press.

McGregor, JoAnn. 1999. Containing Violence: Poisoning and Guerrilla/Civilian Relations in Memories of Zimbabwe's Liberation War. In *Trauma and Life Stories,* edited by K. Lacy Rogers and S. Leydesdorff, 131–59. London: Routledge.

———. 2002. The Politics of Disruption: War Veterans and the Local State. *African Affairs* 101 (402): 9–37.

Mugabe, Robert Gabriel. N.d. Inside the Third Chimurenga. Manuscript.

Nkayi District Zanu(PF) Committee. 2000. Zimbabwe's Elections—Yr. 2000. Post-Mortem Roundup. Manuscript.

Nkomo, Nicholas. 1996. Between the Hammer and the Anvil: The Autobiography of Nicholas Nkomo. Manuscript.

Progress Review on the 1979 Grand Plan. N.d. Photocopy.

Raftopoulos, Brian. 2003. The State in Crisis: Authoritarian Nationalism, Selective Citizenship, and Distortions of Democracy in Zimbabwe. In *Zimbabwe's Unfinished Business: Rethinking Land, State, and Nation in the Context of Crisis,* edited by Amanda Hammar, Brian Raftopoulos, and Stig Jensen, 217–42. Harare: Weaver Press.

Ranger, Terence. 2004a. Nationalist Historiography, Patriotic History, and the History of the Nation: The Struggle over the Past in Zimbabwe. *Journal of Southern African Studies* 30 (2): 215–34.

———. 2004b. The Politics of War Veterans. Review of *Guerrilla Veterans in Post-war Zimbabwe: Symbolic and Violent Politics, 1980–1987,* by Norma Kriger. *Journal of African History* 45 (1):165–66.

Werbner, Richard. 1998. Smoke from the Barrel of a Gun: Postwars of the Dead, Memory, and Reinscription in Zimbabwe. In *Memory and the Postcolony,* edited by Richard Werbner, 71–102. London: Zed Books.

White, Luise. 2003. *The Assassination of Herbert Chitepo: Texts and Politics in Zimbabwe.* Bloomington: Indiana University Press.

Zimbabwe Human Rights NGO Forum. 2002. Vote ZANU (PF) or Starve. Harare.

———. 2003. Monthly Reports. www.hrforumzim.com.

Memory and Violence in Postgenocide Rwanda

**Timothy Longman and
Théoneste Rutagengwa**

> Do you think that I could truly forget? When I sleep or when I am awake,
> I think of it. I and the rest of the population have felt the weight and
> consequences of this destructive war.
> —Hutu man, Butare, Rwanda, 8 September 2001

> If you do not forget, you cannot forgive. That is my opinion.
> What has happened has happened. It is necessary to move on.
> —Hutu woman, Byumba, Rwanda, 27 March 2002

IN societies seeking to rebuild after mass atrocity, collective memories of violence pose a major obstacle to reconciling divided populations and constructing a durable peace. Memories of persecution and suffering sustain group identities and, after festering for years or even decades, can become a basis for future violence. Memories may retain their power even as they are passed down from one generation to the next (Danieli 1998). In Yugoslavia, for example, the collective Serbian memory of defeat at the hands of the Ottoman Empire in the fourteenth century remained an important part of the narrative of national identity and served to justify violence against Bosnian and Kosovar Albanian Muslims in the twentieth century (Sells 1996).

Yet the nature of collective memory is not predetermined. Memories are not mere accurate recollections of past incidents but, particularly in reference to major public events, socially constructed. As Maurice Halbwachs, who coined the phrase *collective memory,* argued more than fifty years ago, "It is in society that people normally acquire memories. It is also in society that they recall, recognize, and localize their memories" (Halbwachs 1992, 38). Liisa Malkki has compellingly demonstrated through her study of collective memory among Burundian Hutu refugees in Tanzania that social contexts greatly affect how memories are constructed and retained (Malkki 1995). While in a setting such as a refugee camp memories of persecution may remain intense and inspire people to support continued violence, in other settings, such as among refugees integrated into local communities, memories may dissipate. Hence, how collective memory is constructed following violent events has a major impact on the likelihood that violence will recur in the future.[1]

The war and genocide that shook Rwanda in 1994 represent the most intense violent conflict to have swept across an African state in recorded history. From April to July, between 500,000 and 800,000 people, mostly members of the Tutsi minority group, died in the genocide,[2] while the civil war between government forces and the Rwandan Patriotic Front (RPF) killed tens of thousands more civilians and drove nearly four million of the country's inhabitants from their homes, including two million who sought exile in neighboring countries. Thousands more civilians died in RPF attacks on refugee camps in Zaire in 1996.[3]

Any government taking power after such extensive disorder and violence would face the difficult task of restoring order and preventing future outbreaks of violence, but the RPF found itself in a particularly challenging position when it took over Rwanda in July 1994. As a rebel movement that took power through military victory and that was dominated by and identified with a Tutsi minority that constituted at most 15 percent of the population, the RPF faced a population that was potentially hostile to its authority. The former regime had organized popular support for the genocide by appealing to a collective memory of the colonial and precolonial era that depicted the Tutsi as foreign conquerors who dominated the country and exploited the Hutu majority, and it claimed that the RPF was seeking to reestablish Tutsi dominance.[4]

Seeking to broaden its popular appeal, the RPF created a Government of National Unity, which included representatives of predominately Hutu political parties, and ministerial positions were divided almost evenly between Hutu and Tutsi. The government has also sought to reshape collective memory both of Rwanda's past and of recent events, using trials, public addresses, commemorations and memorialization, school programs, reeducation camps, and changes in the national symbols. By reshaping the popular understandings of the past, the government hopes to change how Rwandans understand themselves as a nation, creating a new unified national identity that will prevent future outbreaks of ethnic violence.

While seeking to promote national unity, the RPF has also sought to secure its own authority, and this latter goal has sometimes contradicted and undermined the former. The RPF's official narrative of the past glosses over historical conflicts and exploitation and whitewashes the RPF's own violent acts. This violence—not simply the arrest of thousands under suspicion of involvement in the genocide and military operations in Rwanda and neighboring Democratic Republic of Congo (formerly Zaire), but ongoing repression of those who criticize the government—continues to create political tensions and to divide the country. As the regime becomes entrenched in power, its efforts to shape collective memory appear to many Rwandans to be cynical attempts to gain the quiescence of the population.

In this essay, we analyze how the competing goals of the RPF-dominated regime are playing themselves out within the Rwandan population. We studied three local communities over the two-year period 2001–03, using a variety of research methods to understand how the population was responding to the government's social policies. Our particular focus here is the discourses of memory and their impact on social identities.

The Research Project

In order to understand the official historical narrative, during the period of our research we monitored the local and international press, including the radio, for speeches, official statements, laws passed, and other official declarations, and we have gathered government reports and publications and other documentation that provides indications of the official interpretations of Rwanda's past. We also conducted interviews with numerous government, political-party, and civil-society officials, including representatives from the Ministries of Local Government and Administration; Internal Security; Foreign Affairs; Youth, Sports, and Culture; Education, and Finance; as well as the attorney general; members of the Supreme Court; the heads of the Electoral, Constitutional Reform, and Legal Reform Commissions; leaders of the Rwandan Patriotic Front, the Rwandan Democratic Movement, the Social Democratic Party, and the Christian Democratic Party; representatives of the National Unity and Reconciliation and Human Rights Commissions; Catholic, Protestant, and Muslim religious leaders; and leaders of groups for human rights, economic development, genocide survivors, the Twa minority, women, and youth.

In addition to this national-level research, we conducted local case studies in three communities that represent several of the important vectors of diversity in Rwandan society. Although an administrative reform in early 2001 created new local-government units known as districts, we chose to work with the units that had been in place at the time of the genocide, known as communes.[5] We chose to do this both because the political organization of the districts remained in flux throughout the period of our research and because the genocide was organized by commune. The three communes reflect Rwanda's diversity according to region, level of urbanization, ethnic distribution, and experience in the genocide and after. Ngoma, the commune for Butare, Rwanda's second largest city and home to the national university, is located in the south of the country and has a comparatively large Tutsi population. Our other two case studies were in rural communes: Mabanza, in the central-western prefecture of Kibuye, and Buyoga, in the northern prefecture of Byumba. These three communes experienced the violence in 1994 in distinct ways. Since much of Buyoga was in the demilitarized zone that fell rapidly under RPF control, only a few sectors experienced genocide, but there were extensive massacres carried out by the RPF. Ngoma (Butare) experienced both the genocide and postgenocide massacres and revenge killings, while Mabanza experienced the genocide, but as part of the French-controlled Zone Turquoise, few massacres or revenge killings.

In each of these communes we employed a range of data-collection methods. Focusing on a selection of sectors within the communes,[6] we carried out intensive interviews with 25–35 individuals in each community, and we conducted focus-group interviews with genocide survivors, women, youths (aged 18–30), and older adults (55 and older) in each commune.[7] A total of 104 individuals participated in the focus groups. We also conducted a survey of 2,091 individuals in these three communes (plus one additional commune, Mutura, in the north), with at least 500 surveyed in each community.[8] A project on the role of schools in social reconstruction studied schools either in these communes or in neighboring communes in the same provinces. Finally, we carried out ethnographic observation in each community, including visits to genocide memorials and massacre sites and observation of *gacaca* courts, a new system of local justice, and of elections.

The study was limited in several ways. Since the research covered only three communes, the study obviously has certain geographic limitations, but we felt it important to have greater depth in our research, and the communes were selected to represent the most important vectors of Rwandan social diversity. The political climate in Rwanda at the time of the research created the greatest limitations for the study. The topics discussed were politically sensitive, and although Rwanda has made some important advances toward the development of a democratic political system, civil liberties remain seriously restricted and politically motivated violence continues to stifle free expression. Hence, participants in both the interviews and the focus groups demonstrated some reluctance to speak frankly. Nevertheless, the diversity of methodologies used and the fact that activities were carried out by several research teams created a wealth of data that helped to correct for the politically sensitive nature of the topics discussed.

The Official Narrative of Memory

The official interpretation of Rwanda's past promoted by the government is rooted in an understanding of Rwanda's history developed among Tutsi living as refugees outside Rwanda prior to 1994. Government officials frequently bring this interpretation into their speeches, and it informs the establishment of memorials and commemorations. This historical narrative can also be found in a growing number of government documents and locally published academic journals, such as the journal *Cahiers lumière et société,* published by the Dominican Center, produced by a group of returned refugees occupying university, government, and religious posts in Rwanda who have undertaken the project of reinterpreting and rewriting Rwanda's history.

According to the official historical interpretation, the 1994 genocide cannot be understood without looking at Rwanda's colonial experience. In this narrative, Rwandan society was essentially unified before the arrival of colonial rulers. The categories Hutu, Tutsi, and Twa had limited social significance, representing mere occupational divisions. The three groups were unified by religion, language, multiethnic clan membership, and the unifying influence of the king; conflicts that arose within the Rwandan kingdom reflected other lines of social demarcation, such as clan. A presidential commission made up of both politicians and intellectuals that was part of a series of discussions on Rwanda's future produced a report titled *The Unity of Rwandans.* According to the report, "The King was the crux for all Rwandans. . . . After he was enthroned, people said that 'he was no umututsi anymore,' but the King for the people. . . . In the programme of expanding Rwanda, there was no room for disputes between Hutus, Tutsi and Twas. The King brought all of them together" (Office of the President of the Republic 1999, 6). Similarly, in an article titled "The Family as the Principle of Coherence in Traditional Rwandan Society," Déogratias Byanafashe writes of the consolidation of the state of Rwanda under the Nyiginga dynasty,

The result of this centralism and this uniformization of the management of the country was a consciousness of the population's unity. "One king, one law, one people," that was Rwanda in this precolonial "nyiginya" period. This step of development of the country was the supreme realization of Rwanda as a family whose members were named the Rwandans or Rwandan people. In fact, it required the recent colonial intervention to break this people into three sections called "ethnicities." (1997, 20, trans. Timothy Longman)

According to the official narrative, the divisions imposed on Rwanda by colonial rule were the root cause of the genocide. Colonial rule and the Catholic Church divided Rwanda's population and transformed Hutu, Tutsi, and Twa into ethnic identities. The attacks that took place in 1959 and began the exodus of Tutsi into exile were not a "revolution," as claimed by previous regimes, but represented the beginning of genocide in Rwanda, and they are directly attributable to the cynical manipulations of Catholic missionaries and colonial administrators who wanted to guarantee their continued influence even after formal independence.[9] The postcolonial governments continued to use ethnicity as a wedge, falsely teaching that Tutsi were foreign invaders who had always subjugated and exploited the Hutu majority. These false teachings created hatred of the Tutsi among the Hutu, who came to view Tutsi as less human and less deserving of basic rights. At the same time, the authoritarian regimes encouraged obedience and docility from the population. This combination of an ideology that fostered ethnic hatred and an obedient population was key to the genocide.[10] The genocide itself is the defining event in the history of Rwanda and represents the culmination of the failed policies of international exploitation, ethnic division, and authoritarian government.

Given this interpretation of Rwandan history and the sources of genocide, reconciliation requires the country to "recover national unity" that existed in precolonial Rwanda. People should reject the myth of ethnicity and instead put "Rwandan citizenship first" (Office of the President of the Republic 1999, 64, 63). Reconciliation also requires the development of a democratic political culture, so that people will think independently and be resistant to irresponsible leaders who want to manipulate them to undertake future ethnic violence. The Rwandan people need to develop "respect of human rights" (Office of the President of the Republic 1999, 63), which requires the population to take responsibility for their actions during the genocide and to judge those who participated in atrocities in order to fight impunity.

The government has used a variety of methods to promote these ideas. Solidarity camps, called *ingando,* are intensive reeducation programs that politicians, entering university students, returned refugees, and released prisoners, among others, have been required to attend for one to three months. In addition to providing paramilitary training, the camps spend much time discussing Rwandan history and the genocide, as participants are led to embrace the government interpretation of the past. Memorials and commemorations are used to preserve the memory of the genocide and to show the dangerous results of ethnic divisions. At a number of massacre sites, bodies of victims have been left exposed, either in the rooms where the massacres took place or in semienclosed tombs. Each year, on 7 April, a national gathering is held at one of these sites, at which the president and other dignitaries speak about the genocide and how to avoid similar tragedies in the future. An annual national Day of Heroes highlights courageous individuals, primarily those who have fought ethnic division. Both national trials and the new *gacaca* courts are important tools for asserting the reprehensibility of the genocide and demonstrating that persecuting Tutsi has negative consequences.[11] In 2001 the government adopted a new flag, a new anthem, and a new seal, claiming that the old national symbols had associations with the genocide and the new symbols could mark a break with the past.[12]

Contradictory Messages

While the desires to promote national unity and foster responsible citizenship have motivated many government policies, other interests have tempered the government's social agenda. The RPF leaders have a strong desire to hold onto power, driven by a well-developed sense of their own moral rectitude and right to rule, and a lingering distrust of the population. This pushes them to maintain tight control on the political system even as they create limited democratic openings. They see themselves as enlightened leaders who liberated Rwanda from tyranny and ended the genocide and regard criticism and disagreement as indicators of a lack of political maturity and continuing "divisionist" ethic. While supporting free political choice in principle, the regime does not yet have confidence in the population. In practice, the only way the population can demonstrate its readiness for democracy is to choose the RPF. Even articulating a different vision for the country's future becomes evidence of political irresponsibility and continued divisiveness. These concerns lead the government to continue to use considerable political repression and to retain tight control on the inner circles of power, even as they talk about democracy and civil rights and maintain a government that appears diverse on the surface.[13]

The government is particularly sensitive to implications that it is guilty of human-rights abuses or that it is discriminatory. Although abundant evidence implicates the RPF for carrying out massacres as it advanced across Rwanda in 1994, after taking power, and in its two military incursions in Congo,[14] the government vociferously rejects any suggestion that it has engaged in systematic human-rights abuses. Government officials claim that any abuses their troops may have engaged in were in opposition to official policy, were not systematic, and have been dealt with already by the RPF, so they have no moral equivalency to the genocide.[15] While the government maintains numerous genocide memorial sites, there is not a single site commemorating the victims of RPF massacres, though research clearly indicates that tens of thousands of people were killed in such attacks. Officials rarely, if ever, refer to massacres in their speeches, and very few cases of involvement in massacres have been tried. The *gacaca* courts are expressly forbidden from treating cases of human-rights abuses by the RPF or its supporters. In addition, those who criticize the RPF for its own record of exclusion are brutally silenced. For example, former president Pasteur Bizimungu was harassed and then arrested after he criticized the RPF for being the cabal of a small minority and formed a new political party that he claimed would be truly inclusive (International Crisis Group 2002, 11–12). In 2003, during the runup to presidential and parliamentary elections, the government targeted the largest and most viable opposition party, the Democratic Republican Movement (MDR), for being "divisionist," effectively preventing it from posing a real political challenge (Human Rights Watch 2003). The RPF seeks to enforce consensus on civil and political society, even where real consensus does not exist, which unintentionally may contribute to greater division and contradict the party's own assertions about how to avoid future violence.

Popular Narratives of Memory

While the RPF-dominated government has a clear idea of how it wants the population to understand the Rwandan past, this agenda is challenged both by contradictions in the RPF's own program and by the experience of the population, which does not always coincide with the official interpretation. Since the RPF is plainly invoking Rwanda's history selectively and with obvious political intent, Rwanda presents an interesting case study of the limits of a government's ability to shape the collective memory of a population. In our individual and focus-group interviews, we asked people about their understanding of Rwandan history and their perspectives on the war and genocide, both in their community and at the national level. By employing a variety of research methods, we developed a good sense of how the populations in the three communities we studied interpret Rwandan history, the genocide, and the way to achieve reconciliation.

Rwandan History

A detailed account of Rwandan historiography is beyond the scope of this chapter. It is important to note, however, that the account of Rwanda's past offered by most specialists in Rwandan history differs substantially not only from the history taught by those in power prior to 1994 but also from the version of history promulgated by the current regime and its supporters. The pre-1994 governments taught a version of history developed during the colonial era that claimed that the Twa, Hutu, and Tutsi were distinct racial groups that had migrated into Rwanda at different times.[16] Although this account was discredited by extensive scholarship,[17] the idea that the Tutsi were foreign invaders who had conquered Rwanda several centuries earlier and had since oppressed and exploited the larger Hutu population was a key element in the ideology used to promote the genocide, as organizers of the genocide claimed that the invading RPF sought to reestablish Hutu servitude.[18]

Yet the account of history promulgated by the current regime and its supporters also differs substantially from the view shared by most historians. These differences suggest the degree to which current interpretations of the Rwandan past are also being shaped by ideology, albeit an ideology that may be intended to promote national unity rather than division. For example, the current regime argues that Rwanda was historically unified and that ethnic divisions emerged during colonial rule, yet substantial evidence challenges the idea of the essential unity of precolonial Rwanda.[19] Very few scholars would support the idea that Rwanda represented a nation-state, however, given the diversity of regional and other identities and the complexity of political arrangements.[20] On ethnicity, the scholarly community is more divided. Nearly all scholars agree that the meaning of Hutu and Tutsi as social categories changed during the colonial period, but many scholars reject the idea that colonial rulers "created" ethnic categories. Catharine Newbury, for example, has demonstrated how the last precolonial regime used ethnic differentiation as a means of dividing and dominating the population of regions being integrated into the Rwandan kingdom (1988), while Jan Vansina, the dean of Rwandan historians, goes so far to assert that armed conflicts in the late precolonial period took on an ethnic character (2001). As Timothy Longman has argued elsewhere, the key impact of colonial rule on identities in Rwanda was to racialize them and remove their mutability (Longman 2001).

Despite the contested nature of the historical account currently being promoted, we found that the population was remarkably familiar with this official narrative. In response to questions about their impressions of Rwandan history and of the development of ethnic conflict, research subjects overwhelmingly reported that Rwandans, historically, had been unified, and that it was colonial rule that had created the divisions. A man in Kibuye reported that he had heard the country's leaders talk about the past. "They say that before the colonization of Rwanda, the people were unified . . . and that this changed with the arrival of missionaries and colonialists who pulled the people away from the king, and the problems began from there."[21] An elderly man in Butare told us:

Everything began in the colonial period with the introduction by the Belgians of identity booklets called during the time "amabuku." Before no one officially distinguished between the ethnicities. Humanity and integrity was at heart and each person could have it. The king could offer goods to everyone without any distinction and without taking into account membership in an ethnic group. Also the situation changed with the inauguration of political parties in 1959–1962 after the death of King Rudahigwa.[22]

A Tutsi man, a former refugee, offered a similar analysis of colonial rule:

I hear it said that everything began with the arrival of the whites, above all the Belgians. They created division between King Musinga and the population. They divided the population to dominate them. It is thus that the ethnic criteria were defined, saying that there were those who were born to rule, in favor of the Tutsi at first then turning toward the Hutu, telling them that they were dominated by the Tutsi.[23]

Although respondents were almost universally familiar with the official narrative of Rwanda's past, many also questioned the development of a new official narrative. Many expressed skepticism about the ways in which history has been interpreted and manipulated by those in power. One man in Byumba told us:

I deplore the tendency that there is to want to re-write history, because this revision could generate other conflicts over misunderstandings and interpretations. . . . I would like [to teach my children about history] but the problem is that the official version differs from my own beliefs. For example, officially they say there are no more ethnic groups in Rwanda. I myself want my children to know how to identify themselves according to their ethnicity in relationship to others but above all to respect others.[24]

When asked about the teaching of history in schools, a young man in Butare expressed his frustration at attempts by both sides in Rwanda's conflicts to manipulate history:

Personally I think that there have been some gaps, because the version [of history taught in class] depended on the ethnicity of the professor. You would say that there is no true history! That which used to be good is considered bad today. We need a true history and unbiased. Whatever its version, it is our history and we ought to accept it as such and not put ourselves to transforming it from one day to the next.[25]

In our survey, 49.2 percent of respondents agreed or strongly agreed with the statement, "Whoever is in power rewrites Rwandan history to serve their own interests"; only 21.7 percent disagreed or strongly disagreed.

Furthermore, only a minority of respondents volunteered historical explanations for the genocide unless asked specifically about history and ethnicity. While politicians regard the genocide as deeply rooted in Rwandan history, our respondents were more likely to blame the genocide on immediate causes, such as bad politicians and greed. This divergence may be explained in part by the different attitudes toward the role of ideology. While the current regime sees ideology as a key factor that inspired popular participation in the genocide, a majority of the people we interviewed saw the genocide as an affair more of the elite, with people participating primarily out of fear and ignorance. Those we interviewed generally agreed that the previous regime had taught a biased version of history that encouraged ethnic hatred and division, but they did not volunteer this as a major cause of the genocide.

The War and Genocide

In our interviews and focus groups, we asked about the specific events that had taken place at both the community and the national level. We found a substantial difference between the discourse used to discuss these events by genocide survivors and that used by others, particularly Hutu. For example, when we asked, "Can you explain in your own words what happened in Rwanda in 1994?" survivors almost universally invoked the Kinyarwanda phrase that the government and survivors' organizations have adopted for genocide, *itsemba bwoko,* literally "to decimate an ethnic group," an expression that did not exist in Kinyarwanda prior to 1994. Hutu were more likely to refer to *intambara* (war), *ubwicanyi* (killings), or, more vaguely, *ibyabaye* (happenings) or *amahano* (horror, tragedy). Some Hutu did employ the term *itsemba bwoko,* but many used it only secondarily. In addition, some Hutu spoke of *itsemba tsemba* (massacres), a term that very few Tutsi, whether survivors or repatriated refugees, mentioned. The language of most interviewees indicated awareness of the official explanation of events. One man's response is typical: "They've said that it was a genocide and massacres, so I call it like that as well."[26]

While the official genocide discourse emphasizes the mass nature of the violence, people in the three communities we studied interpreted the violence as an affair of the elite, particularly national leaders, while deemphasizing the role of popular participation. Political explanations for the violence were most common. Many respondents discussed the greed for power and wealth and the desire of those in power to keep their positions. A man in Butare said that the genocide was caused by "the desire to monopolize all wealth and the struggle for power." Many people mentioned the expansion of political-party activity in the 1990–94 period as something that had divided the country and created instability. For example, one young man in Butare explained, "It all got worse with multiparty politics. Then the different members of the political parties confronted each other often and in most cases, this had an ethnic connotation. They said that there were parties of Hutu and those of Tutsi fanatics of the RPF who were in war against the Habyarimana regime."[27]

Many other respondents mentioned the RPF and its attempt to reenter Rwanda as a cause for the genocide. For example, a young man in Butare said that "the principal cause of the genocide was the refusal by those in power at the time for the former refugees to return to their country."[28] While this response may seem innocent enough, the official discourse does not relate the genocide to the RPF and its attack on Rwanda. The suggestion that the RPF's actions might have contributed to the genocide in any way is highly politically charged, and most respondents approached such interpretations delicately. A young man in Kibuye, for example, explained:

What happened in Rwanda in 1994 was nothing other than a genocide. This genocide was undertaken and nourished as a part of the war of 1990 which divided the Rwandan political class of which one part did not want to hear talk of the peaceful return of those who had attacked Rwanda. There was at the same time this multiparty politics that was aborted and confounded with rivalries between ethnic groups.[29]

A young woman in Byumba similarly explained the source of the genocide as "the thirst for power on one side and the will to return to the country on the side of the RPF."[30]

When discussing their own communities, respondents almost universally said that the violence initially had come from elsewhere. In Butare, people claimed that the violence had begun with the arrival of presidential-guard troops and the intervention of interim president Sindikubwabo or with attacks by people from neighboring Gikongoro Prefecture. In Mabanza, people insisted that there had not been militia training in Mabanza and claimed that local violence had begun with attacks by militia groups from other communes. People attributed the violence to the Bakiga, whose name means "People from the North," a term used derisively to refer to unsophisticated mountain folk, in this case, to people from the Ramba and Gaseke communes in President Habyarimana's home prefecture Gisenyi, and from Rutsiro, the Kibuye commune bordering it. For example, people in the community of Rubengera reported that the violence had begun with attacks by pillaging groups that drove Hutu and Tutsi alike from their homes.[31] In Buyoga, people claimed that it was soldiers fleeing from the RPF's advance on the town of Byumba that had brought the violence into their commune.[32] Genocide survivors sometimes spoke about the violence as beginning with anti-Tutsi massacres in 1959, 1963, and 1973, while most Hutu asserted that ethnic relations had been peaceful in their communities prior to 1994, or at least prior to 1990, and that only the intervention of outside forces had led to violence.

While portraying the violence as organized by national elites and initiated by outside groups, most people we interviewed did not deny that people in their communities ultimately had participated in the genocide, but the degree to which they held the local population responsible varied. Genocide survivors were more likely to emphasize local participation and to hold the local population responsible, as an exchange in one of our focus groups demonstrates. A Hutu man claimed, "The fact that the situation went on for two months made it so that some people from Rubengera [Mabanza], weak in spirit, of course, in the end were implicated in the massacres. But the population at the beginning refused to give into temptations." And a Tutsi genocide survivor responded: "I find, all the same, that we should not minimize too much the role played by the local population in the massacres. There was also a certain complicity evident on the part of some people, because the killers from, for example, Gisenyi or Rutsiro couldn't have known the Tutsi in Gacaca Sector if people hadn't served to indicate. That is a sign of the previous existence of a certain mistrust or interethnic hatred in Rubengera."[33]

Many respondents blamed popular participation on simple "evil" or "meanness." Others said that the ignorance of the population had allowed them to be misled by corrupt authorities. Interviewees also claimed that many had been intimidated by the authorities into participating, for fear of being labeled *ibiyitso* (accomplices). A number of people mentioned the radio as an important influence,[34] and some people mentioned the role of displaced persons, fleeing the advance of the RPF, who had spread rumors about the RPF attacks or had played the leading role in organizing attacks. People also identified greed and poverty as major factors driving participation. A woman in Butare asserted, "It was the search for riches. Those who killed had need of the property of the victims."[35] Significantly, however, few people mentioned hatred of Tutsi as a cause for the genocide. Consistent with the claim that ethnic relations had been good prior to the genocide, Hutu in particular tended to attribute the anti-Tutsi violence to nonideological causes.

Justice, Commemoration, and Reconciliation

The people in communities we studied were nearly unanimous in the perception that Rwanda needs reconciliation, and they generally shared a common understanding of the meaning of reconciliation. They disagreed sharply, however, on how reconciliation might be achieved. While nearly everyone agreed on the need to judge those who had participated in the violence and on the need for those who had committed offenses to admit their errors and receive forgiveness, they differed over how these practices should be operationalized. Furthermore, people disagreed about the effect of commemoration and memorialization, and on the need to change the flag, the national anthem, and the national seal.

As one older man told us, "Reconciliation is part of Rwandan culture. It is for forgetting the wrong committed or suffered. Without this, Rwandans will arrive at nothing."[36] The word for reconciliation in Kinyarwanda is *ubwiyunge,* which comes from the same root as that for the word meaning "to set a broken bone," and this Rwandan concept of bringing together people whose relations have been ruptured was widely shared among the people we interviewed. As one survivor in Kibuye explained, "Reconciliation is the fact that those who did wrong ask forgiveness from those whom they offended, and thus the two parties renew their social relations as before."[37] A Hutu man in Byumba offered a similar assessment, saying that reconciliation was "speaking the truth, recognizing responsibilities in public, confessing and asking for forgiveness, and above all to be able also to benefit from this forgiveness. Because it is not enough only to ask; it is necessary to receive forgiveness in return. Otherwise, it is frustrating."[38] People understand reconciliation to mean bringing together the victims and the victimizers in order to rebuild community.

While there is general agreement on the concept of reconciliation, there are subtle differences in how Tutsi survivors and Hutu understand the means of bringing people together. For survivors, admitting the wrong done and asking forgiveness is essential. Some genocide survivors expressed concern that they are being called upon to simply offer forgiveness, without first being asked to do so by their victimizers:

The problem is that they ask us for reconciliation. It is true that it is necessary, because we can't continue with cyclical massacres. But you feel bad when you see those who killed your family strolling around with impunity. I say this, because it is the case for me. I lost all my family in the genocide. My home was destroyed, and I live badly. But I feel bad when I know that the author of all this lives in Kigali. I know that [when he visits] he arrives at night and leaves early the next day [to avoid arrest]. How can I reconcile with him when he doesn't come to ask my forgiveness or at least to reimburse my goods that he destroyed?[39]

For many survivors, the role of judicial action is important only insofar as it brings people to account for the wrongs they committed and facilitates the process of compensation. Survivors are less interested in punishing those who killed their families and destroyed their homes than in having them come forward and admit their wrongdoing. Survivors also express considerable interest in compensation, because this is consistent with historical practices of reconciliation in Rwanda and also because so many survivors have been left in dire financial straits. One survivor in Byumba, for example, said that reconciliation requires "a true justice, equitable and one that permits those who deserve it to have reparations for their losses."[40] Since cases in classical courts do not require penitence on the part of the convicted, do not facilitate face-to-face contact between victims and their victimizers, and lack the means for providing compensation, survivors express quite negative attitudes toward the classical court system. In contrast, many survivors felt that *gacaca* courts could encourage positive confrontation with the accused and help bring reparations, though many expressed concerns about *gacaca* as proposed. At the same time, a substantial number of survivors we interviewed also expressed a desire to see those who had wronged them punished.

Meanwhile, Hutu in general expressed greater support for judicial action, but they emphasized the role that trials, whether in classical courts or *gacaca* courts, could play in releasing the innocent. When they spoke of judging the guilty, many Hutu seemed to emphasize the importance of identifying those who were actually responsible for the wrong done, thereby eliminating collective guilt. Many Hutu did discuss the need for those who had done wrong to come forward and ask forgiveness, but they tended to see survivors as obligated to forgive. At the same time, very few Hutu spoke of reparations or compensation as an aspect of reconciliation. A minority of Hutu did speak of the one-sided nature of postgenocide justice as a stumbling block to reconciliation. For example, a woman in Buyoga asserted, "Personally, I think there will not be reconciliation. It is not possible. How do you expect there to be reconciliation with a one-sided judicial system that pursues only one group and protects the others? . . . It pursues only one part of the population while there are assassins on the other side. True justice is one that judges all sides in the same manner."[41]

Some respondents complained of another type of bias in the Rwandan judicial system—favoritism of the rich over the poor:

Our justice will contribute to the reconstruction of the country the day when it becomes impartial. We have seen that when they imprison a leader, they give him more
advantages. His trial advances very quickly, and often he is quickly liberated, while
at the same time the poor peasants spend years and years in prison without even having a case file. We are greatly astonished when we hear that there are social classes in
prison. There are some prisoners who employ others as grooms or washers. It's truly
astonishing![42]

Respondents were deeply divided over the impact of genocide memorials and commemoration on reconciliation. Many expressed a belief that memorials and commemoration served an important function in keeping alive
the memory of the violence that Rwanda had experienced. The comments
of genocide survivors in a focus group in Butare are typical. Said one: "You
can't forget the genocide and its consequences. These are living facts of what
was committed in the light of day. Children who are born today ought to
learn that Rwanda experienced a massacre and that it is bad. Forgetting is not
possible, but I want commemoration to continue and to be done regularly."
Another added: "Another thing is that the fact of remembering our innocent
victims is in itself a moral obligation. One should construct and manage memorial sites in a more impressive fashion, in a fashion where everyone would
notice and understand their significance."[43]

Others, however, expressed objections to such commemoration on several
grounds. Some felt that memorialization was divisive, filling survivors with
anger and Hutu with fear and shame. For example, one Tutsi survivor told
us, "It is better to forget, because [remembering what happened] brings back
to life hatreds in some people."[44] Some Hutu complained that commemoration has been one-sided, that it has taken into account only the suffering of
Tutsi. This was particularly true in Buyoga, where the genocide was limited
but where many Hutu died at the hands of the RPF. For example, one woman
reported, "They commemorate the genocide of the Tutsi, but the experience
of those who went to the camps [in Congo] is put to the side."[45] Another re-
spondent told us that both Tutsi and Hutu who suffered in 1994 should be
considered victims. "It is not bad to speak about [what happened], but the
problem is that arouses from time to time tensions and disagreements. Above
all, when it concerns the definition of who is a victim or not of this war. The
victims should not be differentiated in my opinion."[46] Related to this sentiment
is a feeling expressed by some survivors that they are the only ones who bother
to commemorate the genocide. A widow in Buyoga, for example, complained:
"We do it, but the others remain at home, pursuing their work in the fields as
if they have forgotten what happened to us just a few years ago."[47]

Some Rwandans we interviewed expressed concern that continually re-minding people of what happened keeps injuries fresh and prevents vic-tims—and society—from moving on. For example, a woman in Butare claimed, "The commemoration done each year could damage the process [of reconciliation]. Hearts remain injured with this repeated commemoration."[48] Interestingly, while Tutsi were generally more supportive of commemoration and memorialization, attitudes did not break down clearly along ethnic lines. For example, a genocide survivor in Kibuye had similar concerns about com-memoration: "To continue to talk about what happened risks infecting your children, who didn't even see it. It is better that they don't hear that there were others who killed with machetes."[49]

While people debate the merits of commemoration, they also impart di-verse meanings to commemorations and memorial sites. Survivors almost universally believe that these events and sites are intended to honor their suf-fering and loss. Hutu, meanwhile, are divided in their interpretations. Some express anger or frustration over the one-sided nature of commemoration that focuses on the suffering of Tutsi while ignoring the suffering of Hutu.[50] Others recognize that the sites focus on the Tutsi but feel that this is just, given what happened in the country.[51] Many other Hutu simply interpret the commemorations and memorials in an inclusive fashion. For example, a Hutu woman in Rubengera, Kibuye, whose husband was in prison, accused of participation in the genocide, explained, "Personally, I commemorate what happened. I think I have suffered like others have suffered. I suffer because I can't raise my children well. . . . I find that what I had happen has a place in the commemorations, because we commemorate the suffering that every-one suffered. If it hadn't been for the war, we wouldn't have suffered."[52] An older man in the same commune expressed a similar generalized interpreta-tion of commemoration: "We should not forget that a genocide was commit-ted against members of the Tutsi ethnic group and that thousands of innocent Hutu are dead in exile in Zaire. It is thus necessary each time to remember this, so that such filth is never reproduced."[53]

People were also divided over changing the national symbols. Many sur-vivors made claims similar to those of government officials, that the old na-tional seal, which contained a machete, brought back negative memories of the machetes used to kill during the genocide, and that the mention of eth-nicity in the national anthem was dangerous, and many Hutu were sympa-thetic.[54] Others, however, regarded the changes as a cynical political manipu-lation with little serious impact on the society. In a focus group in Byumba, one woman claimed, "They make these changes without the opinion of the people. We need a referendum. For the majority of the population, the RPF has taken power and has imposed their national anthem and their flag." Another added, "Few people know this new national anthem. The people think that they simply wanted to erase anything pertaining to Habyarimana."[55]

Memory, Identity, and Culture

Our research in three local communities in Rwanda provides a mixed picture of the ability of the government to reshape memory and culture after violence. On the one hand, we found that the government has done a very good job of disseminating its message about Rwandan history and culture. People we interviewed were widely aware of the government's interpretation of Rwanda's essential unity in the precolonial era and the artificiality of ethnic identities. They also knew the new term used for genocide, *itsemba bwoko,* and nearly everyone condemned the violence that took place. On the other hand, many people seem to feel that calls to remember the genocide and to come together for national unity have been cynically manipulated by the ruling elite, who are more concerned with their own positions of power than with truly unifying the country. People feel severely constrained in their ability to discuss the social and political situation openly. As one person in Kibuye told us, "We can't speak freely, only in whispers. It is this fear that stays in people's hearts. They are afraid that if they speak about ethnicity, they may be accused of supporting hostilities."[56] Others expressed the need to talk openly about what had happened in Rwanda, and especially about ethnicity. "I don't see why one should not talk about what exists," said one person.

You exist, I exist. We say in Kinyarwanda, "Someone who does not want people to talk about him should have stayed in his mother's womb." So why not talk? That's reconciliation. It is between you and me. It is between Tutsi and Hutu, between Hutu and Hutu, between Tutsi and Tutsi, between all the different ethnic groups. So how can you arrive [at reconciliation] without talking about what is good or bad, what is favorable or not for this reconciliation?[57]

A small number of people we interviewed, particularly genocide survivors, were willing to criticize the current regime directly, but most others challenged the regime only indirectly. Interviewees often prefaced their responses with statements such as, "We have been told," or "I have heard on the radio," while responses later in the interviews revealed that their own ideas about history, ethnicity, reconciliation, and other issues were not in complete accord with the official positions.

Ultimately, it becomes clear that while the current regime has been able to dominate public discourse about what went wrong in Rwanda and how to achieve reconciliation, other discourses are being formed privately. The regime's attempts to fashion a collective memory of the violence of 1994 have been undermined by the perception that the presentation of the past is self-serving. Most people publicly espouse essential elements of the official discourse, yet they mix this with elements drawn from the discourse of the previous regime, or from their own experience. For example, ethnicity clearly remains a central factor for Rwandan social identity. Some people with whom we spoke sincerely and forcefully rejected ethnic differentiation because of the suffering that it has brought upon the country. Yet for many, ethnicity remains central. As one older woman in Kibuye said, "It is true that in the official documents, like the identity card, the ethnic label has been eliminated. Yet the truth is that this ethnic label remains in people's hearts."[58] Many Hutu resent the fact that they cannot discuss their own experiences of suffering. "There will be no reconciliation between Hutu and Tutsi," said one woman in Butare, "because Tutsi have a tendency to see themselves as the only survivors, the only victims of the genocide. When a Hutu dares to say that he is also a victim, he is quickly blamed and made to feel uneasy. So, how can there be reconciliation in such a situation?"[59] Even those who sought to reject ethnic labels found it difficult to leave them behind. Several people we interviewed refused to give their ethnic identity, claiming that ethnicity no longer existed, yet later in the interview, when we asked whether they had relatives from another ethnic group, they would freely volunteer that they had a Hutu sister-in-law or a Tutsi mother.

Continuing ethnic consciousness does not necessarily mean that ethnic hatred remains strong or that an ideology of ethnic division continues to hold sway. Instead, it may reflect the fact that people continue to relate to society differently, depending upon their ethnic background. The substantial divergence in responses in our research between the Hutu and the Tutsi, especially the survivors, provides evidence that the two groups experience the current situation differently. In postgenocide Rwanda, Tutsi genocide survivors generally feel more free to speak, but many of them feel that they lack real influence in a regime that is dominated by former refugees who were not in Rwanda at the time of the genocide. Many survivors feel that problems such as insecurity and poverty are not being adequately addressed. Most Hutu feel limited in their ability to speak freely, particularly to express criticisms, because of fears that they will be accused of participating in the genocide or of promoting division. Those who have dared to claim publicly that the regime is exclusionary and favors a particular ethnic group have faced dire consequences, as in the case of former president Pasteur Bizimungu, who was denounced and then arrested.

The use of repression by the current regime undermines attempts to change the country's political culture. Rather than creating responsible citizens, the regime is actually encouraging the type of obedience that was a factor in public participation in the genocide. One young man's ethnic self-identification is a troubling indication of the degree to which Rwandans may seek to conform to the government's messages: "When I was still in the refugee camps in Zaire, they told us that we were Hutu. Today, on returning to my country, they say that there are no longer Hutu nor Tutsi. So, it is perhaps best to say that I was Hutu until January 1997, and I am Rwandan since I returned to Rwanda."[60] Whether he actually believes that his identity has changed, the effort to adapt to the message of the regime, at least publicly, is common to many of the people we interviewed.

Yet if people still find that ethnicity is important, they also do not see it as the continuing source of their conflicts. We found an overwhelming desire on the part of those we interviewed to find means to avoid future conflicts, and many of the people felt that the population, if left to its own devices, would be able to achieve reconciliation and maintain peace. As one older man in Kibuye claimed,

We folks in the countryside, we have already achieved our reconciliation. The survivors and others share everything together and have even started marrying one another again. But at the same time, we see problems at the top. The ruling class has not arrived at reconciliation, even though it is at the base of this war that has ravaged Rwanda. It [the ruling class] ought to shine as an example. It is enough to hear all the time of someone going into exile, that some other has been arrested, to see that they still need to reconcile at the top. We here have no problems.[61]

In our survey, 76.7 percent of respondents agreed or strongly agreed with the statement, "If Rwandan leaders would leave the population to themselves, there would be no more ethnic problems." While some observers might be troubled that such an attitude reflects a failure on the part of the population to take responsibility for their actions, if we look at the history of the 1994 genocide in these three communities, we may be reassured. In none of the three communities did the genocide happen spontaneously. Instead, in all three communities, military and political officials intervened from outside to organize the genocide and involve the local population. As one survivor in Mabanza claimed, "In reflecting on what happened, you draw the conclusion that these killings were well organized. If it hadn't been reinforcements of gendarmes and authorities, the inhabitants of this region would have been able to defend themselves without fail [against efforts to organize the genocide]."[62] Many people, Hutu and Tutsi alike, seemed to feel that if they were left to their own devices, the population would sort out its own problems and avoid future violence.

It is too early to know the long-term impact of government efforts to shape memory, identity, and culture in Rwanda. If public discourse remains strictly controlled, it may be that younger generations will be more thoroughly influenced, particularly if programs such as solidarity camps continue to be implemented.[63] However, if leaders act in ways that seem to contradict their own arguments and interpretations, the power of their efforts at social engineering seems likely to be reduced. If, for example, the government continues to act in ways that some see as ethnically discriminatory or exclusionary, people will fail to be convinced that ethnicity no longer exists. If the government continues to call on the people to take responsibility for their actions during the genocide, yet fails to take responsibility for its own war crimes and human-rights abuses, people will likely continue to mouth the messages of justice and unity in public while privately decrying continuing injustice and inequality. Clearly, the case of Rwanda indicates that the government can effectively dominate the discourse of memory and reconciliation. Whether this domination can create a collective memory or bring reconciliation remains to be proven.

Notes

The research for this project was funded by the MacArthur Foundation and conducted under the auspices of the Human Rights Center of the University of California, Berkeley, as part of the project, "Communities in Crisis: Justice and Social Reconstruction in the Aftermath of Genocide and Ethnic Cleansing in Rwanda and the Former Yugoslavia."

1. A related argument is made in Herf 1997, in which the very different memories of the Nazi past constructed in the two German states is analyzed.

2. The best source on the genocide is Des Forges 1999.

3. On RPF violence against civilians, see Des Forges 1999; and Reyntjens 1999.

4. On the ideology of the genocide, see Des Forges 1999; and Chrétien 1995a.

5. Until 2001, Rwanda was divided into twelve prefectures, with each prefecture divided into communes, sectors, and cells. The 2001 reforms changed the name of the regional units to *provinces* but made few changes to their territorial limits, while the 165 communes were consolidated into 106 districts. Sectors and cells remained the subcommunal political units.

6. We focused our research in the sectors of Cyarwa-Cyimana, Cyarwa-Sumo, and

Matyazo in Ngoma; Rubengera, Gacaca, Nyarugenge, and Kibirizi in Mabanza; and Zoko, Mutete, Muranzi, and Burenga in Buyoga.

7. We conducted interviews with four focus groups in both Buyoga and Mabanza and five in Butare.

8. For a more extensive discussion of the survey, see Longman et al. 2004.

9. *The Unity of Rwandans,* for example, seeks to demonstrate the hand of the Church in writing the 1957 Hutu Manifesto, an important document in the assertion of Hutu social and political rights (Office of the President of the Republic 1999, 42–46). Similarly, Jean Nizurugero Rugagi completely denies any Hutu initiative in the move toward political influence: "The Administration needed practical arguments to turn the masses away from the Tutsi authorities and to attract their sympathy at the same time. The ploy was not difficult to invent. It was only necessary to create popular discontent and to create at the same time voices that directed this discontent on the backs of the Tutsi authorities" (1997, 49).

10. See Mugesera 1996; Rutayisire and Muzungu 1995; and *Les cahiers evangile et société,* December 1996, devoted to ideologies.

11. For statements of the government position on trials, see Gahima 2002; and Sezibera 2002.

12. The minister of local administration, for example, told us that the national symbols had been changed "because not all Rwandans found themselves in these symbols," which symbolized negative things and encouraged division (interview by authors, Kigali, 8 June 2002).

13. International Crisis Group 2002 presents a detailed account not only of the harassment of non-RPF politicians and members of the civil society but also of the degree to which RPF members retain the key positions in government. A similar documentation of the distribution of power is presented each year in the annual report by Marysse and Reyntjens. While many ministers are either Hutu or non-RPF, they are always backed up by an assistant who is Tutsi RPF.

14. See Des Forges 1999, chapter on the RPF; Prunier 1998, chap. 10; and Reyntjens 1999.

15. In a speech at San Francisco's Commonwealth Club in March 2003, for example, President Paul Kagame strongly rejected the assertion that the International Criminal Tribunal for Rwanda could try members of the RPF, claiming that if there were any evidence of abuses by his troops, the government of Rwanda could deal with them itself.

16. For an articulation of this perspective, see Maquet 1961.

17. The challenge to the colonial historic account began with Vansina 1962 and included numerous works by scholars such as Marcel d'Hertfelt, Jean-Pierre Chrétien, Catherine Newbury, David Newbury, René Lemarchand, Alison Des Forges, and others.

18. On the ideology of the 1994 genocide, see Chrétien 1995b; and Des Forges 1999.

19. David Newbury (2001) presents an excellent review of the literature on precolonial Rwanda and Burundi.

20. The idea of Rwanda as a nation-state is advocated, for example, by Gamaliel Mbonimana (1998). Mbonimana is currently chair of the department of history at the National University of Rwanda.

21. Interview, Kibirizi, Kibuye, 14 September 2001.

22. Interview, Butare, 7 September 2001.

23. Interview, Matyazo, Butare, 2 December 2001.

24. Interview, Buyoga, Byumba, 17 December 2001.

25. Interview, Cyarwa, Butare, 9 September 2001.

26. Interview, Cyarwa-Cyimana, Ville de Butare, Butare, 7 September 2001.

27. Interview, Cyarwa-Sumo, 9 September 2001.

28. Interview, Matyazo, Butare, 2 December 2001.

29. Interview, Kibirizi, Kibuye, 14 September 2001.

30. Interview, Mutete, Kisaro, Byumba, 29 March 2002.

31. Even Tutsi genocide survivors accept this assertion that the violence came initially from outside (focus-group interview with survivors, Mabanza, Kibuye, 10 August 2002).

32. This tendency to attribute violence to people from outside is consistent with research that Timothy Longman conducted in 1995–96 in Butare, Gikongoro, and Kibuye for Des Forges 1999.

33. Focus-group interview with elders, Mabanza, Kibuye, 10 August 2002.

34. For example, a woman in Mabanza claimed that when it was said on the radio that "Radio Rwanda only encouraged people with bad faith in acts of massacres," Radio Rwanda said, "In Bugesera [a region in which massacres had occurred in 1992] they have finished. What are you waiting for?" (focus-group interview with women in Mabanza, 10 August 2002).

35. Interview, Cyarwa, Butare, 8 September 2001.

36. Focus-group interview with survivors, Mabanza, Kibuye, 10 August 2002.

37. Ibid.

38. Interview, Muranzi, Kisaro, Byumba, 17 December 2001.

39. Focus-group interview with survivors, Mabanza, Kibuye, 10 August 2002.

40. Interview, Muranzi Sector, Kisaro District, 27 March 2002.

41. Interview, Muranzi Sector, Kisaro District, 27 March 2002.

42. Focus-group interview with women, Kisaro, Byumba, 1 March 2003.

43. Focus-group interview with survivors, Matyazo, Butare, 17 August 2002.

44. Interview, Muranzi, Kisaro, Byumba, 28 March 2002.

45. Ibid., 27 March 2002.

46. Ibid., 17 December 2001.

47. Interview, Mutete, Kisaro, Byumba, 29 March 2002.

48. Focus-group interview with women, Matyazo, Butare, 17 August 2002.

49. Interview, Gacaca, Mabanza, Kibuye, 23 August 2001.

50. A woman in Kibuye told us, "It would be better to forget. On both sides, there were victims, and so it is better to forget and think about the future" (interview, Mabanza, Kibuye, 23 August 2001).

51. One man, for example, said, "I find that the memorial sites are necessary and that all the ethnicities should think about them in the same manner. I see that at the time of the anniversary of the genocide, all the ethnic groups participate in ceremonies of commemoration. I think that this is a good thing, because we have the chance to pray and to

meditate on a collective memory of these people who, after all, were savagely killed even though they were innocents" (focus-group interview with elders, Mabanza, Kibuye, 10 August 2002).

52. Interview, Rubengera, Kibuye, 23 August 2001.

53. Focus-group interview with elders, Mabanza, Kibuye, 10 August 2002.

54. For example, the minister of local administration, who was ultimately charged with changing the symbols, explained to us at length the negative connotations of the old symbols and their exclusionary and injurious implications (interview, Kigali, 8 June 2002).

55. Focus-group interview with women, Kisaro, Byumba, 1 March 2003.

56. Interview, Rubengera, Mabanza, Kibuye, 24 August 2001.

57. Interview, Kibirizi, Kibuye, 14 September 2001.

58. Focus-group interview with elders, Mabanza, Kibuye, 10 August 2002.

59. Focus-group interview with women, Matyazo, Butare, 17 August 2002.

60. Interview, Cyarwa-Cyimana, Butare, 9 September 2001.

61. Focus-group interview with elders, Mabanza, Kibuye, 10 August 2002.

62. Focus-group interview with survivors, Mabanza, Kibuye, 10 August 2002.

63. For example, a Hutu youth leader in Byumba who had attended several solidarity camps was able to present a nearly perfect version of the government account of Rwandan history and the genocide, and he seemed to have no doubt that the version was true (interview, Buyoga, Byumba, 24 January 2003).

References

Byanafashe, Déogratias. 1997. La famille comme principe de coherence de la société rwandaise traditionelle. *Cahiers lumière et société,* no. 6 (August): 3–26.

Chrétien, Jean-Pierre, ed. 1995a. *Rwanda: Les médias de la haine.* Paris: Karthala.

———. 1995b. *Rwanda: Les médias du génocide.* Paris: Karthala.

Danieli, Yael. 1998. *International Handbook of Multigenerational Legacies of Trauma.* New York: Plenum.

Des Forges, Alison. 1999. *Leave None to Tell the Story: Genocide in Rwanda.* New York: Human Rights Watch.

Gahima, Gerald. 2002. Re-establishing the Rule of Law and Encouraging Good Governance. Address to the 55th Annual DPI/NGO Conference, New York, 9 September.

Halbwachs, Maurice. 1992. *On Collective Memory.* Edited and translated by Lewis A. Coser. Chicago: University of Chicago Press.

Herf, Jeffrey. 1997. *Divided Memory: The Nazi Past in Two Germanys.* Cambridge, MA: Harvard University Press.

Human Rights Watch. 2003. *Rwanda: Preparing for Elections, Tightening Control in the Name of Unity.* New York, 8 May.

International Crisis Group. 2002. *Rwanda at the End of Transition: A Necessary Political Liberalisation.* Brussels, 13 November.

Longman, Timothy. 2001. Documentation and Individual Identity in Africa: Identity

Cards and Ethnic Self-Perception in Rwanda. In *Documenting Individual Identity: The Development of State Practices in the Modern World,* edited by Jane Caplan and John Torpey, Princeton: Princeton University Press.

Longman, Timothy, Phuong Pham, Harvey Weinstein, and Alice Urusaro Karekezi. 2004. Connecting Justice to Human Experience: Attitudes toward Accountability and Reconciliation in Rwanda. In *My Neighbor, My Enemy: Rebuilding Communities in the Aftermath of Genocide and Ethnic Cleansing,* edited by Eric Stover and Harvey Weinstein. Cambridge: Cambridge University Press.

Malkki, Liisa. 1995. *Purity and Exile: Violence, Memory, and National Cosmology among Hutu Refugees in Tanzania.* Chicago: University of Chicago Press.

Maquet, Jaques. 1961. *The Psremise of Inequality in Ruanda: A Study of Political Relations in a Central African Kingdom.* London: Oxford University Press.

Marysse, S., and Filip Reyntjens, eds. 2002. *L'Afrique des Grands Lacs.* Paris: l'Harmattan.

Mbonimana, Gamaliel. 1998. Le Rwanda état-nation au XIXe siècle. Paper presented at a seminar on the history of Rwanda, Butare, 14–18 December.

Mugesera, Antoine. 1996. À l'origine de la desintegration de la nation rwandaise. *Les cahiers evangile et société,* June, 46–58.

Newbury, Catharine. 1988. *The Cohesion of Oppression: Citizenship and Ethnicity in Rwanda, 1860–1960.* New York: Columbia University Press.

Newbury, David. 2001. Precolonial Burundi and Rwanda: Local Loyalties, Regional Royalties. *International Journal of African Historical Studies* 34 (2): 255–314.

Office of the President of the Republic. 1999. *The Unity of Rwandans: Before the Colonial Period and under Colonial Rule; under the First Republic.* Kigali: Republic of Rwanda.

Prunier, Gerard. 1998. *The Rwanda Crisis.* New York: Columbia University Press.

Reyntjens, Filip. 1999. *La guerre des Grands Lacs: Alliances mouvantes et conflits extraterritoriaux en Afrique Centrale.* Paris: L'Harmattan.

Rugagi, Jean Nizurugero. 1997. Décolonisation et démocratisation du Rwanda. *Cahiers lumière et société,* no 7 (October): 43–54.

Rutayisire, Paul, and Bernardin Muzungu. 1995. L'ethnisme au coeur de la guerre. *Cahiers Centre Saint-Dominique* 1 (8 August): 68–82.

Sells, Michael A. 1996. *The Bridge Betrayed: Religion and Genocide in Bosnia.* Berkeley and Los Angeles: University of California Press.

Sezibera, Richard. 2002. The Only Way to Bring Justice to Rwanda. *Washington Post,* 7 April.

Vansina, Jan. 1962. *L'évolution du royaume rwandaise: Des origines à 1900.* Reprint, Brussels: Academie Royale des Sciences d'Outre Mer, 2000.

———. 2001. *Le Rwanda ancien: Le royaume nyiginya.* Paris: Karthala.

CONTRIBUTORS

JOCELYN ALEXANDER is Lecturer in Commonwealth Studies at the University of Oxford. She has researched and published extensively on land, ethnicity, religion, war, and political authority in Zimbabwe and Mozambique. She is coauthor, with JoAnn McGregor and Terence Ranger, of *Violence and Memory: One Hundred Years in the "Dark Forests" of Matabeleland* (2000) and author of *The Unsettled Land: The Politics of Land and State-Making in Zimbabwe* (2006).

EDNA G. BAY is Associate Professor in the Graduate Institute of the Liberal Arts and Director of the Institute of African Studies, Emory University. A historian of West Africa, she has published extensively on the slave-trading state of Dahomey, including *Wives of the Leopard: Gender, Politics, and Culture in the Kingdom of Dahomey* (1998). Her interest in contemporary questions of violence was stimulated by the Sawyer Seminars at Emory in 2001–3.

BELINDA BOZZOLI is Deputy Vice-Chancellor (Research) and Professor of Sociology at the University of the Witwatersrand, Johannesburg. Born in South Africa, she was educated in Johannesburg and the United Kingdom. She is the author of *The Political Nature of a Ruling Class* (1983), *Women of Phokeng* (1991), and *Theatres of Struggle and the End of Apartheid* (2004) and the editor of several volumes of collected essays.

MARTHA CAREY is a doctoral candidate at Emory University. An anthropology graduate of Albion College, she worked with the international emergency humanitarian organization Médecins Sans Frontières from 1993 to 2002. Specializing in the implementation of projects in conflict zones, she has worked in a number of volatile areas, including Somalia, Bosnia-Herzegovina, Timor, Sudan, and Sierra Leone.

JOANNA DAVIDSON is a doctoral candidate in anthropology at Emory University. She carried out more than two years of ethnographic fieldwork in Guinea-Bissau, where she focused on social and religious transformations under way in the impoverished and embattled northwest. Her articles have appeared in

European and American academic journals and edited volumes. Prior to pursuing her doctorate, she worked for several years with various international NGOs, primarily in Latin America, in the fields of indigenous rights, refugee services and advocacy, gender equity, and social entrepreneurship.

DONALD L. DONHAM is Professor of Anthropology at the University of California, Davis. He has carried out long-term field research in Ethiopia and South Africa. His principal publications from his work in Ethiopia are *History, Power, Ideology: Central Issues in Marxism and Anthropology* (2nd ed., 1999) and *Marxist Modern: An Ethnographic History of the Ethiopian Revolution* (1999). He currently is working on a book on the violence that occurred among black workers in a gold mine at the time of the 1994 South African elections. He was Director of African Studies at Emory University from 2000 to 2003, when the Sawyer Seminars were planned and carried out.

TIMOTHY LONGMAN is a political scientist trained at the University of Wisconsin, Madison, who teaches at Vassar College. He has published numerous articles and chapters on the conflicts in Central Africa, and his book *Commanded by the Devil: Christianity and Genocide in Rwanda* has recently been accepted for publication. In addition to his teaching and research, Longman has worked as a consultant for Human Rights Watch and the International Center for Transitional Justice, researching and writing reports on human-rights violations in Democratic Republic of Congo, Burundi, and Congo.

JoANN McGREGOR is Lecturer in Human Geography at the University of Reading, United Kingdom. She is coauthor, with Jocelyn Alexander and Terence Ranger, of *Violence and Memory: One Hundred Years in the "Dark Forests" of Matabeleland* (2000) and coeditor, with William Beinart, of *Social History and African Environments* (2003). She is currently engaged in research on the new Zimbabwean diaspora in the United Kingdom.

WILLIAM RENO, a specialist in African politics and the politics of "collapsing states," is Associate Professor of Political Science at Northwestern University. He is the author of *Corruption and State Politics in Sierra Leone* (1995) and *Warlord Politics and African States* (1998). His current work examines violent commercial organizations in Africa, the former Soviet Union, and the Balkans and their relationships to state power and global economic actors.

THÉONESTE RUTAGENGWA is the Rwanda country director for the Center for Nonviolent Communication. He has been a visiting scholar at the Human Rights Center and the University of California, Berkeley.

ELAINE SALO is an anthropologist and Senior Lecturer at the African Gender Institute (AGI), University of Cape Town, South Africa. Her doctoral dissertation, "Respectable Mothers, Strong Men, and Good Daughters" (2004), examines how notions of personhood and community were shaped by race, gender, and sexuality in Manenberg Township, South Africa, during the post-apartheid transition. Her latest research examines the construction of identity and the meanings of sexuality among youth in Cape Flats townships, in the Western Cape, South Africa.

DANIEL JORDAN SMITH is the Stanley J. Bernstein Assistant Professor in the Social Sciences and Assistant Professor of Anthropology at Brown University. He has conducted research since 1995 focusing on Igbo-speaking southeastern Nigeria, including topics such as relationships between Igbo migrants and their communities of origin, Nigeria's HIV/AIDS epidemic, and popular responses to inequality. His articles on Nigeria have appeared in *Africa, Africa Today, American Anthropologist, American Ethnologist, Cultural Anthropology, Culture, Health & Sexuality, Ethnology, Ethnos, Medical Anthropology, Population and Development Review,* and *World Development.* His book *Corruption and Its Discontents: The Nigerian Factor* is forthcoming from Princeton University Press.

INDEX